THE BIGGEST JOKE BOOK EVER

(No Kidding!)

Michael Pellowski

APPLESAUCE PRESS

Dedicated to Jeanne Yager Snyder & Bernadette Pellowski Strausser

The Biggest Joke Book Ever (No Kidding!)

13-Digit ISBN: 978-1-60433-226-1
10-Digit ISBN: 1-60433-226-3

This book may be ordered by mail from the publisher. Please include $2.95 for postage and handling. Please support your local bookseller first!

Books published by Cider Mill Press Book Publishers are available at special discounts for bulk purchases in the United States by corporations, institutions, and other organizations. For more information, please contact the publisher.

Applesauce Press is an imprint of
Cider Mill Press Book Publishers
"Where good books are ready for press"
12 Port Farm Road
Kennebunkport, Maine 04046

Visit us on the Web!
www.cidermillpress.com

Design by Melissa Gerber
All illustrations courtesy of Anthony Owsley & Theresa Burke
Printed in USA

2 3 4 5 6 7 8 9 0
First Edition

CONTENTS

CHAPTER 1

KOOKY ANIMAL KINGDOM

What's gray, weighs 2,000 pounds and spins around like a top?
A hippo stuck in a revolving door.

....

How can you tell the difference between a zebra corporal and a zebra sergeant?
The zebra sergeant will have more stripes.

....

ATTENTION: Moles sell houses hole sale.

....

What's black and white and red all over?
A sloppy penguin eating tomato soup.

....

What weighs two tons and is gray and lumpy?
A hippo with the mumps.

....

Why do chameleons make great party guests?
Because they always blend in.

....

Knock! Knock!
Who's there?
I adder.
I adder who?
I adder in a trap, but she escaped.

....

ATTENTION: Wild hogs tell boaring stories.

....

What do you get if you cross an antelope with a journalist?
A gnus reporter.

....

What do you call a seasick rhino?
A green horn.

Knock! Knock!

Who's there?

Gecko.

Gecko who?

Gecko-ing or you'll be late for school.

What goes bounce! Bonk! Bounce! Bonk! Bounce! Bonk?

A kangaroo hopping around in a room with a low ceiling.

NOTICE: Rich kangaroos always have deep pockets.

What do you get if you cross an Australian animal with a cheerleader?

A kangarooter.

Why was the lion dripping wet?

He had a water mane break.

What do you call a ram that lives at the top of a mountain?

A hillbilly goat.

Knock! Knock!

Who's there?

Weasel.

Weasel who?

Weasel while you work.

What's black and white and slowly turning blue?

A very cold penguin.

What does a polar bear wear when his head is cold?
An ice cap.

What happens when two zebras crash into each other?

They see stars and stripes.

What kind of sharks live in the desert?

Sand sharks.

....

What kind of sharks eat lions?

Mane-eaters.

....

What kind of shark has no friends?

A lone shark.

....

What sign makes a shark happy?

No fishing.

....

Why are drowning sharks always left to die?

Because who'd give a shark mouth-to-mouth resuscitation?

....

What did the shark say when he saw Moby Dick?

I think I'll have some white meat.

What does a shark call a bunch of fish swimming together?

A school lunch.

....

What did the shark say when he saw an Asian surfer?

Did someone send out for Chinese food?

....

Why did the great white go to the hospital?

He needed shark therapy.

....

What do you get when you cross a kangaroo with a jungle vine?

A jump rope.

....

What do you get if you cross a hyena and a parrot?

An animal that laughs and then asks itself what's so funny.

....

What do you get if you cross frogs with chameleons?

Leapin' lizards.

What do you get if you cross a hippo with a hog?
The world's biggest pork chops.

What do you get if you cross a sheep and a large primate?
A bah-boon.

What do you call a dapper king of the jungle?
A dandy lion.

What do you get if you cross a coyote and a chimp?
A howler monkey.

What kind of exercises do bunnies do?
Hareobics.

What do you get if you spill boiling water down a rabbit hole?
Hot cross bunnies.

What theory did the famous skunk philosopher propose?
I stink, therefore I am.

Where did the actor skunk deliver his monologue?
Scenter stage.

ATTENTION:
Rabbits like to rent garden apartments.

what do space squirrels like to eat?
Astronuts.

What do you get if you cross minks and pines?
Very expensive fur trees.

What do you get when a bunny marries Bambi?
Hare deer everywhere.

Show me two skunks who enlist in the Marine Corps, and I'll show you a phew good men.

What do you call a grizzly that sheds? Bear naked.

What lives in an oak tree and cooks greasy meals?
A frying squirrel.

How do rabbits fly to Europe?
They take a hare plane.

What's soggy and has large antlers?
A rain deer.

How much money do a dozen skunks have?
They have twelve scents.

How can you tell if a tree is a dogwood?
Check out its bark.

What's black and white and green all over?
A sloppy skunk eating pea soup.

Why couldn't the herd of deer buy dinner?
Because they only had one buck.

What did the judge say when lawyer skunk appeared before him?
Odor in the court.

How do you get rid of unwanted rabbits?
Use hare remover.

What did Mr. Beaver say to the oak tree?
It's been nice gnawing you.

ATTENTION:
Skunks use smell phones.
Snake phones have crawler I.D.

Roadrunner phones have speed dial.

What's the slowest way to send a letter?

Snail mail.

Then there was the gopher publisher who printed an underground newspaper.

Why was the fox so depressed?

The hunting dogs kept hounding him day and night.

Knock! Knock!

Who's there?

I flounder.

I flounder who?

I flounder in the shoe department.

What did Ms. Frog wear on her feet?

Open toad shoes.

How did Mr. Turtle pay his bills?

He shelled out cash.

What's worse than buying mittens for an octopus?

Buying sneakers for a centipede.

Which animal lives in the White House and eats fish?

The presidential seal.

What's the best way to save a frog's life?

Clamp his mouth shut so he can't croak.

What did Judge Mole say to the gopher witness?

Remember to tell the hole truth.

....

Why did the boy porcupine follow the girl porcupine everywhere she went.

He was stuck on her.

....

Knock! Knock!
Who's there?
Gopher.
Gopher who?
Gopher a walk to calm your nerves.

....

What kind of bread does a gopher eat?

Hole wheat.

....

What did one porcupine say to the other.

Quit needling me.

....

What does Bullwinkle Moose drink when he has an upset stomach?

Elk-o-seltzer.

What do you get if you cross a turtle with a flock of geese?

A slow-down zone.

....

What did Mrs. Fox say to Baby Fox when she put him to bed?

Pheasant dreams, son.

Quit needling me!

....

Knock! Knock!
Who's there?
Rabbit.
Rabbit who?
Rabbit up. It's an order to go.

....

Why was the little bunny in the timeout chair?

He was having a bad hare day.

Mother: Why did you take your goldfish out of the bowl?

Boy: He needs a bath.

....

What do you call a boy slug that lives in a shell?

Snail male.

....

What happened to the frog that parked near a fire hydrant?

He got toad away.

....

What did the robber porcupine say to his quills?

It's time for a stick up.

....

What is a rabbit's favorite playground game?

Hopscotch.

....

What do rabbits like to eat for dessert?

Carrot cake.

....

What do you call a very athletic hare?

A jock rabbit.

....

Why did Mr. Mole risk all of his poker chips on one hand?

Because he wanted to gopher broke.

....

Why was the lion king sad and lonely?

He had no pride.

....

Why do rabbits never go bald?

They constantly reproduce hares.

....

What do little frogs use to catch fish?

Tadpoles.

How does a skunk get rid of odors?

He uses an ex-stink-guisher.

What did the waiter say to the skunk?
May I please take your odor, sir?

Do rabbits use combs?
No. They use hare brushes.

NOTICE: Sane squirrels live in nut houses.

What do you get if you cross a skunk
with a hand grenade?
A stink bomb.

What kind of stories did Mrs. Rabbit tell her children at bedtime?
Cotton tales.

ATTENTION: Mr. Frog has a bachelor pad at his pond.

What do you call a moose that tells tall tales?
A bull moose.

What is a squirrel's favorite Christmas show?
The Nutcracker.

What do you get if you cross a rabbit with morning mist?

Hare dew.

why did Ms. Bunny go to the beauty parlor?

To get her hare set.

Knock! Knock!

Who's there?

Odor.

Odor who?

Odor men are wiser than younger men.

Knock! Knock!

who's there?

Distinct.

Distinct who?

Distinct of a skunk is awful.

Which skunk girl went to a fancy ball?

Scenterella.

what do you call a skunk that carves figures out of wood?

A whittle stinker.

What do you get if you cross a hot-air balloon with a skunk?

Something that raises a stink.

What has three ears and a cotton tail?
A rabbit eating corn on the cob.

What do you get if you cross a turtle with a pig?
A trailer pork.

ATTENTION: Turtles are shellfish reptiles.

Why did Bambi fail his test?
His teacher didn't want to pass the buck.

How does a snake navigate through a strange forest?
He uses a GPHiss system.

Knock! Knock!
Who's there?
Possum.
Possum who?
Possum some relish on his hotdog.

You tortoise everything we know

What did the little turtles say to their father?
You tortoise everything we know.

In which direction did the turtle move when he saw us watching him?
Tortoise.

Miss Tortoise: Humph! You're a real square.
Mr. Turtle: What do you expect? I'm a box turtle.

HINKY PINKIES
What do you call ...
A rodent's mate? A mouse spouse.
A tadpole's diary of his travels? A frog log.
A big rodent's rug? A rat mat.
Smokey's recliner? A bear chair.

Tim: Any animal that's not tame is a dangerous creature.
Slim: Now that's a wild accusation.

Marty: Have you ever seen a coyote jog?
Artie: No, but I've seen a fox trot.

What do you get if you cross the U.S. Post Office with Smokey Bear?
I don't know, but it stamps out a lot of forest fires all across the country.

What's black and white with splashes of red?
Two skunks having a rotten tomato fight.

Ranger: I saw a grizzly in a nudist camp.
Guide: Was he bear naked?

What do you get if you cross a rattlesnake with a car tire?
A snake that rattles and rolls.

Then there was the hard-working gopher that built his home business from the ground up.

What is a skunk's favorite holiday?

Scent Valentine's Day.

Mr. Lion: A couple of antelopes just moved into the house next door.
Mrs. Lion: Let's go welcome our gnu neighbors.

Why did Ms. Antelope go to the beauty parlor?

She wanted a gnu hairstyle.

Did you hear about the lions that went out on the town and had a roaring good time?

What do you get if you cross a noisy chimp with a prizefighter? A chatter boxer.

What do monkeys use to make their sandwiches?
Banana bread.

What do you get if you cross a needle and a tiger?

A pin-striped jungle cat.

Knock! Knock!
Who's there?
Hyena.
Hyena who?

Hyena tree sits the majestic eagle.

What time is it when you see a hippo sitting on your doghouse?
Time to get a new doghouse.

Which monkey can fly?
The hot-air baboon.

Mr. Antelope: My wife and I just had a baby.
Mr. Warthog: Congratulations on being gnu parents.

what did the hitting instructor say to the python?
Choke up on your bat.

What do you get if you cross a chimp with a noisy beehive?
Monkey buzzness.

KOOKY QUESTION: Do snow leopards like ice cream?

Knock! Knock!
Who's there?
Lion.
Lion who?
Lion will get you into trouble, so be truthful.

Knock! Knock!
Who's there?
Lion.
Lion who?
Lion on a block of ice can send shivers down your spine.

What's black and white and has red cheeks?
An embarrassed zebra.

ATTENTION:
Some jungle animals have beastly luck.

Knock! Knock!
Who's there?
Thea.
Thea who?
Thea later alligator!

What's black and white and slightly green?
A seasick zebra.

What's hairy and hops up and down?
A gorilla on a pogo stick.

What did Mr. Antelope wear to his wedding?
A gnu suit.

Why was the lion comedian a smash hit in Vegas?
The audience was full of laughing hyenas.

Knock! Knock!
Who's there?
A lioness.
A lioness who?
A lioness king of beasts.

What happens when thousands of lions go to a sporting event?

The crowd really roars.

What do you call a lion that gobbles up your father's sister?

An aunt eater.

What did the boa say to the python?
I have a crush on you.

Lion: Do you want to race me?

Leopard: That depends. You're not a cheetah, are you?

What did the ape say when his sister-in-law had a baby?
Well, I'll be a monkey's uncle!

What did the grapes say when the hippo stepped on them?
Nothing. They just let out a little whine.

What's multi-colored, slithers, and has a forked tongue?
A rainboa.

What do you get if you cross solar flares and a leopard?

Sun spots.

Why are chimps awful storytellers?

Because they have no tales to speak of.

Where does a lion keep an antelope?

In a prey pen.

NOTICE: Then there was the rhino that joined the army and traded in his horn for a bugle.

What are antelopes and gazelles?

Just plain African animals.

What did the tiger say to the sailor?

Do you want to be my prey, mate?

ATTENTION: Giraffes are heads above other African animals in every respect.

Why is it difficult for a giraffe to apologize?

Because it takes a long time for a giraffe to swallow its pride.

How does a rhino navigate safely on a misty morning?

He uses his fog horn.

ATTENTION: Moles like ground coffee.

Knock! Knock!

Who's there?

Woodchuck.

Woodchuck who?

Woodchuck come to our party if we invited him?

DAFFY DEFINITION:

Bat: **A mouse with a pilot's license.**

....

What did Mr. Squirrel send his girlfriend when he joined he Army?

Forget-me-nuts.

....

Mr. Turtle: What did you buy for Mr. Snake and Ms. Kitty when they got married?

Miss Pooch: Hiss and Purrs bath towels.

....

What do you get if you cross a bison and a duck?

A buffalo bill.

....

NOTICE: Male lions like to live on the African mane land.

....

What do you get when a fast spotted cat falls in a mud puddle?

A dirty cheetah.

....

What does a gorilla wear in the kitchen?

An ape-ron.

Why did the silly rodents always bump into tree trunks?

They were tree blind mice.

....

How does a zebra travel from place to place?

He hoofs it.

....

What do you call a man who rides an elephant?

A trunk driver.

....

What do you get if you cross a rhino with a footwear salesman?

A rhinoceros with a shoehorn.

Which jungle animal is always pouting?
A whinoceros.

....

What do North Pole stockbrokers read?
The Walrus Street Journal.

....

What happens when a skunk crawls through a flower garden?
He ends up smelling like roses.

....

What did the baseball manager say to the boa?
Let's try the squeeze play.

....

What did the baseball umpire say to the sheep?
Ewe are out!

....

Why did the kangaroo infielder miss the ground ball?
Bad bounce.

....

SIGN ON A MOUSEHOLE EXIT: Creep out.

....

Scientist: I just crossed a duck with a bottom-dwelling fish.
Reporter: If your experiment is a success, it'll be a feather in your carp.

....

What do you get when you subtract rabbits from bunnies?
Hare problems.

....

Knock! Knock!
Who's there?
Gibbon.
Gibbon who?
Gibbon is always better than receiving.

Which rodent makes a good baseball shortstop?
A field mouse.

Which mink was a barbarian warrior?
Chinchilla the Hun.

Knock! Knock!
Who's there?
A rattle.
A rattle who?
A rattle squeal on his friends every time.

Hunter: I spotted a leopard.
Guide: Baloney! They're born that way.

What did one duck football player say to the other duck football players?
Let's puddle up.

How do you bring a rabbit back to life?
Use hare restorer.

What did Mr. Rabbit give Miss Bunny?
A 24-carrot ring.

GOOFY MATCH GAME
They're a perfect match. She eats like a bird ... and he's a bookworm.
They're a perfect match. She's a real thoroughbred ... and he's mule headed.
They're a perfect match. She's as timid as a mouse ... and he's a sneaky rat.
They're a perfect match. She's a little deer ... and he doesn't have a buck to his name.
They're not a perfect match. She's a cute young kid ... and he's a grumpy old goat.

What does an ill rabbit drink?
Hare tonic.

▶ ▶ ▶ ▶ ▶ ▶ ▶ **KOOKY QUESTION:** Do crocodiles wear alligator shoes?

Are giraffes intelligent?

Yes. They're one of the highest forms of animal life.

What happened when the lioness invited the tiger to dinner?
The tiger ate the lion's share of the food.

What do you call an Asian ox that talks too much? A yakety-yak.

Why do fish like to eat worms?
Who knows! They're just hooked on them.

What do you get when a mouse peels onions?

Mouse-ka-tears.

▶ ▶ ▶ ▶ ▶ **What's tiny, gray, has big ears, and a large trunk?**
A mouse on a sea cruise.

KOOKY QUESTION: Do moles and gophers have tunnel vision?

▶ ▶ ▶ ▶ ▶ ▶ ▶ ▶ ▶ ▶ ▶ ▶ ▶ ▶ ▶ ▶ ▶ ▶

Why did the kangaroo tourist put a zipper on its pouch?

It was afraid of pickpockets.

Cowboy: I just saw a baby snake.
Cowgirl: How do you know it was a baby?
Cowboy: It had a rattle.

What is a mouse's favorite dessert? Cheesecake.

ANIMAL TONGUE TWISTERS

Lazy Larry Llama loves lovely Lacy Lion.

Timmy Turtle texted Tillie Tortoise ten times.

Hairy Harry Hound hurries home.

Sheep shouldn't sleep in shaky shacks.

Pretty Pinky Porker pines for Porky Peter Pointer.

Ron Watts runs rat races.

How did the beaver break his teeth?
He wandered into a petrified forest.

What animal can jump higher than the Empire State Building?

Any animal. The Empire State Building can't jump.

What do you get if you cross a zebra and a penguin?
An animal in a striped tuxedo.

◄ ◄ ◄ ◄ ◄ ◄ ◄ ◄ ◄ ◄ ◄ ◄

Knock! Knock!
Who's there?
Asp.
Asp who?
Asp your mother if you can come out.

◄ ◄ ◄ ◄ ◄ ◄ ◄ ◄ ◄ ◄ ◄ ◄

What do you get if you cross a turtle and an ATM machine?
A creature that shells out cash.

► ► ► ► ► ► ► ► ► ► ► ► ► ► ► ►

What's the difference between a comedian and a squirrel?
A comedian cracks nutty jokes and a squirrel just cracks nuts.

◄ ◄ ◄ ◄ ◄ ◄ ◄ ◄ ◄ ◄ ◄ ◄ ◄

What do you get if you cross a frog and a calendar?
Leap year.

► ► ► ► ► ► ► ► ► ► ► ► ► ►

Why was the rabbit with a broken foot so sad?
He had an unhoppy birthday.

◄ ◄ ◄ ◄ ◄ ◄ ◄ ◄ ◄ ◄ ◄

What do you get if you cross a kangaroo with a pirate?
A sailor who jumps ship.

► ► ► ► ► ► ► ► ► ► ► ► ► ►

Todd: A family like yours should be illegal.
Rod: So zoo us.

What has long ears, a bushy tail and chops down trees?
A lumberjack rabbit.

What financial advice did Mr. Mole give to Mr. Gopher?

Don't burrow money.

what kind of punch does a boxer turtle throw?

A slow poke.

Why don't they invent:
Bulletproof vests for animals to wear during hunting season?
A GPS device homing pigeons can use?
Miniature cows that give condensed milk?
Feather toupees for bald eagles?
Tiny waterbeds for pet goldfish?

What do you call an Arctic bear that competes in the Olympics?
A polar vaulter.

What do you get if you cross a seal and a cougar?
A sea lion.

When doesn't a skunk smell?
When its nose is clogged up.

Who has lots of long arms and is a Western outlaw?
Billy the Squid.

What do you get if you cross a Christmas plant with a female deer?
Mistle-doe.

WHAT A WILD NEIGHBORHOOD!
My big brother belongs to the Elks Club.
My father is a member of the Moose Lodge.
My uncle belongs to the Lions Club.
My cousin is a card shark.
My little brother is a weasel.
My grandfather is a real turkey.
My grandmother is an old crow.

what's the worst thing a giraffe can have?
Whiplash.

What is a turtle's favorite game?
The old shell game.

What did Mrs. Skunk say to Mr. Skunk at dinnertime?
Can we odor out tonight?

What do you get if you cross large rodents with small, juicy fruits?
A ratsberry bush.

What did Mr. Turtle say to Miss Tortoise?
Shell we dance?

What happens when silk worms race?
They usually end up in a tie.

Animal trainer #1: How's the giraffe business?
Animal trainer #2: **Things are looking up.**

Which monkey can't keep a secret?
The blaboon.

What do you get if you cross an octopus with a piece of furniture?

An arm, arm, arm, arm, arm, arm, arm, armchair.

What takes tons of wool and years to knit?

A turtleneck sweater for a giraffe.

Instructions on a roadrunner's phone: "Please leave your message after the beep, beep!"

What do you get if you cross a small rodent with an oil can?
A mouse that never squeaks again.

Visitor on safari: **Gulp! I'm seeing spots before my eyes.**
Guide: **Relax. That's just a leopard.**

◄ ◄ ◄ ◄ ◄ ◄

What do you get if you cross a centipede with a piece of furniture?
A foot, foot, foot, foot stool.

CHATTER CHUCKLES
You tell 'em Monkey ... you're a chimp off the ol' block.
You tell 'em Little Chimp ... you're no cheetah.
You tell 'em Alligator...you're tale is no croc.

Knock! Knock!
Who's there?
Whale.
Whale who?
Whale I guess I'll be going now.

What exercise do you get when you cross kangaroos with athletes?
Jumping jocks.

What do you call a turtle soldier?
A helmet with legs.

What did the kangaroo say to the hitchhiker?
Hop in!

Why did the little piggy stay home?
His room was a pigsty and his mother made him clean it.

Why do leopards wear spotted coats?
The tigers bought all the striped ones.

Where do lions bathe?
In the mane stream.

What happens when two frogs try to catch the same bug at the same time?
They end up tongue-tied.

Knock! Knock!
Who's there?
Gopher.
Gopher who?
Gopher a snack while the commercial's on.

Why did the pig athlete go to the trainer?
He hurt his hamstring.

Why did the pig go to the optometrist?
He had pink eye.

Why did the pig farmer call the vet?
He wanted her to cure his ham.

How did the turtle travel to the Orient?
He took a slow boat to China.

Where does a juvenile delinquent fish swim?
In a reform school.

How did the squid get downtown?
It took an octobus.

Elephants

What did Tarzan say when he saw three elephants wearing sunglasses?
Nothing. He didn't recognize them.

What kind of elephant lives in a teepee?
An Indian elephant.

What weighs two tons, has a trunk, and loves pepperoni pizza?
An Italian elephant.

ATTENTION: An elephant is a nosy animal.

What's gray, carries flowers, and visits sick people?
A get wellephant.

What did the label on the back of the elephant's designer jeans read?
Wide load.

Why did the elephant have lots of tiny holes in his nose?
He forgot to put mothballs in his trunk.

What do you get if you cross an elephant with a vacuum?
Something that sucks up a lot of dirt.

What did the polite elephant on the subway do?
He stood up and let five ladies take his seat.

What do you get if you cross a steer and a pachyderm?
A bull elephant.

Where's the best place to watch an elephant pole vault?
As far away from the landing pit as possible

What do you get if you cross an elephant with a shotgun?
A pachyderm with a double barrel trunk.

How did the elephant get his trunk stuck in the drainpipe?
He put his nose where it didn't belong.

What do you get if you cross a bloodhound and a pachyderm?
An elephant with a trunk that can track any scent in the world.

Trainer: Hey! You're an African elephant pretending to be an Indian elephant.
Elephant: So Sioux me.

How do you pick up an elephant?
Be polite. Tell her she's cute and offer to buy her lunch.

What's gray, weighs two ton, and has two wheels?
An elephant on a motorcycle.

Girl: Did Noah take any suitcases on the Ark?
Boy: No. But the elephants brought along two trunks.

What did the peanut vendor say to the elephant?
Keep your nose out of my business.

Boy: Are peanuts fattening?
Girl: Have you ever seen a skinny elephant?

Why do cowboys ride horses instead of elephants?

Elephants take too long to saddle.

Why do cowboys tame wild horses, but not wild elephants?

Would you want to ride a bucking elephant?

Why don't Eskimos keep elephants as pets?

Elephants can't squeeze into igloos.

What do elephants bring to a sauna bath?

Swimming trunks.

Why didn't Mr. Elephant get rich?

He always agreed to work for peanuts.

What has red lips, three tongues, and a trunk?

A girl elephant wearing lipstick and sneakers.

What's gray, has big ears, and is ten feet tall?

A mouse on stilts.

What did Detective Elephant do at the crime scene?

He nosed around looking for clues.

What do you get if you cross a woodpecker and an elephant?

Something that pecks holes in giant Redwood trees.

What does an elephant need to pull heavy loads?

A tow trunk.

What is an elephant's motto?
Keep on trunkin'.

What's blue, has big ears, and weighs two tons?

A spoiled elephant holding its breath.

....

Why do elephants have white tusks?

They brush after every meal.

....

Knock! Knock!

Who's there?

Harry.

Harry who?

Harry up. I don't want to miss the elephant parade.

....

How do you make a gray elephant blue?

Tell him a sad story.

....

How do you can an elephant?

Just say, "You're fired!"

....

How do you can pink elephants?

Hand them pink slips.

....

What weighs two tons and has a million red dots on it?

An elephant with the measles.

How do you make an elephant float?

Throw him a very big life preserver.

....

Man: **I used to have a pet elephant, but I had to get rid of him.**

Guy: **Why?**

Man: **I was spending too much time cleaning out the litter box.**

....

Why did the elephant fail his Army physical?

He had flat feet.

....

How did the elephant plastic surgeon get rich?

He performed thousands of nose jobs.

Why was the sailor elephant so sad?

His trunk was lost during a storm at sea.

....

What do you get if you cross pachyderms with tiny insects?

Eleph-ants.

....

What do you get if you cross an elephant and a turtle?

I don't know, but you should see the size of its shell.

....

Knock! Knock!

Who's there?

Howell.

Howell who?

Howell I feed my pet elephant?

....

Knock! knock!

Who's there?

Dozen.

Dozen who?

Dozen anyone want to see the circus elephants?

....

Why are elephants so smart?

They have tons of gray matter.

....

What do you get when an elephant steps on a can of corn?

Creamed corn.

....

What's as big as an elephant, looks like an elephant, but doesn't weigh an ounce?

An elephant's shadow.

How did an elephant get stuck in a tree?

His parachute got caught.

Why did the elephant become a reporter?

He had an uncanny nose for news.

How can you tell if an elephant is snobby?

A snobby elephant walks around with its nose stuck up in the air.

How do you know when an invisible elephant is behind you?

You'll smell the peanuts on his breath.

What makes an elephant feel sick?

A pachygerm.

Why did the elephant miss his flight to Europe?

Because they took too long searching his trunk at the airport.

What has a trunk, weighs two tons, and is red all over?

An elephant with a bad sunburn.

What climbs trees, buries nuts, and weighs two tons?

An elephant who thinks he's a squirrel.

Why did the little elephant spend two hours in the bathtub?

His mother ordered him to wash behind his ears.

Why do elephants make fantastic reporters?
They have a great nose for news.

Why was the boy elephant mad at his date?
She took too long to powder her nose.

Why didn't the elephant tip the bellboy?
Because he dented his trunk.

What do you get if you cross an elephant with an octopus?
An animal that has trunks everywhere.

What do you get if you cross a prehistoric elephant and a flock of sheep?
A very woolly mammoth.

What weighs two tons and plays baseball? A Cleveland Indian Elephant.

What's gray, has big ears, and weighs 500 pounds?
A very obese mouse.

What has a glove compartment and two trunks?
A car being driven by an elephant.

What lives in the jungle, has spots, and weighs two tons?
An elephant with the measles.

What do you get if you cross a centipede and an elephant?

You get out of the way!

Why do elephants have trunks?
Because they'd look ridiculous with suitcases on their faces.

What do you get if you cross a pachyderm with Rudolph the Red-Nosed Reindeer?

An elephant with a trunk that glows in the dark.

Knock! Knock!
Who's there?
Ella.
Ella who?
Ellaphant.

Why do elephants have squinting eyes? From reading the small print on peanut packages.

A man took his trained elephant to the circus. "Dance," he said as the band began to play. Instantly, the elephant began to dance around as the owner of the circus watched closely. When the number ended, the trainer turned to the circus owner. "Well," he said, "are we hired?" "No," replied the circus owner. The trainer was stunned. "Why not?" he asked. "Because," the circus owner snapped, "the band played a waltz and your elephant did a mamba."

Why did the herd of elephants get a ticket?
Because their tail lights didn't work.

What do elephants use bowling balls for? To play marbles.

Why were the elephants the last animals to board Noah's ark?
Because it took them a long time to pack their trunks.

What do you get if you cross an elephant with an anteater?
The world's best and fastest bug exterminator.

Barry: **Why do elephants paint themselves purple?**
Larry: **I don't know.**
Barry: **So they can hide on grapevines.**
Larry: **I've never seen an elephant on a grapevine.**
Barry: **That's because they do such a good job.**

Ike: I went on safari in Africa and late one night I shot an elephant in my pajamas.
Spike: Don't be ridiculous! How could an elephant fit in your pajamas?

Why do elephants have unlimited credit?
No one is brave enough to stop them from charging.

What do you get if you cross an elephant and a cornfield?
Giant ears of corn.

Do elephant musicians read sheet music?
No. They play by ear.

Elephant: Was that an earthquake? I feel tremors.
Rhino: No. It's just the hippos playing leapfrog.

What do elephants wear on the beach?
Bathing trunks.

What do you get if you cross an elephant with a mouse?
I don't know, but it makes big holes in the wall.

Absurdaphants ▶▶▶▶▶▶▶▶▶▶▶▶▶▶▶▶▶

Of all the animal jokes out there, why are elephant jokes the silliest? For example:

Why did the elephant wear blue tennis shoes?
Because his white ones always got dirty.

While some elephant jokes are puns or word play (including many in this section), the craziest ones put elephants in situations we don't normally think of them in. The question above is silly because we know elephants don't wear shoes. The answer is funny because not only doesn't it answer the question as to why the elephant is wearing shoes in the first place, but it says the elephant has white tennis shoes, too! It's impossible, absurd, and it makes us laugh! These sorts of elephant jokes have been popular for nearly fifty years, and thankfully, elephants have a good sense of humor, because these jokes are fun to tell and even more fun to come up with. Here are some more. After reading them, try making up some of your own.

How do you get an elephant in the refrigerator?
Open the door, put in the elephant, and then close the door.

How do you know there's an elephant in the refrigerator?
Footprints in the butter.

How do you know there are two elephants in the refrigerator?
You hear giggling when you close the door.

How can you tell when an elephant is hiding in your closet?
You won't be able to get the door shut.

What's gray and bounces?
An elephant on a trampoline.

What's gray, weighs 2,000 pounds, and floats?
An elephant wearing a life jacket.

What has two wheels, giant ears, and wobbles?
An elephant learning to ride a bike.

Can elephants fly?
Yes. But only if they have a pilot's license.

How do you make an elephant float?
Pour soda into a glass, add a scoop of ice cream, and dump in an elephant.

For the Birds

What do you get if you cross two blobs of raw pastry and an ostrich?
A dough-dough bird.

....

What do geese do when they get caught in a traffic jam?
They honk a lot.

....

Who do you get if you cross a water fowl with a Western hero of the O.K. Corral?
Duck Holiday.

....

Why didn't the nervous rooster cross the road?
Down deep he really was really a chicken.

....

What do you get if you cross an eagle and a minister?
A bird of pray.

....

What do you get if you cross pigeons in a coop with pigs?
Roost pork.

....

Show me a canary who swallows a loaded gun ...
and I'll show you some cheep shots.

....

What do you get if you cross a stork with Sasquatch?
A bird that stands on one big foot.

....

What do you get if you cross a rooster with a parrot?
A bird that yells, "Get up!" at the crack of dawn.

Society Sue: My pet canary is so spoiled she refuses to sing unless she's accompanied by a pianist.

Snobby Robbie: My pet dog is so spoiled, when I command him to sit, our butler has to pull out a chair for him.

....

What did Ms. Flamingo say to Mr. Crane?

Quit storking me.

....

What do you get if you cross a centipede with a myna bird?

A walkie talkie.

....

Why couldn't Mr. Goose buy a house?

He didn't have a down payment.

....

Which bird skydives out of airplanes?

The parrot trooper.

....

Hen: I don't have much of a nest egg.

Duck: Why is that?

Hen: Because all of my life I've worked for chicken feed.

....

What does a bird maid use to keep the nest clean?

A feather duster.

....

What do crows use to make their sandwiches?

Corn bread.

....

What did the mallard wear to his wedding?

A duckcedo.

Then there was the owl who became a mystery writer and penned several who-done-its.

What happens when pigeons have a hot coop?
They roost themselves.

NOTICE: Acme Bird Phones—We tweet you right!

What did the duck feathers say to the goose feathers?
It's down time at last.

Ollie: **I'm a wise old owl.**
Robin: **So, who gives a hoot?**

Knock! Knock!
Who's there?
Owl.
Owl who?
Owl be back in a minute.

DAFFY DEFINITION:
Bird nest: Cheep housing.

How does a crow know who's trying to contact him?
He checks his cawler I.D.

What do you get if you cross a pigeon with a bat?
A bird that roosts upside-down.

What do you get if you cross a rhino with a goose?
A bird with a horn to honk.

What do you get if you cross an owl and a coyote?

A hoot and howler.

What do you get if you cross a coyote with a rooster?

A canine that crows at daybreak or a bird that howls when the moon rises.

Knock! Knock!

Who's there?

Ammonia.

Ammonia who?

Ammonia bird in a cage.

What kind of bird insults people?

A mockingbird.

Where did the little bird go after elementary school?

To junior fly school.

Why was Mr. Duck upset?

His bill was in the mail.

What did Ms. Duck get after her nose job?

A big medical bill.

What game do mother hens play with their chicks?

Peck a boo.

NOTICE: Buy a duck feather iPod and get free down loads.

Which bird works at the construction site?
The crane.

What birds work underground.
Coal mynas.

Which owl has a band of merry men?
Robin Hoot.

Mr. Pigeon: I need to go out tonight.
Mrs. Pigeon: Why?
Mr. Pigeon: I've been cooped up at home all week.

How do you post a canary?
Use bird class mail.

What has feathers and holds up banks?
A robber ducky.

What do you call a couple of keets?
Parakeets.

Knock! Knock!
Who's there?
Wottle.
Wottle who?
Wottle I do now? asked the turkey.

What do you get if you cross a tortoise and a pigeon?
A turtle dove.

What do you get if you cross wooden shoes with song birds?

Dutch tweets.

What do you get if you cross ducks with popcorn?

Quacker Jacks.

What do you call a baby bird?
A chirp off the old block.

Mr. Duck: Are those new feathers?
Mr. Goose: No. It's hand me down.

What do you call an in air collision between two birds?
A feather bender.

What two birds are in the story of Alice in Wonderland?

Tweeter Dee and Tweeter Dum.

What's black and white and red on the bottom?

A baby penguin with diaper rash.

NOTICE: Birds snack on potato chirps.

Worm #1: What's the best way to avoid getting eaten by an early bird?
Worm #2: Sleep late.

What do you get if you cross a canary with a chimp?

A chirp monk.

Knock! Knock!
Who's there?
Egos.
Egos who?
Egos are big birds with keen eye-sight.

Knock! knock!
who's there?
who?
who who?
what are you, some kind of owl?

When does a black bird seek psychiatric help?
When it's a raven maniac.

Where do adult birds go for a friendly drink?
A crow bar.

What do you get when you clone a duck and cross the results with a hoagie?
A double ducker sandwich.

What do you get if you cross a tall pink bird with a roadrunner?
A flamingo-go-go.

Knock! Knock!
Who's there?
Hens.
Hens who?
Hens up! We've got you surrounded.

What do you call a wacky chicken?
A cuckoo cluck.

Knock! Knock!
Who's there?
A bird talon.
A bird talon who?
A bird talon fibs is a serious matter.

Knock! Knock!
who's there?
Wren.
Wren who?
Wren in Rome, do as the Romans do.

How did the goose earn a free vacation?
He accumulated a lot of frequent flyer miles.

Which bird was a star baseball player?
Chirper Jones.

Who has feathers and won the lottery?
The Lucky Duck.

DAFFY DEFINITIONS:
Condor: A prison entrance.
Goblet: A baby turkey.

....

Knock! Knock!
Who's there?
Robin.
Robin who?
Robin people is a felony crime.

....

Mr. Toucan: **Who are those two old birds?**
Mrs. Toucan: **They're my grand-parrots.**

....

What does a 300-pound parrot say?
Polly wants a cracker—so move it!

....

Who has feathers and is a basketball star?
Larry Birdie.

....

Mr. Vulture: **What's for dinner?**
Mrs. Vulture: **Leftovers.**

....

Mr. Vulture: **What would you like to order for dinner?**
Mrs. Vulture: **I'm not hungry. I'll just peck.**

Knock! Knock!
Who's there?
Wren.
Wren who?
Wren you're smiling, the whole world smiles with you.

....

Knock! Knock!
Who's there?
N-M-T
N-M-T who?
N-M-T nest makes a mother bird sad.

....

What has feathers and plays jazz music?
A Ducksey-Land Band.

Mr. Goose: **You talk crazy.**
Mr. Duck: **That's why they call me Wild Bill.**

....

Why did Mr. Duck have a lot of mouths to feed?
He was a bill collector.

What did the old tree say to the sapsucker?
Quick pecking on me.

Jack: Why are those storks flying so fast?

Mack: Maybe they're hurry cranes.

ATTENTION: A hen that invests wisely will always have a secure nest egg.

What happened to the flock of geese that landed in a hot spring?
They cooked their own gooses.

Where do pelicans shop for food?
At the fish market.

What has webbed feet and carries a gun?
A duck hunter.

Larry: I named my pet parrot Paulie.

Barry: Paulie want a cracker?

Mr. Goose: Dr. Duck, I think you're a quack physician.

Why do baby birds squawk a lot at mealtime?
You'd squawk too if your mother fed you bugs and worms.

What do you get if you cross a gopher and a robin?
A miner bird.

What do you get if you cross owls and mixed breed mutts?
Who curs?

What do you get when geese fly headfirst into a brick wall?
Goose bumps.

What do you get if you cross a magician and a canary?
A trick or tweeter.

What do you get if you cross a mime with duck feathers?
Quiet down.

What kind of pie can fly?
A magpie.

What do you get when you cross a crow with dynamite?
Caw-boom!

What does an owl say when its caller ID isn't working?
Who's calling?

What did the crow say when he saw three ears of corn?
Humm ... which one should I peck?

Horsey Ha Ha's

Which horses wear military uniforms?
Pony soldiers.
....

What did the racehorse say when the temperature reached 100 degrees?
I'm too hot to trot.
....

DAFFY DEFINITION:
Zebra: A horse in a pinstripe suit.
....

How can you prove a horse has six legs?
First count his back legs and then count his fore legs.
....

What do you call a herd of camels packed tightly together?
Humper to humper traffic.
....

Knock! Knock!
Who's there?
Cayuse.
Cayuse who?
Cayuse your bathroom? I gotta go.
....

What does a pony put on his deli sandwich?
Horseradish.
....

What do you get if you cross a giraffe with a thoroughbred horse?
Something that wins a lot of races by a neck.

How can you make a slow racehorse fast?
Stop feeding him.

Farmer: **How is my sick horse?**
Vet: **He's in stable condition.**

Why are horses bad dancers?
They have two left feet.

What do you call a male deer and a wild horse standing side by side?
A buck and bronco.

What's the quickest way to ship a small horse?
Use pony express.

Then there were the newlywed horses that checked into the bridal suite.

Mack: I heard you wrote a book about how to stop a stampede of wild horses.
Zack: Yes. It's a tale of whoa.

What do you call a vet with laryngitis?
A hoarse doctor.

What did the racehorse say to the stable?
Is my fodder in there?

DAFFY DEFINITION:
Centaur: a man with good horse sense.

DAFFY DEFINITION:
Thoroughbred racehorse: a barn athlete.

▶ ▶ ▶ ▶ ▶ ▶ ▶ ▶ ▶ ▶ ▶ ▶ ▶ ▶ ▶ ▶

Billy: When your young thoroughbred colt grows into a horse, are you going to race him?
Willy: Heck no! He's already faster than I am.

◀ ◀ ◀ ◀ ◀ ◀ ◀ ◀ ◀ ◀ ◀ ◀ ◀ ◀ ◀ ◀

SIGN ON A STABLE: We rent mules and donkeys, but we refuse to give kickbacks to our patrons.

▶ ▶ ▶ ▶ ▶ ▶ ▶ ▶ ▶ ▶ ▶ ▶ ▶ ▶ ▶ ▶

Tim: Pegasus is a flying stallion with wings.
Jim: That's a lot of horse feathers.

◀ ◀ ◀ ◀ ◀ ◀ ◀ ◀ ◀ ◀ ◀ ◀ ◀ ◀ ◀ ◀

Knock! Knock!
Who's there?
Mare E.
Mare E. who?
Mare E. Christmas everyone!

▶ ▶ ▶ ▶ ▶ ▶ ▶ ▶ ▶ ▶ ▶ ▶ ▶ ▶ ▶ ▶

What do you call a camel locked in a famous church in France?
The humpback of Notre Dame.

◀ ◀ ◀ ◀ ◀ ◀ ◀ ◀ ◀ ◀ ◀ ◀ ◀ ◀ ◀ ◀

ATTENTION: Camels have a dry sense of humor.

▶ ▶ ▶ ▶ ▶ ▶ ▶ ▶ ▶ ▶ ▶ ▶ ▶ ▶ ▶ ▶

Horse: Don't look so sad, Bronco.
Bronco: Okay. I'll try to buck up.

◀ ◀ ◀ ◀ ◀ ◀ ◀ ◀ ◀ ◀ ◀ ◀ ◀ ◀ ◀ ◀

SIGN ON A HORSE FARM: America needs a more stable economy.

It's Raining Cats & Dogs

What kind of work does a weary cat do?
Light mousework.

Which holiday do dogs like best?
Howl-o-ween.

Bob: Look. That dog is chasing his tail.
Rob: He's having trouble making ends meet.

ATTENTION: Our neighborhood is so bad our watchdog has a burglar alarm on his dog house.

Which state has the most cats and dogs?
Petsylvania.

What do you get if you cross a poodle and a guppy?
A dog fish.

What do you call a cat that casts spells?
A magic kit.

Don: Can I take a picture of your dog doing a trick?
Ron: Sure. Spike will gladly be a roll model.

What do you get if you cross a barking dog and the ocean?
Ruff Seas.

What did one cat neighbor say to the other?
Our neighborhood is going to the dogs.

Our neighborhood is going to the dogs!

Zack: What do you do when you take your pet dog for an automobile ride?

Mack: We put him in a cur seat.

Why did the pooch go into the clothing store?

He wanted to buy a houndstooth jacket.

Which dog marks test papers?
The Grade Dane.

What did the cowboy say to the two toy poodles sitting before him?
Get along little doggies.

Judy: Where are you going in such a rush?
Rudy: I'm running away from trouble.
Judy: You can't run away from trouble. You have to face it.
Rudy: You face him. Trouble is the name of our neighbor's pit bull and here he comes!

Knock! Knock!
Who's there?
Ken L.
Ken L. who?
Ken L.s are dog hotels.

Knock! Knock!
Who's there?
Tabby.
Tabby who?
Tabby or not tabby, that is the question.

What do you get if you cross spirits with mixed breed dogs?
No body curs.

Boy to Girl: My pet dog is so sophisticated he doesn't speak. He recites poetry instead.

ATTENTION: K9 police make dog collars.

Why do cats climb trees?
Because they don't know how to use ladders.

Knock! Knock!
Who's there?
Irish.
Irish who?
Irish your dog would stop barking.

What is the theme song of the president's dog?
Heel to the Chief.

what do you get if you cross a cantaloupe and Lassie?
A melon-collie dog.

Knock! Knock!
Who's there?
Coincide.
Coincide who?
Coincide and let the dog out.

SIGN ON AN ITCHY DOG: Welcome to the Land of the Flea.

Boy: My dog is a police dog.
Girl: He doesn't look like one.
Boy: He's doing undercover.

what do you get if you cross a fishing rod with a kitten?
A pole cat.

Why did the cat buy a computer?
So it could play with the mouse.

What do you get if you cross a kitten with crushed tomatoes?
Catsup.

What kind of dogs do angels keep as pets?
Saint Bernards.

What do you get if you cross a dog with a boomerang?
A pet that runs away, but always comes back.

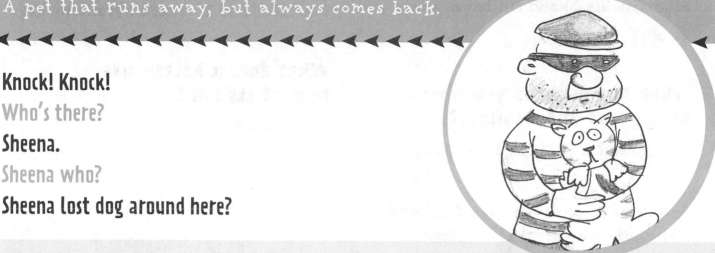

Knock! Knock!
Who's there?
Sheena.
Sheena who?
Sheena lost dog around here?

How can you tell if a cat burglar has been in your house?
Your cat will be missing.

Jim: My pet hound used to be a great hunting dog.
Tim: What happened?
Jim: Someone told him it's impolite to point.

Lady: I like this little dog, but I think his legs are too short.
Pet Store Clerk: They're not too short. They all reach the floor, don't they?

First Dog: Bark! Bark!
Second Dog: Meow! Meow!
First Dog: What's wrong with you? A dog doesn't say "meow!"
Second Dog: I'm learning a foreign language.

Knock! Knock!
Who's there?
Noah kitten.
Noah kitten who?
Noah kitten who wants to play with me?

What kind of pet does the Abominable Snowman have?

A chilly dog.

....

What do you get if you cross a hungry cat and a canary?

A cat that's no longer hungry.

....

Show me a snow leopard ... and I'll show you a real cool cat.

....

Ken: **Your dog has a loud, scary bark.**

Len: **Yup. It sure is a big, bad woof.**

....

What dog lives at a baseball stadium?

The catcher's mutt.

....

Knock! Knock!

Who's there?

Design.

Design who?

Design said beware of dog!

....

What do you call mail sent to female cats?

Kitty letter.

....

What kind of car has a motor that purrs?

A catillac.

Girl: Have you ever seen a catfish?

Boy: No. But I've seen a hunting dog.

....

What does a kitten use to part its fur?

A catacomb.

....

....

What did one itchy dog say to the other?

You scratch my back and I'll scratch yours.

....

When is it bad luck to have a black cat cross your path?

When you're a mouse.

....

ATTENTION: All young cats must swim in the kitty pool.

....

Why did Miss Kitty and Mr. Tom Cat get married?

They were a purrfect match.

WANTED: Trained cat to work with bird act. Must know how to keep mouth shut.

....

Knock! Knock!
Who's there?
Kit.
Kit who?
Kit busy and stop asking silly questions.

....

What does a cat put on a hot dog?
Moustard.

....

What do you get if you cross a lemon tree and a cat?

A sour puss.

....

What happens when a watchdog eats garlic?

His bark becomes worse than his bite.

....

What do you get if you cross a canine with a skunk?

A Scent Bernard.

....

Mack: How did your dog break his front paws?

Zack: He did it burying a bone.

Mack: Really? Where?

Zack: In a parking lot.

Then there was the sheepdog that got into trouble for crying "woof" all the time.

Girl: Why is your pet dog lying outside your front door?

Boy: He's our welcome mutt.

....

When is a bloodhound dumb?
When he has no scents.

....

What did the weary watchdog say to his master?

I'm tired of you making me sic.

....

Mother: **Our new pet dog can't sleep in the house tonight.**

Boy: **But we haven't finished building his doghouse.**

Mother: **Well go out and buy him a pup tent.**

DAFFY DEFINITION:

Greyhound: A stock cur racer.

....

They're a perfect match ... he's a watchdog and she has lots of ticks.

....

What did the French chef say to his pet pooch at meal time?

Bone appetite!

....

Knock! Knock!
Who's there?
Ty.
Ty who?
Ty up the dog before he runs away.

....

Knock! Knock!
Who's there?
Annette.
Annette who?
Annette is used to catch stray dogs.

....

What do you get if you cross a keg of black powder and a mixed breed dog?

Dynomutt.

....

What do you get if you cross a chili pepper, a gopher, and a pooch?

A hot diggity dog.

....

What do you get if you cross a cat and a cobbler?

Puss in boots.

Why was the little kitten so irritable?
She needed a cat nap.

Which feline always enters a room after a drum roll?
The tom-tom cat.

Where did the kittens go on their class trip?
To a science mewseum.

Chester: My parents got me a turtle for a pet instead of a dog.
Lester: Is having a pet turtle fun?
Chester: Not really. Watching him fetch a stick is kind of boring.

KOOKY QUESTION:
Do watchdogs get time off for good behavior?

What do you get when a pet pooch sees a ghost?
A dog fright.

Why was Mr. Doggie late for work?
He got tied up at home.

What do you do with a very sick dog?
Put him in an intensive cur unit.

What kind of parent does a mixed breed dog have?
A mutter.

Why did the boy give his dog a cell phone?
To make it easier to call him.

What did the owl say when he saw the kennel was empty?
Who let the dogs out?

Why was the old dog so happy?
He had a new leash on life.

Old Man: I'm taking our sick dog to the vet.
Old Lady: How can we afford to pay the bill?
Old Man: Don't worry. We have medicur.

Boy to Girl: My pet dog is a snazzy dresser. He wears a heavy coat in winter and pants in the summer.

How did the dog get splinters in his tongue?
He ate table scraps.

How do you make a dog dizzy?
Give it a tail spin.

What do you get if you cross a canine and a canary?
A doggie tweet.

 Which dog weighs the most?
The heavyweight boxer.

Boy: Where is my pet pooch?
Mom: He ran away.
Boy: That's a doggone lie.

Ken: I took my dog to a pet psychologist, but it didn't do much good.
Len: Why not?
Ken: My dog is so well trained he refused to get on the couch.

How did Tom Cat learn he was a father?
His wife sent him a certified litter.

What does a pet pooch use to write a letter?
A dog pen.

Lady: My pet cat has a live bird in its mouth.
Vet: What kind of bird?
Lady: Swallow.
Vet: Don't say that!

What do you get if you cross a rabbit and two cats?
Hare! Kitty! Kitty!

Knock! Knock!
Who's there?
I Major.
I Major who?
I Major watchdog run away.

What do you get if you cross a male cat with a giraffe?
A tom that peeps in third-story windows.

ATTENTION: Did you hear about the dog that went to medical school and became a famous heeler.

Uncle: How do you wake your son up in the morning?
Mother: I throw the neighbor's cat on his bed.
Uncle: How does that wake him up?
Mother: My son sleeps with his pet dog.

What did the dog say when he saw two tree trunks?
Bark! Bark!

Then there was the weary police dog who had a ruff day on the job.

What do you call a dog that is book smart?
A well read Rover.

What do you call an old dog that can't see?
A blind spot.

What trick do you get when you cross a dog and an acrobat?
A bark flip.

what did Momma cat do after kitty soccer practice?
She picked up her litter.

Lana: I have a very cunning cat.
Donna: What makes you say that?
Lana: She eats a piece of cheese and then waits by a mouse hole with baited breath.

Mrs. Dog: Do you want to go to the flea market?
Mr. Dog: Yes. I'm itching to get there.

Pat: **Look at all those happy dogs walking in single file.**
Matt: **That's the first time I ever saw a waggin' train.**

What kind of dog tracks down new flowers?
A bud hound.

Farm Funnies

Why did the herd of sheep call the police?
They'd been fleeced by a con man.

DAFFY DEFINITION: Shepherd: a sheep walker.

Why did Mr. Duck get arrested?
The police caught him quacking a safe.

What do you call a hen from Georgia who changes the color of her feathers?
Southern dyed chicken.

What do you get if you cross an armored military vehicle with a sheep?
Tank ewe.

What did the pig marshal say to the hog outlaw?
"Reach for the sty, pardner."

What do you call a cow that always has bad luck?
A barn loser.

What do you get if you cross a hog with a frog?
A hamphibian.

What is a pig's favorite ballet?
Swine Lake.

Lester: Is Shakespeare the real name of your hog?

Chester: Nah. It's just his pen name.

· ·

Farmer: **Do you know how long cows should be milked?**

City Fella: **They should be milked the same as short cows are.**

· ·

What do you get if you cross a lemon grove and a herd of cows?

Lots of sour cream.

· ·

What do you get if you cross a cow with a tiger?

Something that's too dangerous to milk.

· ·

Knock! Knock!

Who's there?

Eject.

Eject who?

Eject the chicken coop and all the hens are gone.

· ·

Rooster: Would you like to give a speech to the hens?

Duck: I'll take a quack at it.

· ·

What do you do after you walk up to the front door of a bovine's home?

You ring the cow bell.

what's pigskin used for?

To hold the pig together.

· ·

Why did the rooster stick its head in the sand?

It was a beachcomber.

· ·

Then there was the exhausted shepherd who couldn't sheep at night.

· ·

Why did the pig get a bad grade in school?

He had sloppy penmanship.

· ·

what do you get if you put a dairy cow in a garden?

Milkweed.

· ·

Why was the farmhouse full of rabbits?

It had central hare conditioning.

· ·

What do you get if you cross a pig with a truck that says "wide load?"

A road hog.

· ·

Knock! Knock!

Who's there?

Mule.

Mule who?

Mule be sorry if you don't open the door.

What do you get if you cross a toad and a pig?

A wart hog.

....

Why couldn't the good egg lend the poor rooster five bucks?

Because the egg was broke.

....

Bunny Breeder: Some of my rabbit are kind of old.

Dairy Farmer: Having a few gray hares is nothing to be ashamed of.

....

What do you get if you cross a holy relic with a bovine?

A sacred cow.

....

Knock! Knock!
Who's there?
Hence.
Hence who?
Hence lay eggs in chicken coops.

....

What did Barbie do when she directed the hens in a play?

Barbie cued the chickens.

....

Poultry farmer: I bought fifty mail-order baby chickens and they haven't arrived yet.

Sales clerk: Relax. The chicks are in the mail.

When do baby hens leave their hotel?

At chickout time.

....

Farmer: I own a skunk farm.

Reporter: Now that's a stinkin' way to earn a living.

....

Farmer: Do you want to hear how I started my rabbit farm?

Reporter: No. I don't care for hare-raising tales.

Mr. Bull: I'm falling in love with you.

Ms. Cow: The feeling is mootual.

....

Farmer: My donkey loves classical music.
Reporter: What's your donkey's name?
Farmer: Braytoven.

What sounds do you hear when you feed little chickens firecrackers?

Chick-a-boom! Chick-a-boom! Chick-a-boom! Boom! Boom!

Cow #1: Two bulls got into a savage fight yesterday.

Cow #2: Spare me the gory details.

Where does a hog leave its car when it takes the train to work?

In a pork and ride.

What do you get if you cross a pig and an angel?

Hog heaven.

Why do cows give milk?

They're not smart enough to sell it.

What do you call a sheep that squeals on her pals?

Ewe dirty rat.

What did Mr. Pig say to his girlfriend when he proposed marriage?

"Sty with me forever."

Mrs. Sheep: Anything interesting in tonight's newspaper?

Mr. Ram: No. It's all baa news.

Where do sheep get their hair cut?

At the local baa-baa shop.

Who was the strongest sheep in the ancient world?

Hercufleece.

Knock! Knock!
Who's there?
Ox.
Ox who?
Ox me nice and I'll take you out for ice cream.

Ram: A sheep that always butts in.

What do you call a sheep from outer space?
A Ewe-F-O.

Karate Pig: How'd you like a pork chop?
Boxer Sheep: No thanks. How'd you like a wool sock?
Tough Bunny: Knock it off before I rabbit punch both of you.

DAFFY DEFINITION:
Goat Herder: A person who likes to work with kids.

What did Captain Cattle say to Sergeant Steer?
Let's beef up our defenses.

What do you get if you cross a hog and a Texas lawman?
A pork ranger.

Then there was the dairy cow that started a lawn-mooing business.

What sound do you hear when you cross a cow with an owl?
Moo-who.

What did the umpire yell when the pig slid into home?
"Pig out!"

Tex: Was the All-Steer band any good?

Rex: Not really, but they had a good horn section.

▶ ▶ ▶ ▶ ▶ ▶ ▶ ▶ ▶ ▶ ▶ ▶ ▶ ▶ ▶ ▶ ▶ ▶ ▶ ▶

What do you get if you put a sheep in a steam room?
A wool sweater.

◀ ◀ ◀ ◀ ◀ ◀ ◀ ◀ ◀ ◀ ◀ ◀ ◀ ◀ ◀ ◀ ◀ ◀ ◀ ◀

Where do the Rockette Cow dancers perform?

Radio City Moosic Hall.

▶ ▶ ▶ ▶ ▶ ▶ ▶ ▶ ▶ ▶ ▶ ▶ ▶ ▶ ▶ ▶ ▶ ▶ ▶ ▶

Man: What do you do for a living?
Farmer: I raise female pigs and male deer.
Man: Is that profitable?
Farmer: I already have one hundred sows and bucks.

◀ ◀ ◀ ◀ ◀ ◀ ◀ ◀ ◀ ◀ ◀ ◀ ◀ ◀ ◀ ◀ ◀ ◀ ◀ ◀

what's the best way to keep milk fresh?

Leave it in the cow.

▶ ▶ ▶ ▶ ▶ ▶ ▶ ▶ ▶ ▶ ▶ ▶

NOTICE: Dairy farmers want to make moo money.

◀ ◀ ◀ ◀ ◀ ◀ ◀ ◀ ◀ ◀ ◀ ◀

What do Wall Street cows invest in?

Mootual funds.

▶ ▶ ▶ ▶ ▶ ▶ ▶ ▶ ▶ ▶ ▶ ▶

Elsie: Are you a newlywed cow?
Dulcey: Yes. I'm a honeymooer.

◀ ◀ ◀ ◀ ◀ ◀ ◀ ◀ ◀ ◀ ◀ ◀

what did the sailor say when he saw ewes swimming in the ocean?

Sheep ahoy!

▶ ▶ ▶ ▶ ▶ ▶ ▶ ▶ ▶ ▶ ▶ ▶ ▶ ▶ ▶ ▶ ▶ ▶ ▶ ▶

What does a rooster on a dairy farm shout at dawn?
Cock-a-doodle moo!

Why did the nanny goat quit her job?
She had too many kids to take care of.

◄ ◄ ◄ ◄ ◄ ◄ ◄ ◄ ◄ ◄ ◄ ◄ ◄ ◄ ◄ ◄ ◄ ◄

What do you call a goat that takes religious vows?
A nunny goat.

► ► ► ► ► ► ► ► ► ► ► ► ► ► ► ► ► ►

When do cows make the most noise?
When the feel moo-dy.

◄ ◄ ◄ ◄ ◄ ◄ ◄ ◄ ◄ ◄ ◄ ◄ ◄ ◄ ◄ ◄ ◄ ◄

What did the bull say to his horns after they were trimmed?
"Having you around is pointless."

► ► ► ► ► ► ► ► ► ► ► ► ► ► ► ► ► ►

What did the pasture say after the herd of cows left?
"I'm not completely shot. They just grazed me."

◄ ◄ ◄ ◄ ◄ ◄ ◄ ◄ ◄ ◄ ◄ ◄ ◄ ◄ ◄ ◄ ◄ ◄

Knock! Knock!
Who's there?
Cow.
Cow who?
Cow much longer are you going to put up with all this knocking?

► ► ► ► ► ► ► ► ► ◄ ◄ ◄ ◄ ◄ ◄ ◄

**what do you get if you cross a flock
of woolly animals and angels?**
Sheep in heavenly peace.

◄ ◄ ◄ ◄ ◄ ◄ ◄ ◄ ◄ ◄ ◄ ◄ ◄ ◄ ◄ ◄

What has four wheels, two horns, and give milk?
A cow on a skateboard.

► ► ► ► ► ► ► ► ► ► ► ► ► ►

Shepherd #1: **I heard wolves attack flocks at night.**
Shepherd #2: **So have I, but I'm not losing any sheep over it.**

What has a woolly fleece and is combat ready?
A battle sheep.

Did you hear about the two shepherds who became best friends even though they had mutton in common?

Where do young cows eat their lunch?
In a calf-eteria.

What do you get if you cross a flock of sheep with a steer?
A woolly bully.

Why was Ms. Cow upset?
Her boyfriend was in a bullfight.

Why couldn't the dairy cow give milk?
She was an udder failure.

What's the easiest way to count your farm animals?
Use a cowculator.

Where do bovines go to enjoy fun in the sun?
Cowlifornia.

Knock! Knock!
Who's there?
A cow pasture.
A cow pasture who?
A cow pasture house on its way to the barn.

What do you get if when you leave dairy cows in the sun too long?

Evaporated milk.

What do you get if you cross a bovine and an ocean marker?

A cow buoy.

What do you get when a herd of dairy cows is caught in an earthquake?

Milkshakes.

Len: **My uncle earns a living with his pen.**
Ben: **Is he a famous writer?**
Len: **No. He's a pig farmer.**

What did Mr. Pig say to Ms. Hog?

"I wanna hold your ham."

What do you call a pig that robs houses?

A ham burglar.

Where does a ham burglar go if he gets caught?
To the state pen.

Knock! Knock!
Who's there?
Sty.
Sty who?
Sty home from school if you feel ill.

DAFFY DEFINITION:
Pig Farming: A real pork grind.

What kind of express train did the pig ride on?
Ham track.

SIGN ON A PIG STY: Visitor porking only.

What do you call a slow hog?
Pokey Pig.

Who was the most famous royal swine?
Queen Pigtoria.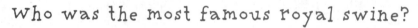

What do you get when a pig eats an herb garden?
Spiced ham.

What do you call a possessed pig?
Deviled ham.

Knock! Knock!
Who's there?
Pig.
Pig who?
Pig on someone your own size.

What do you get if you cross hogs and eagles?
The day when pigs fly.

What does a pig eat after a big meal?
An after dinner oinkmint.

What do you call a pig that gets fired from its job?
A canned ham.

What does a pig eat on a hot day?
A slopsicle.

What did the hog say after it laid in the hot sun too long?
"I'm bacon out here."

What did the hog farmer name his three silly pigs?
Moe, Larry, and Curly Tail.

What do you get if you cross a hog, a dog, and a Ferris wheel?
A piggy-bark-ride.

What do you get if you cross a pig with a fir tree?
A porky pine.

What do you get when a pig falls down a steep hill?
Pork roll.

What do you call a royal castle owned by a male deer and a little pig?
Buck and Ham Palace.

What does a pig bet in a game of cards?

Porker chips.

Mother Hen to her chicks at midnight: "Now go to sleep and I don't want to hear another peep out of you."

What farm animal comes in handy after a snowstorm?

The plow horse.

Zeke: I know a hog that ate 100 dill cucumbers.
Deke: That's quite a pickled pig's feat.

How do you safely handle a baby goat?

Use kid gloves.

Where does a pig go to pawn his watch?

To a ham hock shop.

Who has webbed feet and captures criminals?

Duck Tracy.

SIGN ON A CHICKEN COOP: No fowl language!

What do you get if you cross a pig with a gerbil?

A hamster.

Knock! Knock!
Who's there?
Aware, aware.
Aware, aware who?
Aware, aware have my little sheep gone?

What do you get if you cross a young sheep with a lumberjack?

Lamb chops.

What do you get if you cross a shelled nut with a ram?

A peanut butter.

SIGN ON A ROAD TO A SHEEP FARM: No ewe turns.

What did the sheep say to the ram?

Hey, move your butt!

What hen was the first chicken in space?

Cluck Rogers.

Sheep: I'm going to tell you about the most powerful sheep in history.

Goat: Oh no. Not more bleats of strength.

Why did the two flocks of sheep have an accident?

They rammed into each other.

Why was the rooster upset?

He couldn't find his comb.

NOTICES:

Acme Wool, Inc.: **We're a tightly-knit company.**

Acme Wool Products: **We're the best and it's the darn truth.**

The little pig who lived in a house of bricks: We made the Big Bad Wolf so mad he left in a huff!

NOTICE: All cattle in the American West have a brand name.

....

Why did Mr. Pig go to the casino?

He wanted to play the slop machines.

....

Why didn't the rooster cross the road?

Because deep down he was really a chicken.

....

What do you find at a hog mall?

Pork shops.

....

What do you call a chicken that eats hard clay?

A brick layer.

....

What do you get when a sow has a cranky baby pig?

The ham that rocks the cradle.

....

NOTICES:

Computer sheep use ewe tube.

Cows have Hay-T-M cards.

Crows have cawling cards.

Cavalry horses have charge cards.

....

What did Captain Pig shout to his crew?

All hams on deck.

What kind of bird insults people?

A mocking bird.

....

What does a bison bet in Las Vegas?

Buffalo chips.

....

How does a poultry farmer keep track of newborn chickens?

He makes notes in his chick book.

....

Knock! Knock!

Who's there?

Ewe.

Ewe who?

Ewe look familiar to me.

....

What happens when you talk to a cow?

It goes in one ear and out the udder.

....

CHAPTER 2

SCHOOL SNICKERS

What class did the demolition crew take?
Home wreckonomics.

. . . .

What do you get if you cross a teacher and a golf coach?
Book clubs.

. . . .

What comes at the end of a jail sentence?
A free period.

. . . .

Why did the clock get detention?
It kept tocking in class.

. . . .

What school activity does Jack Frost like best?
Snow and Tell.

. . . .

Teacher: Did your father help you with these math problems?
Student: No, teacher. I got them wrong all by myself.

. . . .

Knock! Knock!
Who's there?
Ivan.
Ivan who?
Ivan sent to the office three times today.

. . . .

Basketball Coach: Today I'm giving you a test on how to make assists.
Player: What do we have to do?
Basketball Coach: Just pass and you'll pass.

. . . .

Why didn't the biology teacher marry the physics teacher?
The chemistry just wasn't right.

Jenny: I'm reading a sob story.

Penny: Can I borrow it when you're finished?

Jenny: Yes. You're welcome to read it and weep.

....

Why didn't the French teacher ask the Spanish teacher to marry him?

He didn't know how to speak the language of love.

....

How do bee students get to class?
They take a school buzz.

....

What's the difference between a locomotive engineer and a school teacher?

One minds the train and the other trains the mind.

....

Why did the rabbit try out for high school sports?

He wanted to go to the Varsity Hop.

....

Why did the comedian tell school jokes?
He wanted to have a class act.

....

Teacher: Our president is married to the First Lady.

Girl: I thought Adam was married to the first lady.

Knock! Knock!
Who's there?
Alda.
Alda who?
Alda kids in my class are taller than me.

....

Boy: Do you get marks for laying eggs?

Girl: No, but they grade the eggs.

What do you get if you cross a math teacher and a clock?
Arithmaticks.

....

What English college did the bull go to?
Oxford.

....

What did the teacher say to the rabbit student?
Sit hare.

....

Why do elephant students always get good grades?

Because elephants never forget to study.

How does a gym teacher keep evil spirits out of the gym?

He exorcises them.

....

Gym Teacher: **What is your favorite aquatic sport?**

Student: **Channel surfing.**

....

What's the first class a snake takes in school?

Hisstory.

....

What do pig students bring home at the end of a semester?

Repork cards.

Why does it take snails six years to graduate from high school?

Snails are slow learners.

Why was the student Jolly Green Giant so sad?

He didn't do well on his pea SATs.

....

Zack: Why did you go to boarding school?

Mack: Dude! I thought it was a surfer's college.

....

Music Teacher: **Why did you sign up for violin lessons?**

Student: **I just wanted to fiddle around.**

....

Why did the sailor play high school sports?

Because he wanted to be elected captain.

....

Knock! Knock!
Who's there?
Weevil.
Weevil who?
Weevil heard enough about the Civil War for one day.

....

Cara: **Basket-making class is cancelled.**

Lara: **Why?**

Cara: **The teacher took a weave of absence.**

NOTICE: Troll Students are gnome schooled.

What comes out at night and hoots whom? What? Where?
A wise owl showing off his vocabulary.

Why did the baby genius take geometry?
He wanted to learn about formulas.

Why did the farmer take a math class?
He wanted to learn about square roots.

Student: Do you have any books on gambling casinos?
Librarian: You bet we do.

Jack: I read a book on how they made the Holland and Lincoln tunnels.
Mack: Boring!

In a Catholic school the librarian is a Sister. She's also an expert on nun-fiction.

Boy: Can you help me pick out some good books to read?
Librarian: I'm sorry, but this is a shelf-service library.

What flies around a kindergarten class at night?
The alphabat.

Which fish is always last?
The one in the after-school program.

Which cartoon skunk is a college bound student?
Preppy Le Phew!

Where did the smart cat go to college?
Purr-due.

What is Mickey's job at school?
He's the mice principal.

Mom: How did you manage to get an A in art class?
Daughter: I was picture perfect.

"Hi!"

Why didn't 2 go out with 3?
He was a little odd.

Boy: **Summer vacation is getting to be too short.**
Girl: **What do you mean?**
Boy: **It's not long enough for me to forget what I learned in school all year.**

Girl: **I want to take my college classes on a cruise ship.**
Advisor: **First you have to go to boarding school.**

Father: Did your chemistry teacher like your class project?
Boy: He loved it. In fact, it blew him away.

Why are fish great at doing math?
They multiply fast.

Teacher: **What was Samuel Clemens' pen name?**
Student: **Convict?**

Boy: **My teacher talks to herself.**
Father: **Does she know that?**
Boy: **Nah. She thinks we're listening to her.**

Teacher: Today we're having an I.Q. test.
Dork: Oh no! I forgot to study for it.

▶ ▶ ▶ ▶ ▶ ▶ ▶ ▶ ▶ ▶ ▶ ▶ ▶ ▶ ▶ ▶ ▶ ▶ ▶

What did the astronaut give the school bully?

His launch money.

◀ ◀ ◀ ◀ ◀ ◀ ◀ ◀ ◀ ◀ ◀ ◀ ◀ ◀ ◀ ◀ ◀ ◀ ◀

What do you do with a naughty principal?
Make him sit in a corner office.

▶ ▶ ▶ ▶ ▶ ▶ ▶ ▶ ▶ ▶ ▶ ▶ ▶ ▶ ▶ ▶ ▶ ▶ ▶

Why did the banker become a teacher?
She wanted to check papers.

◀ ◀ ◀ ◀ ◀ ◀ ◀ ◀ ◀ ◀ ◀ ◀ ◀ ◀ ◀ ◀ ◀ ◀ ◀

Johnny: I want to study sources of energy in college.
Lonnie: Maybe you'll win a fuel scholarship.

▶ ▶ ▶ ▶ ▶ ▶ ▶ ▶ ▶ ▶ ▶ ▶ ▶ ▶ ▶ ▶ ▶ ▶ ▶

Knock! Knock!
Who's there?
Will Hugh.
Will Hugh who?
Will Hugh all pass in last night's homework, please?

◀ ◀ ◀ ◀ ◀ ◀ ◀ ◀ ◀ ◀ ◀ ◀ ◀ ◀ ◀ ◀ ◀ ◀ ◀

Why wouldn't numbers 9 and 3 play ball against numbers 5 and 7?
Because the teams weren't even.

▶ ▶ ▶ ▶ ▶ ▶ ▶ ▶ ▶ ▶ ▶ ▶ ▶ ▶ ▶ ▶ ▶ ▶ ▶

Then there was the absent-minded conductor who
frequently lost his train of thought.

◀ ◀ ◀ ◀ ◀ ◀ ◀ ◀ ◀ ◀ ◀ ◀ ◀ ◀ ◀ ◀ ◀ ◀ ◀

How do you paint a research facility?
First put on a lab coat.

SIGN IN GYM: Watch your step. No class trips.

◀ ◀ ◀ ◀ ◀ ◀ ◀ ◀ ◀ ◀ ◀ ◀ ◀ ◀ ◀ ◀

Knock! Knock!
Who's there?
Water.
Water who?
Water you waiting for? Get to class.

▶ ▶ ▶ ▶ ▶ ▶ ▶ ▶ ▶ ▶ ▶ ▶ ▶ ▶ ▶ ▶

Father: **Does my son fool around in school?**
Principal: **Let me put it this way. He has a reserved seat outside my office.**

◀ ◀ ◀ ◀ ◀ ◀ ◀ ◀ ◀ ◀ ◀ ◀ ◀ ◀ ◀ ◀

Teacher: **Today we're going to watch a history lesson on TV and I don't want anyone changing the subject.**

▶ ▶ ▶ ▶ ▶ ▶ ▶ ▶ ▶ ▶ ▶ ▶ ▶ ▶ ▶ ▶

NOTICE: Student umpires who want to learn how to call balls and strikes are home schooled.

◀ ◀ ◀ ◀ ◀ ◀ ◀ ◀ ◀ ◀ ◀ ◀ ◀ ◀ ◀ ◀

Why did the architect become a school teacher?
He wanted to draw up some lesson plans.

▶ ▶ ▶ ▶ ▶ ▶ ▶ ▶ ▶ ▶ ▶ ▶ ▶ ▶ ▶ ▶

Why did the teacher bring birdseed to school?
She had a parrot-teacher conference after class.

◀ ◀ ◀ ◀ ◀ ◀ ◀ ◀ ◀ ◀

Where did the plum go to college?
U. of Pitt.

▶ ▶ ▶ ▶ ▶ ▶ ▶ ▶ ▶ ▶

Knock! Knock!
Who's there?
Sum.
Sum who?
Sum math teachers are harder than others.

What did the bully say to his instructor?
Go ahead. I dare you to teach me a lesson.

What does the person in charge of a school eat a noontime?

The principal meal of the day.

How much schooling did the famous detective Sherlock Holmes have?

Just elementary stuff.

Teacher: How did you like our lesson about the Atlantic Ocean?
Student: I couldn't absorb all of the information.

What do you call a TV set outside of class?
A hall monitor.

Girl: **What are you reading?**
Boy: **A mystery.**
Girl: **But that's a math textbook.**
Boy: **It's a mystery to me.**

Grandfather: How could you do so badly in history? I always excelled in this class.
Grandson: That's because there was less history to study when you were in school.

Teacher: What grade are you in, soldier?
Military School Student: Sixth, sir. But I'm expecting a promotion at the end of the year.

SIGN IN ART CLASS: Fingerpaints ... a hands-on activity.

What do you get if you cross a rat with a best-selling author?
A rodent with a lot of tales.

Student Chef: I took a course on how to prepare tender steak. It was a tough class to pass.

◄◄◄◄◄◄◄◄◄◄◄◄◄◄◄◄◄◄◄◄◄◄◄◄◄◄◄◄◄◄◄◄◄

NOTICE TO COMMERCIAL FISHERMEN: No school today.

Harry: I want to go to lumber school.
Barry: First you have to pass your college boards.

Why did the student with the flu have to stay after school?
His nose kept running in the halls.

What was the name of the Quiz Kid's father?
Pop Quiz.

►►►►►►►►►►►►►►►►►►►►►►►►►►►►►

Knock! Knock!
Who's there?
Gino.
Gino who?
Gino the answer to my question or not?

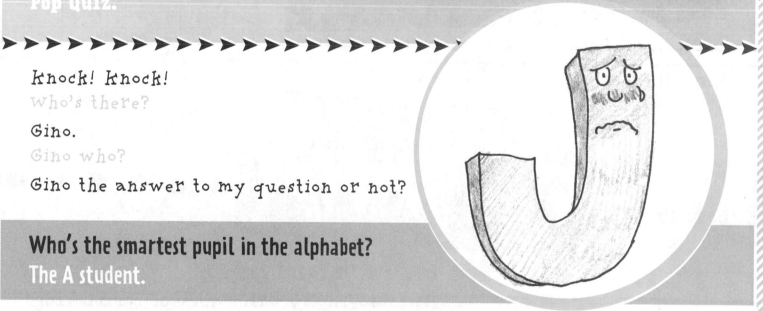

Who's the smartest pupil in the alphabet?
The A student.

Who's the saddest letter in the alphabet?
The blue J.

Which two letters of the alphabet announce who the smartest pupil in your class is?
I-M.

►►►►►►►►►►►►►►►►►►►►►►►►►►►►►

Why was the math teacher upset?
His son was a problem child.

What did the junior high basketball team do at snack time?
They dunked doughnuts.

Jack: My teacher always picks on me and makes fun of me.
Mack: So transfer to another class.
Jack: I can't. I'm home schooled.

Why was Miss Smith's class a total circus?
Too many of her students were class clowns.

Where do convicts go to college?
Penn State.

Business Student: I took a cashier's course.
Clerk: Yeah, so?
Business Student: Now I want to change class.

DAFFY DEFINITION:
Autobiography – the story of car making.

What do poker players do in art school?
They draw cards.

What do you need to pass med school? Lots of patients.

Why did the medical student get expelled?
He paid someone to doctor his grades.

What is the worst bug you can find in a medical school dorm?
The flu bug.

Lily: What are you going to do in the school talent show?
Billy: I'm going to pretend to be a bird flying.
Lily: In other words, you're going to act up.

Knock! Knock!
Who's there?
Adopt.
Adopt who?
Adopt my pen on the floor and it rolled away.

Bill: Did you climb the ropes in gym?
Will: Yes. For a few minutes I was alone at the top of my class.

Student: What grade did I get on The Old Man and the Sea?
Teacher: You're the Young Man and the C.

Latin Student: Are you good in Spanish class?
Spanish Student: Si!
Latin Student: Oh well, we can't all be "A" students.

Gym Teacher: Tomorrow we're going to jump rope.
Girl: Yahoo! I finally get to skip class.

Boy: Why did you drop out of remote control school?
Girl: There were too many clicks.

Boy: I'm a lot like my dad when it comes to school.

Teacher: What do you mean? You're dad is a businessman.

Boy: I know, but we both always need extra credit to get by.

....

DAFFY DEFINITION:

Addition Problem — Sum Fun.

....

What do you get if you cross teachers and lawyers?

A class-action suit.

....

What class does Mr. Soda Pop teach?

Fizz Ed.

....

DAFFY DEFINITION:

Drama School Play – a class act.

....

Why did the police detective go to school?

To investigate the student body.

....

Coach: Will you please pass the mustard?

Teacher: I show no favoritism at grading time.

....

How does an acrobat read a school book?

He flips through the pages.

....

What does teacher Santa mail to homes?

Christmas report cards.

....

Why did the geek take his report to the school dance?

The teacher told him to date his paper.

Why are teachers like bank robbers?
They both want everyone to raise their hands.

Then there was the large math teacher who wore plus-size clothes.

What is a kangaroo student's favorite part of the year?
Spring break.

What's yellow, has wheels, and attends classes?
Bus students.

Why did the dentist go back to medical school?
He wanted to brush up on his studies.

What did the fish give his teacher?
A crabapple.

Jenny: Why did you drop out of medical school?
Lenny: I'm sick of doing homework.

Why did the surgeon become a watchmaker?
He wanted to be a big-time operator.

What does it take to pass a course on intestines?
A lot of guts.

KOOKY QUESTION:
Does a gymnastics coach take roll call?

And then there was the history teacher who insisted on living in the past.

DAFFY DEFINITION:

Female Astronaut – a launch lady.

Ted: I got an "A" for cutting class.
Fred: What? How's that possible?
Ted: I go to barber school.

What do you use to catch a school of fish?
Bookworms.

What does a real-estate student do after school?
He has lots to study.

Where do rabbits go to medical school?
They go to Johns Hop-kins.

Robbie: Someday I want to help build the perfect fighting man.
Bobbie: Study marine biology.

Knock! Knock!
Who's there?
Anita.
Anita who?
Anita borrow a pencil and some paper.

Why did the caddy go back to school?
He wanted to study golf courses.

What do band students sit on?
Musical chairs.

Why couldn't the student flyer become a test pilot?
His grades weren't high enough.

What is a home-schooled student's first class?
Home room.

Why is a school like a kingdom?
They both have many subjects.

NOTICE: I don't mind being sent to the office so much … it's the principal of the thing that really bugs me.

What do you get if you cross a sorcerer with a class instructor?
A wiz ed teacher.

DAFFY DEFINITION:
School Library – a silence museum.

Why was the cat student given an award at the end of the year?

It had a purrfect attendance record.

Why is a schoolyard larger at recess than at any other time?

Because at recess there are more feet in it.

. . . .

Why did an alarm sound when a monk walked into school?

It was time for a friar drill.

. . . .

Student: **What do I have to do to graduate from this music school?**

Teacher: **Just pass notes.**

. . . .

Why did the girl get a bad grade in cooking class?

Her dog ate her homework.

How To Tell a Joke!

Making people laugh isn't as easy as it looks—though messing up a joke is incredibly easy! Comedians practice telling their jokes over and over until they have them just right. Follow these tips and your audience will be giggling and guffawing!

1. Know your joke by heart. Practice it out loud before telling it to your audience. And then tell it with confidence.

2. The lead up to a joke is important. Don't tell your audience you're about to tell the joke. Just tell it. Surprise is a big part of the humor. Also, don't tell them ahead of time how funny (or dumb or not funny) your joke is. (There's nothing funny about that.)

3. Practice timing your punch line. It's called punch line for a reason!

4. Provide just enough details so that the joke works. Don't overdo it.

5. Don't tell jokes you don't get.

6. Watch the pros tell jokes and mimic their styles while you develop your own style.

TEACHER SEZ ...

Today we're going to study about growing a garden. Take out your weeding books.

Today we're going to study pigs. Does everyone have a pen?

Today I'm going to put a new spin on computer learning. Take out your lap tops.

Today we're going to talk about death. And this will be on your final exam.

How does a clam open its hall locker?

It uses a seafood combination.

Boy: **Two of my classes at school are brothers.**
Father: **Which two?**
Boy: **Jim Class and Art Class.**

What did the teacher say to the pirate during the test?

Keep your "ayes" on your own paper.

Why did the bulldozer operator become a teacher?

He wanted to grade exams.

Knock! Knock!

Who's there?

Ozzie.

Ozzie who?

Ozzie absent from class today?

What's the best way to pass a chef's exam?

Cook up some great answers.

What do you call a teacher's assistant who's from another country?

Foreign aide.

What do you call a part-time music instructor who gives trumpet lessons?

A substi-toot teacher.

Teacher: What do you like best about bakery school?
Student: Roll call.

Why was the student sheep so sad?
She flunked her baaology test.

What did the gangster say to the wrong answer he wrote down?
I'm gonna rub you out.

Why did the carpenter sign up for math class?
He wanted to study up on home additions.

What do three classroom feet equal?
A school yard.

Boy: Dad, I think I'm in a dumb school.
Dad: What makes you say that?
Boy: On the road that leads to the building there's a sign that reads, "Slow School Ahead."

Hal: We're all going to join the school math club.
Cal: Well, count me out.

What did the computer say when the student asked it a homework question?

Search me!

▶ ▶ ▶ ▶ ▶ ▶ ▶ ▶ ▶ ▶ ▶ ▶ ▶ ▶ ▶ ▶ ▶

ATTENTION: No tennis classes — In-service day.

◀ ◀ ◀ ◀ ◀ ◀ ◀ ◀ ◀ ◀ ◀ ◀ ◀ ◀ ◀ ◀ ◀

Why did the military school student point his rifle at his textbooks?

His teachers told him to cover his books.

▶ ▶ ▶ ▶ ▶ ▶ ▶ ▶ ▶ ▶ ▶ ▶ ▶ ▶ ▶ ▶ ▶

Why did Romeo and Juliet study Spanish and French?

Because Spanish and French are romance languages.

◀ ◀ ◀ ◀ ◀ ◀ ◀ ◀ ◀ ◀ ◀ ◀ ◀ ◀ ◀ ◀ ◀

Teacher: **Start counting at five and keep going.**

Student: **Five, six, seven, eight, nine, ten, jack, queen, king, ace.**

Teacher: **Whoa! You've been watching too many poker shows on TV.**

▶ ▶ ▶ ▶ ▶ ▶ ▶ ▶ ▶ ▶ ▶ ▶ ▶ ▶ ▶ ▶ ▶

Knock! Knock!

Who's there?

Weird.

Weird who?

Weird you get the answers to this test?

◀ ◀ ◀ ◀ ◀ ◀ ◀ ◀ ◀ ◀ ◀ ◀ ◀ ◀ ◀ ◀ ◀

What kind of book should you bring to music class?

A note pad.

▶ ▶ ▶ ▶ ▶ ▶ ▶ ▶ ▶ ▶ ▶ ▶ ▶ ▶ ▶ ▶ ▶

What did the math student say to the algebra problem?

I just can't figure you out.

What did the math student say to the geometry teacher?
You know all the angles!

Why did the young teacher take diving lessons?
He wanted to work as a sub.

NOTICE: Then there were the two music students who fell in love and sent romantic notes to each other.

ASSIGNMENT IN A CHINESE COOKING CLASS: Do your home wok.

Boy: My teacher doesn't know the difference between math and grammar.
Father: What do you mean?
Boy: She keeps talking about add-verbs.

Teacher: Is Morgan Matthews here?
Melanie: Morgan is absent, teacher.
Teacher: Quiet, Melanie. Let Morgan speak for himself.

What has four wheels and discovered America?
Christopher Colum-bus.

What did the student give his music teacher?
A note from home.

Teacher: In order for their species to survive, animals must breed.
Student: Duh! If animals didn't breed, they'd suffocate.

SOME SILLY TEACHERS:

Mr. Mark R. Exams

Ms. Kim S. Tree

Mr. M. T. Halls

Mr. Tex Booker

Mr. Hugh Flunk

Why did the zombie student take Latin Class?
Because Latin is a dead language.

Why was the astronaut late for school?
He forgot his launchbox and had to go back for it.

Teacher: How do you think you did on the test?
Student: You'll be surprised. Mark my words.

What kind of essay does a tough judge write?
One that has lots of long sentences.

What has feathers and gives yearly physicals?
The school ducktor.

What do you get if you cross an addition problem with a rabbit's foot?
Sum luck.

What do you get if you cross an art teacher with a math teacher?
A color-by-numbers project.

What happened to Miss Cherry?
She graduated at the top of her sundae school class.

Teacher: What are the three words I never want to hear spoken in my class?

Student: I don't know.

Teacher: That's correct.

What color should a good book be?

A good book should be well red.

Knock! Knock!

Who's there?

Chauffeur.

Chauffeur who?

Chauffeur this semester I've received two As and a B.

What goes caw, caw, caw and does jumping jacks?

A crow-ed gym class.

Knock! Knock!

Who's there?

Luke.

Luke who?

Luke over all the notes I gave you.

What do you get if you cross an exam with a trunk?

A test case.

Millie: I went to school to learn how to shop better.

Tillie: What did you study?

Millie: Buyology.

Willie: I'm going to clown college.

Nilly: Did you get a fool scholarship?

What do you get if you cross a sheep with a clown?

Ewe make me laugh.

What did the school nurse say to the sick students at Clown College?

Remember, laughter is the best medicine.

Brad: I met my girlfriend at Clown College.

Chad: How was the romance?

Brad: It was a funny story of kiss, fight, and make-up.

Judy: How did you manage to graduate from Clown College?

Rudy: The teachers always laughed at my exam answers.

Why did a duck play the bass drum on the school band?

He was an expert on the down beat.

What do you get if you cross a clown college with a school for accountants?

Funny business.

How do you find a clown college on the Internet?
Google Giggles.

Knock! Knock!
Who's there?
Chuckle.
Chuckle who?
Chuckle make you laugh, won't you Chuck.

Professor: When I give a test at Clown College, I expect a lot of funny business during the exam.

What do you get if you cross a clown with Big Foot?
Laugh tracks.

Benny: How did you guys pass your test at Clown College?
Lenny: We crammed together for the clown car exam.

Knock! Knock!
Who's there?
I Rhoda.
I Rhoda who?
I Rhoda book and I hope it becomes a bestseller.

Larry: I wrote a book about rating basements.
Barry: What's it called?
Larry: The Best Cellar List.

Jim: I wrote a book about the Prince of England.
Tim: Did the publisher offer you a good deal?
Jim: Yes. I got a royalty contract.

....

Mick: I knew an author who wrote a funny book about wood carving.
Rick: What kind of book is that?
Mick: A joke and whittle book.

....

FUNNY FORGETTABLE TITLES:

BATHROOM HUMOR by Hugo Potty
OLD FURNITURE by Anne Teek
EASY DANCE LESSONS by B.N. Stepp
LIVING ALONE by Buzz Hoff
DIRTY JOKES by Anita Bath

....

What did the drum say to the drumstick?
You think you're so tough just because you can beat me.

....

What do you get if you cross a school band
and football spikes?
A halftime shoe.

....

Where does a cat band march?
In purr-ades.

....

What did the infielder play in the school band.
A base fiddle.

....

**What should you give a drum majorette who
skins her knee?**
A Band-aid.

What did Teacher Clock say to the student clocks?

Keep your hands to yourselves.

Mr. Bird: **What are you studying in school?**

Little Bird: **Owl-gebra.**

What do you get if you cross band members and sports fans?

Musical cheers.

Bessie: **What do the students do at Clown College?**

Tessie: **We just fool around.**

NOTICE: Clown College is the place where every student is a class clown.

Why did the cat go to Clown College?

It wanted to be a giggle puss.

Why did the hare go to Clown College?

It wanted to be a funny bunny.

Why is Clown College a pleasure to attend?

The classes are like a three-ring circus.

Why did the student take an anatomy class at Clown College?

He wanted to learn how to tickle the funny bone.

Knock! Knock!

Who's there?

Grin.

Grin who?

Grin you're smiling, the whole world smiles with you.

What animal is the mascot of the Clown College?

A laughing hyena.

Teacher: **How did you like the story of Dr. Jekyll and Mr. Hyde?**
Student: **It was good and bad.**

Art Teacher: This work of art depicts fall sports.
Student: What's it called?
Art Teacher: Collage football.

How do you get to be a cosmetologist?
Take a makeup test.

What did the dork study in college?
Geek mythology.

What pirate skipped school a lot?
Captain Hookey.

What do you get if you cross a sardine with a math teacher?
A herring problem.

Barry: **That parrot is talking about American history, math problems, and English literature.**
Larry: **That's because it used to be a teacher's pet.**

Why didn't the little nose like going to school?
Because everyone there picked on him.

Why did the mime student get detention?
He talked in class.

What did Buffalo Bill say when his boy left for college?
Bison.

How did the Hobbit learn to read?
He studied the elfabet.

What are the instructions for a mime test?
Words fail me.

Uncle: **I heard you studied art and logic at college.**
Nephew: **Yes. Now I'm able to draw my own conclusions.**

How do you become an A-plus carpenter?

Do a lot of homework.

....

NOTICE: Bilbo Baggins was gnome schooled.

....

Teacher: Have you read any Dr. Seuss books?

Boy: Hey! I'm a middle school student, not a medical school student.

....

Why couldn't the pig get a student loan?

His parents had a bad credit repork.

....

Teacher: George Washington went down in history.

Student: So did I. I dropped from a B to a C plus.

....

Mother: How do you like learning addition in school?

Son: Every day it's the sum old story.

....

What do you get if you cross a music teacher with a mechanic?

Someone who knows how to tune up a car engine.

....

Teacher: What did Caesar say when Brutus stabbed him?

Boy: Ouch!

Knock! Knock!
Who's there?
Ken Hugh.
Ken Hugh who?
Ken Hugh help me with my book report?

....

ATTENTION: Old school principals never get senile...they just lose their faculties.

....

Teacher: Why are you late for gym class?
Student: I sprained my ankle in the hall.
Teacher: That's a lame excuse.

....

Teacher: Why is your report on milk so short?

Boy: I wrote it on condensed milk.

Boy: **I added up these same numbers ten times.**

Teacher: **That's the way to check your work. Now what did you get?**

Boy: **Ten different answers.**

KOOKY QUESTION: If teachers are so smart, why do they spend the school day asking so many questions?

Preschool Teacher: Where does milk come from?
Little Girl: The dairy case.

Teacher: What are taxes?
Boy: Small nails.

Teacher: The law of gravity keeps us from falling off the earth.
Girl: What kept us from falling off before the law was passed?

Boy: My teacher can't read my handwriting.
Father: That's bad. Write more clearly from now on.
Boy: No, it's good. If I write more clearly she'll find out I can't spell.

Boy: Did you say ice cream?
Teacher: No. You always speak softly.

Gary: Did you hear the news? My algebra teacher just divorced your calculus teacher.
Mary: Humph! Go figure.

What kind of soup does a student studying for exams eat?
Cram chowder.

Teacher: How much is eight minus eight?
Student: I have nothing to say.

Denny: This new math looks fishy to me.
Lenny: Maybe they're herring problems.

Lilly: I heard that the algebra teacher likes the geometry teacher, but she likes the calculus teacher.
Millie: Gosh! What a wacky love triangle.

What did the algebra teacher say to the morning mist?
Dew the math.

Girl: I'm so good at jump rope class my gym teacher let me skip a year.

Teacher: What's topsoil?
Boy: A dirty word.

Teacher: What does it mean when the barometer falls?
Boy: It means the person who put it up did a lousy job.

Algebra Teacher: **And so in conclusion we find that X is equal to zero.**
Student: **Oh brother! All that work for nothing.**

What do you get if you cross a teacher and a lawyer?
A test case.

Teacher: Do you take the school bus home?
Boy: I'd like to, but it won't fit in our garage.

Music Teacher: Can you play the trumpet?
Boy: You're darn tooting I can!

History Teacher: When Abe Lincoln lived in Washington he had a goatee.

Boy: Gosh. Wasn't that a strange pet to keep in the White House?

▶ ▶ ▶ ▶ ▶ ▶ ▶ ▶ ▶ ▶ ▶ ▶ ▶ ▶ ▶ ▶

Professor: Today I'll lecture on the heart, liver, kidneys, and lungs.

Medical Student: Oh no! Not another organ recital.

◀ ◀ ◀ ◀ ◀ ◀ ◀ ◀ ◀ ◀ ◀ ◀ ◀ ◀ ◀ ◀

Marty: I have a sister and two brothers.

Teacher: Are you the oldest in the family?

Marty: No way. My mom and dad are older than I am.

▶ ▶ ▶ ▶ ▶ ▶ ▶ ▶ ▶ ▶ ▶ ▶ ▶ ▶ ▶ ▶

Mindy: How did you do on your pastry chef exam?

Cindy: I passed with flying crullers.

◀ ◀ ◀ ◀ ◀ ◀ ◀ ◀ ◀ ◀ ◀ ◀ ◀ ◀ ◀ ◀

SIGN IN A SCHOOL FOR STUDENT MIMES: Absolutely no talking.

▶ ▶ ▶ ▶ ▶ ▶ ▶ ▶ ▶ ▶ ▶ ▶ ▶ ▶ ▶ ▶

Teacher: Jamie your drawing of a stagecoach is very good, but it has no wheels. What holds it up?

Jamie: Outlaws.

◀ ◀ ◀ ◀ ◀ ◀ ◀ ◀ ◀

Teacher: Who are the Eskimos?

Student: They're God's frozen people.

▶ ▶ ▶ ▶ ▶ ▶ ▶ ▶ ▶

Teacher: Are all classrooms getting new blackboards before school opens?

Principal: Yes. We want every student to start the year with a clean slate.

Teacher: Did you read the book about trees I gave you?

Student: I leafed through it.

Sam and Pam walked into a deli. They were both philosophy students at a nearby college. When a waiter came over, Sam ordered a chicken sandwich and an egg salad sandwich for himself. After the waiter left, Pam asked Sam. "Why did you do that?" Sam grinned. "It's an experiment," said he. "I wanted to see which comes first, the chicken or the egg."

Fred: My health teacher said that exercise will kill germs.

Ed: I guess he knows what's he's talking about.

Fred: But how do you get germs to exercise?

Student: When rain falls, does it eventually go back up into the sky?

Teacher: Yes. In dew time.

Why do math teachers make good detectives?

They're great at putting two and two together.

A teacher asked her third grade students to write down what each one thought was the greatest mystery of nature. Barney Barns wrote that he thought a bear's coat was the greatest mystery of nature. "Why do you think a bear's coat is the greatest mystery of nature Barney?" asked the teacher. Replied the student. "Because God only knows where it's buttoned."

Who do you get if you cross a phys. Ed teacher and a famous western scout?

Gym Bridger.

Teacher: Do you know the name of this Scandinavian country?

Surfer: Nor way, dude.

Teacher: Are you going to finish your woodcarving project for art class?
Student: No. And let the chips fall where they may.

What kind of theology students wear ice skates?
Hockey prayers.

A college theology student was given an exam on biblical holidays. He was stumped by an essay question so he wrote; "Only God knows the answer to this question. Merry Christmas!" Three days later he got back his exam. Next to his essay question his professor wrote, "God gets an A, but you get an F. Happy New Year!"

Principal: **Why are your students buzzing?**
Teacher: **They're getting ready for a spelling bee.**

Teacher: Can you name the four seasons?
Boy: Pepper, salt, vinegar, and mustard.

Why was the inchworm angry?
Its teacher was making him convert to the metric system.

Why didn't the math teacher buy a farm?
He thought some problems might crop up.

What happened to the geometry teacher who became a sailor?
She got lost in the Bermuda Triangle.

"Class I want you to use the word 'bean' in a sentence," said the teacher.

"My father raised a bean crop," said the farmer's son.

"My mother made a three-bean casserole last night," said the chef's daughter.

"You're all bean brains," said the boy whose father was a comedian.

A pessimist is a student who puts a zero on his exam when his teacher hands him the test.

Why did the teacher let the firefly leave the classroom?

Because when you've got to glow you've got to glow.

A little boy came home from his first day at a new school. "How do you like your teacher?" his mother asked him. "I don't like her," the boy quickly replied. "But why not?" questioned the mom. "Because she told me to sit up front for the present," he huffed, "and then she never gave me the gift."

Lunchtime Laughs

Why wasn't the astronaut's son in the cafeteria?
He went home for launch.

....

Where does Jack Frost sit in the cafeteria?
With the cool kids.

....

Teacher #1: **I usually skip lunch and jog instead.**
Teacher #2: **I jog at lunchtime, too, but I eat on the run.**

....

When does a sandwich ask a lot of questions?
When it's made with why bread.

....

NOTICE: The food at the medical school cafeteria is so bad that with every meal you get a free prescription!

....

Where do math teachers go for their noonday meal?
To a lunch counter.

....

Teacher: **If you had six potatoes to divide between twelve people. What would you do?**
Student: **Mash the potatoes.**

....

Principal: **Why are you late for school?**
Student: **I'm not late for school, I'm early for lunch.**

What do you get if a ghost flies into the school cafeteria?
A food fright.

What do members of the school baseball team eat their lunches on?
Home plates.

What did the clumsy student say after he spilled his soup?
Don't worry everyone, lunch is on me.

What does a horn player use to brush his teeth?
A tuba toothpaste.

SIGN IN A SCHOOL LUNCHROOM: Ask for our senior discount.

Teacher: I'd like to know what's in the stew you're serving for lunch today.
Cook: Oh, no you wouldn't.

Student #1: What's the best thing to have in our school cafeteria?
Student #2: A brown-bag lunch.

The food in our school cafeteria is so bad the mice order takeout lunches.

What do dance school students drink with their lunches?
Tap water.

How did the plate get a crack in it?
It had a lunch break.

What do you call a young Scot who works in a school cafeteria? The lunch laddie.

Knock! Knock!
Who's there?
Mister E.
Mister E. who
Mister E. meat is what they're serving for lunch today.

What did the Abominable Snowman Lunch Lady serve to her students? Cold cuts.

Which is the best day of the week to serve hamburgers for lunch? Fry day.

What did the school bowling team order for lunch? Spare ribs.

What's a grumpy salad made with? Lettuce alone.

What kind of cheese did the lunch lady serve to the school basketball team? Swish cheese.

What kind of cake should you never eat for dessert? A cake of soap.

What is a down-to-earth sandwich made of? Ground beef.

What did the geometry teacher have for lunch?

A square meal.

What did the slice of bread say to the sweet roll?

Will you be my honeybun?

What is an author's sandwich made of?

Lots of baloney on write bread.

Where's the worst place to sit in the school cafeteria?

At the cruel kids' table.

What did the tennis player say to the lunch lady?

What are you serving today?

Why did the school principal hire a tightrope walker to prepare lunch?

He wanted her students to have balanced meals.

New Teacher: **Do they have good food in the school cafeteria?**

Old Teacher: **Yes. Until somebody cooks it.**

Cook: I'm tired of everyone kidding me about the meals I serve.

Principal: Don't take offense. They're just tasteless jokes.

How did the butter knife get into trouble in the cafeteria?

It kept cutting up at the lunch table.

Why did the dumb student eat a five-dollar bill?

His mother told him it was his lunch money.

What do you get if you eat your lunch too fast?

A meal ticket.

What did the leopard say to the lion when the lunch bell rang?

Save me a spot at our table.

Why did the student throw his lunch in the garbage?

It was nothing but junk food.

Knock! Knock!

Who's there?

Sieve.

Sieve who?

Sieve me a seat in the lunchroom.

What did the Drivers' Ed teacher have for lunch?

Park chops.

What did the math teachers do in the cafeteria?

They divided their lunches among them.

Student: For crying out loud! Are we having alphabet soup for lunch again?

Lunch Lady: Yes. Read it and weep.

Why did the dog go to school at noon?

He was part of the flea lunch program.

Why was the math teacher overweight?

Every day at lunch he added a few pounds.

Why did the student bring scissors into the cafeteria?

He wanted to cut the lunch line.

Boy: Does this cafeteria food taste as bad as it looks?

Girl: No. It tastes worse.

Knock! Knock!

Who's there?

Hiatus.

Hiatus who?

Hiatus lunch and now the school bully is after me.

Lunch Lady: Why do you have a pickle behind your ear?

Dork Student: Oh no! I must have eaten my pencil!

Smart Alecks

Teacher: Richard, find North America on the wall map.

Richard: There it is.

Teacher: Correct. Now class, who discovered North America.

Class: Richard!

....

Principal: Don't you enjoy going to school?

Debbie: Of course I enjoy going to school. It's the being there that bugs me!

....

Teacher: What do you want to get out of high school?

Student: I just want to get out.

....

Teacher: How would you find the square root of 144?

Student: I'd ask the kid sitting next to me.

....

Teacher: Robert, did you miss school yesterday?

Robert: No way! I didn't miss it one bit.

....

Teacher: Why aren't you using your pencil to take the exam?

Student: It's pointless.

....

Teacher: What are you laughing at, Henry?

Henry: Sorry, teacher. I was just thinking of something funny.

Teacher: From now on when you're in my class, don't think.

Teacher: How would you feed twenty people with ten apples?
Girl: Make applesauce.

....

Principal: Why don't you ever take any books home?
Boy: Because they're school books not home books.

....

Teacher: What can you tell me about the English Channel?
Boy: Nothing. We don't have satellite TV.

....

Principal: Do you come to school just to make trouble?
Bully: No. I also like recess, lunch, and gym.

....

Teacher: Do you know what the word extinct means?
Student: It means a skunk died.

....

Bob: What are you going to do during your summer vacation?
Rob: I'm going to review everything I learned in school the past year.
Bob: And what are you going to do on the second day of vacation?

....

Teacher: Take a seat. Rupert.
Rupert: Where do you want me to take it, teacher?

....

Teacher: Morgan, what do you consider to be the most important date in history?
Morgan: June 28th.
Teacher: What's so special about June 28th?
Morgan: It's my birthday.

....

Principal: Why are you always a perfect idiot?
Student: Everyone is good at something, and I also practice a lot.

Girl: Let's play school. I'll be the teacher.

Boy: Okay. I'll be absent.

....

Mom: Why is your report card soaking wet?

Son: Because all of my grades are below C-level.

....

Teacher: James! I'm happy to see that you've finally raised your hand.

James: Thank you teacher. Now, can I go to the bathroom?

....

Father: Gah! You flunked every class.

Boy: Well, I might not be smart, but at least I'm consistent.

....

Teacher: Does anyone know the name of the First Lady?

Girl: Eve.

....

Teacher: How long did Thomas Edison live?

Boy: He lived until he died.

....

Mom: Summer vacation is not the time to stop learning.

Son: Right. I did that the week before school ended.

Principal: You were late every day this week.

Student: That's not true. I was only late four times. The other day I played hooky.

....

Girl: Why don't you like history class?

Boy: It's always the same old story.

....

Teacher: Neatness counts on the test you just took, class.

Maggie: In that case, I should get a good grade. My paper doesn't have a mark on it.

Instructor: What's the most common cause of dry skin?

Medical student: Towels.

Father: Why do you hate the first day of school so much?

Son: Because it's followed by the second day of school and the third day and on and on.

....

Mother: Why are your grades so low after Christmas vacation?

Girl: You know how it is, Mom. Everything gets marked down after the holidays.

....

Teacher: What do you know about the Grand Canyon?

Student: It's America's greatest depression.

....

Teacher: How did you like our lesson about the Pacific Ocean?

Student: All of the facts are just starting to sink in.

....

Father: How did you find school today?

Son: It was easy. The bus dropped us off at the main entrance.

....

Teacher: Zeke, name six wild animals that live in Africa.

Zeke: Three lions, two zebras, and a giraffe.

Teacher: What comes before March?

Military Student: Forward.

....

Music Student: What are those papers the orchestra leader is looking at?

Music Teacher: That's the score.

Music Student: Oh. Who won?

....

Girl: I know English good.

Boy: I know English "well."

Girl: Then I guess we'll both do okay on the exam.

....

Girl: That's Mr. Smith. He wants to be a member of the school board.

Boy: I'm already a member.

Girl: What do you mean?

Boy: I'm bored with school.

Mother: What did you learn in school today?

Son: Not much. They expect me to go back for more tomorrow.

Teacher: Class! If you don't stop making all this racket, I'll go crazy.

Student: Too late, Teach. We quieted down ten minutes ago.

Teacher: What did you write your research paper on?

Student: On my laptop.

Teacher: Do you know what procrastination is?

Student: Ask me again later.

Bob: I didn't know anything until I started school.

Rob: Neither did I. And I still don't. But now they test me on it.

Teacher: Would you like to do some addition for me?

Student: I don't have a problem with that.

Mother: How do you like doing homework?

Daughter: I like doing nothing better.

Teacher: Why did you stop referring to that dictionary?

Student: Words no longer have any meaning for me.

Teacher: What do you expect to be when you get out of high school?

Student: Retired.

Teacher: What's a polygon?

Student: Something that eventually turns into a frog.

Teacher: How long does it take you to do your homework?

Student: About two hours ... three if Dad helps me.

Teacher: Why are you crawling into my classroom?

Student: Because you said anyone who walks in late gets detention.

Student: I don't think I deserved a zero on this exam.

Teacher: I agree, but it's the lowest mark I can give you.

Teacher: What's the difference between one yard and two yards?

Marty: A picket fence.

Robert: Teacher, would you punish me for something I didn't do?

Teacher: Or course not.

Robert: That's good, because I didn't do my homework.

Teacher: Did you think band practice would be nothing but fun?

Student: Yes. I came here to play.

Chemistry Teacher: What do you know about nitrates?

Student: Sometimes they're cheaper than day rates.

Father: I want you to have all of the things I didn't have as a boy.

Son: You mean like "A's" on my report card?

▶ ▶ ▶ ▶ ▶ ▶ ▶ ▶ ▶ ▶ ▶ ▶ ▶ ▶ ▶ ▶ ▶ ▶

English Teacher: Have you read much Shakespeare?

Student: No. I'm waiting for his new book to come out.

◀ ◀ ◀ ◀ ◀ ◀ ◀ ◀ ◀ ◀ ◀ ◀ ◀ ◀ ◀ ◀ ◀ ◀

Teacher: A noun is a person, place, or thing.

Student: Well, make up your mind. Which is it?

▶ ▶ ▶ ▶ ▶ ▶ ▶ ▶ ▶ ▶ ▶ ▶ ▶ ▶ ▶ ▶ ▶ ▶

Teacher: What will you do when you're as big as your father?

Boy: Diet.

◀ ◀ ◀ ◀ ◀ ◀ ◀ ◀ ◀ ◀ ◀ ◀ ◀ ◀ ◀ ◀ ◀ ◀

Teacher: Did you know Henry Hudson discovered the Hudson River?

Student: Wow! What a coincidence.

▶ ▶ ▶ ▶ ▶ ▶ ▶ ▶ ▶ ▶ ▶ ▶ ▶ ▶ ▶ ▶ ▶ ▶

Teacher: How many feet are there in a yard?

Boy: It depends on how many people are standing in the yard.

◀ ◀ ◀ ◀ ◀ ◀ ◀ ◀ ◀ ◀ ◀ ◀ ◀ ◀ ◀ ◀ ◀ ◀

Teacher: Billy Smith, all of the other students in class forgot to do their homework. Did you forget, too?

Billy: No teacher. But tomorrow I'll try harder.

▶ ▶ ▶ ▶ ▶ ▶ ▶ ▶ ▶ ▶ ▶ ▶ ▶ ▶ ▶ ▶ ▶ ▶

Teacher: Did your father write this composition for you, Marty?

Marty: No teacher. He started it, but my mom had to write the whole thing over.

Teacher: Who was Homer?

Boy: The person Hank Aaron made famous.

Teacher: Can you tell me how fast light travels?

Boy: I don't know, but it always gets here too early in the morning.

Boy: I know the capital of North Carolina.

Teacher: Oh, really?

Boy: No. Raleigh.

Sunday School Teacher: **The Three Wise Men followed a big star.**

Boy: **Oh! They were like biblical paparazzi.**

Teacher: Michelangelo painted the Sistine Chapel on his back. Isn't that amazing?

Boy: Big Deal. My uncle is a sailor and he had a battleship tattooed on his chest.

Teacher: I heard you went to the Grand Canyon on vacation. What did you think of it?

Girl: It was just gorges.

Teacher: Does anyone know Samuel Clemens' pen name?

Boy: No. And we don't know the name of his pencil either.

CHAPTER 3

MONSTER MIRTH!

Monster 1: I just devoured a gym teacher, a fitness expert, and an aerobics instructor.

Monster 2: Gosh! You sure eat a lot of health food.

- -

Where do you go to gas up a monster truck?
To a villain station.

- -

Monster 1: Last night I had my new neighbors for dinner.

Monster 2: How was the meal?

Monster 1: Great! They were delicious.

- -

Why does Frankenstein walk funny?
Monster wedgie.

- -

Why did the Frankenstein Monster go to a psychiatrist?
He thought he had a screw loose.

- -

Why did Dr. Cyclops close his ophthalmology school?
He only had one pupil.

- -

Who do you call to clean a filthy haunted house?
The Ghost Dusters.

- -

Ghostbuster: How much will you charge to haunt my boss?

Ghost: For ten bucks I'll scare the wits out of him.

Ghostbuster: Here's five dollars to do the job. My boss is a half-wit.

- -

What do you get if you cross hot oil with a wizard?
A frying sorcerer.

What do you feed a baby witch?
A magic formula.

What's ten feet tall, creepy, and glows?

The Frankenshine Monster.

NOTICE: Boris the Hangman always watches the nightly noose report.

Knock! Knock!
Who's there?
Logan.
Logan who?
Logan see if there's a full moon out.

Knock! Knock!
Who's there?
Zelda.
Zelda who?
Zelda house! I think it's haunted.

NOTICE: Big Foot drives a monster toe truck.

What did Godzilla say when he saw a NASCAR race?
Oh boy! Fast food.

Why did the Invisible Woman go to the beauty parlor?
Her hair had no body at all.

Harry: I'm tired of studying magic.
Wizard: Maybe you should rest a spell.

What's ghastly and cleans floors?
The Grim Sweeper.

Who haunts the chicken coop?
The Grim Peeper.

Knock! Knock!
Who's there?
I scream.
I scream who?
I scream tastes cool on a hot day.

Igor: Where did you learn to write horror stories?
Boris: In a little red ghoul house.

Why did Baby Frankenstein ask so many questions?

After the Mad Doctor charged him up, he was full of watts.

....

Why did Little Frankenstein go to the playground?

He wanted to ride the scary-go-round.

....

Show me a very sophisticated witch ... and I'll show you a charm school graduate.

....

Knock! Knock!
Who's there?
Weaver.
Weaver who?
Weaver alone, you horrible monster!

....

Which dinosaur likes to play golf?

Tee Rex.

....

What feat did the ghoul gymnast perform?

He did a cemetery vault.

....

Why was the Egyptian pharaoh in a time-out chair?

He disobeyed his mummy.

....

KOOKY QUESTION: Do witches and wizards participate in spelling bees?

What did Dr. Frankenstein say to his exhausted monster?

Lie down. You're in for a shock.

....

Why did the tough little ghosts get detention after school?

They were frighting at recess.

....

What weapon does Indiana Bones carry?

A boo whip.

....

Where is the best place to bury a monster?

In a fiendish plot.

....

What did the ghoul say when he saw a new grave?

Yo! I can dig it.

KOOKY QUESTION: Do monsters wear ghoulashes on rainy days?

Why did the ghost go to the pond?
He was a duck haunter.

NOTICE: Most ghosts like spiritual music.

Boris: Uh-oh! The Invisible Man is taking a shower.
Lady Monster: EEK!
Boris: Relax. There's nothing to see.

What kind of evergreen trees grow in Transylvania?
Frankenpine monsters.

Artifact Dealer: Would you like to purchase an Egyptian mummy?
Customer: Yes. And could you gift-wrap it.

What do you get if you cross Bambi with a ghost?
Bamboo.

What's green, slimy, and scares people?
Kermit the Boo-Frog.

What do you call a ghost who tracks down elephants and rhinos?
A big-game haunter.

NOTICE: Never lend money to the Invisible Man. He'll disappear with your cash.

What do you get if you cross a fisherman with Harry Potter?
Someone who knows how to cast spells.

what do you get if you cross a ghost with a rodent?
A haunted mouse.

What's creepy, clingy, and green?
The Frankenvine Monster.

Knock! Knock!
Who's there?
Shepherd.
Shepherd who?
Shepherd a monster outside.

NOTICE: Fashionable ghosts wear designer boo jeans.

Why doesn't death ever miss a phone call?
He has a grim beeper.

Why did Godzilla eat a volcano?
He wanted a hot lunch.

Why did Godzilla devour the Eiffel Tower?
He was in the mood for French food.

Why did Godzilla consume Alaska?
He wanted a cold supper.

ATTENTION: When Godzilla travels to Great Britain, he eats fish and ships.

▶ ▶ ▶ ▶ ▶ ▶ ▶ ▶ ▶ ▶ ▶ ▶ ▶ ▶ ▶ ▶ ▶ ▶

How do you measure a cemetery?
Use a graveyard stick.

◀ ◀ ◀ ◀ ◀ ◀ ◀ ◀ ◀ ◀ ◀ ◀ ◀ ◀ ◀ ◀ ◀ ◀

Who cleans up a dirty dungeon?
The torture chambermaid.

▶ ▶ ▶ ▶ ▶ ▶ ▶ ▶ ▶ ▶ ▶ ▶ ▶ ▶ ▶ ▶ ▶ ▶

Ivan: We'll have to do something about the hot-tempered monster you created.

Mad Doctor: Why?

Ivan: It keeps losing its head.

◀ ◀ ◀ ◀ ◀ ◀ ◀ ◀ ◀ ◀ ◀ ◀

Which letter of the alphabet turns into a monster when the full moon rises?
The Evil I.

▶ ▶ ▶ ▶ ▶ ▶ ▶ ▶ ▶ ▶ ▶ ▶

Knock! Knock!
Who's there?
Eerie.
Eerie who?
Eerie go again!

◀ ◀ ◀ ◀ ◀ ◀ ◀ ◀ ◀ ◀ ◀ ◀ ◀ ◀ ◀ ◀ ◀ ◀

Mad Doctor: How can I create monsters if I have no parts to work with?
Boris: Don't blame me if you're having an out-of-bodies experience.

▶ ▶ ▶ ▶ ▶ ▶ ▶ ▶ ▶ ▶ ▶ ▶ ▶ ▶ ▶ ▶ ▶ ▶

Where does the Abominable Snowman hide his secret money?
In a slush fund.

What is a yeti's biggest medical problem?

Cold sores.

What does a yeti put in his coffee?

Cold cream.

What did the yeti say when he found a frozen Roman soldier?

Oh boy! Italian ice.

How does Godzilla buy things at the undersea mall when he's out of cash?

He uses a depth charge card.

Why did Godzilla eat the burning apartment building?

He likes home cooking.

What did the people say after Godzilla devoured their apartment building?

That beast ate us out of house and home.

What does the Frankenstein Monster do when he runs short of energy?

He uses his monster charge card.

What did Godzilla say after he ate a dozen armored vehicles?

Tanks for dinner.

Why did Godzilla eat Fort Knox?

He wanted an after-dinner mint.

Where do monsters go to buy a used car?

In the Boris Car Lot.

Knock! Knock!
Who's there?
Karlof.
Karlof who?
Karlof your dogs, monster hunters. I surrender.

Boris: **I know a girl named Wanda who can cast spells.**
Igor: **Gee, she must be a magic Wanda.**

What creature did Mad Dr. Cheese invent?
The Frankenstein Muenster.

Mad Doctor: **Yesterday I created a rope monster.**
Igor: **Did knot!**

Monster: **My fingers don't work right.**
Mad Scientist: **I knew I shouldn't have used second-hand parts when I made you.**

Vampire: **Hello, stranger. Where are you from?**
Frankenstein Monster: **Parts of me are from New York, Texas, Ohio, Maine, Alabama, New Jersey, and other places.**
Vampire: **Wow, you're a real all-American guy.**

Movie Director: Your metal robot monster is too nice.
Mad Doctor: Can I help it if he has a heart of gold?

What is the Abominable Snowman's favorite treat?
Snowcones.

What kind of craft does a space ghost fly?
A BOO-F-O.

How do you clean a dirty space monster?
Chase it through a meteor shower.

....

Which sea serpent is very sloppy?
The Loch Mess Monster.

....

Invisible Man: I'm sick, Doc. I have a skin rash.
Mad Doctor: Don't worry. I'll clear it up.

....

Psychologist: Why are you sad, Ms. Skeleton?
Ms. Skeleton: I have no body to love.

....

What kind of candy do mummies eat after dinner?
Parch-mints.

....

Which mummy has a static problem with his wrapping?
Cling Tut.

....

Boris: That corn plant only grows when it's dark out.
Ivan: Maybe it's a night stalker.

....

What do you get if you cross a ghoul with a cobbler?
A creep shoe.

....

Why did the mummy wear a kilt and carry bagpipes?
Because he was Scotch taped.

....

Mad Scientist: I plan to create a giant rabbit monster.
Igor: Humph! Now that's a hare-brained scheme.

Knock! Knock!
Who's there?
Egypt.
Egypt who?
Egypt me when he sold me this phony magic potion.

NOTICE: Dr. Frankenstein overcharged his monster for his operation.

FRANKENSTEIN FRIGHT SIGHTINGS:

Beware! Here comes the Frankenpine Monsters and there's tree of them.

Beware! Here comes the Frankensty Monster and he's going hog wild.

Beware! Here comes the Frankensteam Monster and he's boiling mad.

Beware! Here comes the Frankenstair Monster and he's climbing up to get us.

Pat: I just saw a horror movie about a monster Leprechaun.
Matt: Lucky you.

What kind of vegetables do monsters eat?
Human beans.

Knock! Knock!
Who's there?
Ooze.
Ooze who?
Ooze afraid of monsters? Not me!

What is a monster baseball player's favorite movie?
The Rocky Horror Pitcher's Show.

Which mummy was a football quarterback?
King Hut!

Boy Ghost: What game do you want to play?
Girl Ghost: Hide and shriek!

How do you make a gingerbread monster?
Use weird dough.

Knock! Knock!
Who's there?
Weird.
Weird who?
Weird you hide the monster
you made last night?

Knock! Knock!
Who's there?
Wail.
Wail who?
Wail find your monster if we have to
search every inch of your castle.

Godzilla eats real submarine sandwiches.
Vampires hate stake dinners.

Boris: I penned a horror story about an axe murderer.
Ivan: Big deal. So now you're a hack writer.

Knock! Knock!
Who's there?
Talon.
Talon who?
Talon monster stories scares little kids.

Knock! Knock!
Who's there?
I'm Gladys.
I'm Gladys who?
I'm Gladys spooky story is finally over.

NOTICE: The old gypsy bank has fortune tellers.

Why did the monster go to the hospital?
To have his ghoulstones removed.

Why don't ghosts star in cowboy movies?
Because they always spook the horses.

Knock! Knock!
Who's there?
Ditty.
Ditty who?
Ditty see a monster outside or not?

Knock! Knock!
Who's there?
Sheena.
Sheena who?
Have you Sheena big ugly monster around here?

Monster #1: Grr! I'm really angry. The Mad Doctor who created me forgot to give me a brain transplant.

Monster #2: Calm down and I'll give you a piece of my mind.

◄◄◄◄◄◄◄◄◄◄◄◄◄◄◄◄◄◄◄◄◄◄◄◄◄◄◄◄◄◄◄◄◄◄

What do you get if you cross Sasquatch with a centipede.
A big foot, foot, foot, foot, foot, foot.

What's the first sounds you hear after Godzilla sees a flock of turkeys?
Gobble! Gobble!

►►►►►►►►►►►►►►►►►►►►►►►►►►►►►►►►►►►►

What does Godzilla do when he sees a flock of geese?
Chow down.

What does a creepy person get when he learns to fly?
A high ghoul diploma.

Which creepy general was the victor of the monsters' civil war?
Gholysses S. Grant.

Boy: How did you get a role in that new ghost movie?
Girl: I did well in the scream test.

►►►►►►►►►►►►►►►►►►►►►►►►►►►►►►►►►►►►

How did the ghost keep his haunted house?
In a frightful mess.

What do you get if you cross a dinosaur with the ruler of the Emerald City?
The Giant Lizard of Oz.

Which dinosaur loves to wear plaid clothing?

Tyrannosaurus Chex.

What makes dinosaurs itch and scratch?

A fleahistoric bug.

Who is the biggest dinosaur crook?

The Gangsta' Raptor.

What do you get if you cross a wild horse with a dinosaur?

A Broncosaurus.

Yeti: Did you date the Abominable Snowgirl?

Sasquatch: No. I asked her out, but she gave me the cold shoulder.

Witch: The stick of my magic broom is broken.

Wizard: Don't worry, I'll handle it.

Ghost pirate: How will I know where the treasure is buried?

Sea witch: That's easy. Hex marks the spot.

What kind of horse does a cowboy ghost ride?

A night mare.

Knock! Knock!

Who's there?

Wilma.

Wilma who?

Wilma howling keep you awake all night?

Mother Witch to Daughter: If you don't study hard at charm school, you'll never learn to spell correctly.

What kind of weapon does a witch from space use?

A hex-ray gun.

What do you get when you cross cheddar cheese with a sorcerer?

Cheese Whiz.

Where's the best place for a mummy to live?

In an old, old, old, old, old age home.

....

what do ghosts eat with roast beef and gravy?

Monster mash potatoes.

....

Why didn't the mummy take a vacation?

He was wrapped up in his work.

....

What does a construction ghost drive?

A boodozer.

....

What does BFF mean to a monster?

Beast Friends Forever.

....

what kind of novels does the Abominable Snowman write?

Chilling tales of suspense.

....

What does a yeti grow in his Himalayan garden?

Llama beans.

....

How does a dumb monster count up to fifteen?

It uses its fingers.

Dracula: I'll see you later.
Invisible Man: No you won't.

....

What zombie makes marital arts movies?

Dead Lee.

....

How do you produce a zombie song?

Kill the music.

....

What do you put on a zombie wanted poster?

Wanted Dead or Not Alive.

....

Where does a zombie keep a skeleton bird?

In a rib cage.

Vampires

What do you call a two-headed vampire?

A twilight double header.

What do you call Dracula's unruly children?

Vampire brats.

What happened to the vampire grape who got caught out in the sun?

He turned into a raisin.

When does Dracula visit with his children's teachers?

On bat-to-school night.

Vampire: How much did you pay for the lining in the bottom of your coffin?
Dracula: I got it dirt cheap.

Knock! Knock!
Who's there?
Zealous.
Zealous who?
Zealous an amulet to protect us from vampires.

Which vampire flew a kite during a thunderstorm?
Benjamin Fanglin.

When do vampires attack geeks and dweebs?
On dork nights.

Villager 1: Do you think we can burn down Dracula's castle and get away with it?

Villager 2: Yes. But it'll be a torch and go situation.

- -

Show me a vampire who loves to play golf ... and I'll show you a monster who enjoys night clubbing.

- -

What did Judge Dracula say as he got into his coffin at daybreak?

It's time to close this case.

- -

Which vampire whines too much?

Pout Dracula.

- -

What does a vampire wear on his head when he flies around?

A batting helmet.

- -

How does a gal vampire flirt with a guy vampire?

She bats her eyelashes at him.

- -

Igor: **Is Dracula a conceited vampire?**

Boris: Yes. He's a vein monster.

- -

SIGN ON A VAMPIRE FAST FOOD STORE: Stop in for a quick bite!

- -

Why did the school ghoul get her vampire addition problem wrong?

Because she didn't count Dracula.

- -

What do you get if you cross Dracula with a cashier?

Count Yourchange.

NOTICE: Vampires who play baseball like to go to batting cages.

Who is Count Dracula's favorite superhero?
Vampire Batman.

Boris: Why is that baby vampire chewing on your neck?
Bride of Dracula: He's teething.

Nurse: What is your blood type?
Vampire: I'm not fussy. I'll drink anything.

Who is the leader of the vampire ducks?
Count Down.

Why did the girl go to the doctor after her date with Dracula?
He gave her a sore throat.

Does Dracula like sailboats?
No. But he's very fond of blood vessels.

Villager: We know you sleep in a coffin filled with the soil of your native land.
Dracula: That's a dirty lie!

Igor: I just saw a ten foot vampire.
Boris: Now that's unusual. Most vampires only have two feet.

What do vampire bats order at I-Hop?
Flapjacks.

NOTICE:

Where is the most dangerous place to live in Transylvania?
Necks-door to Count Dracula.

NOTICE: **Mr. & Mrs. Vampire have undying love for each other.**

Knock! Knock!
Who's there?
Dewey.
Dewey who?
Dewey have enough garlic to repel a vampire attack?

What makes an African vampire bat very happy?
Flying into a herd of giraffes.

Why did the vampire bat fly into a cave?
She wanted to hang out with her friends.

What is one job a vampire can never have?
A day laborer.

What do you call two male vampires who have the same mother?
Blood brothers.

Igor: **Why are you doing somersaults?**
Vampire: **I'm training to be an acro-bat.**

What do you call a baby vampire who is too little to walk?
A night crawler.

What do you get if you cross a vampire bat with a pig?
A hampire.

▶ ▶ ▶ ▶ ▶ ▶ ▶ ▶ ▶ ▶ ▶ ▶ ▶ ▶ ▶ ▶

Which vampire is always on a diet?
Count Calories.

◀ ◀ ◀ ◀ ◀ ◀ ◀ ◀ ◀ ◀ ◀ ◀ ◀ ◀ ◀ ◀

Where do vampires play tennis?
At a night court.

▶ ▶ ▶ ▶ ▶ ▶ ▶ ▶ ▶ ▶ ▶ ▶ ▶ ▶ ▶ ▶

Why did the vampire take an art class?
He wanted to learn how to draw blood.

◀ ◀ ◀ ◀ ◀ ◀ ◀ ◀ ◀ ◀ ◀ ◀ ◀ ◀ ◀ ◀

What do you call a vampire who can stalk victims for twenty-four hours straight?
An all-day sucker.

▶ ▶ ▶ ▶ ▶ ▶ ▶ ▶ ▶ ▶ ▶ ▶ ▶ ▶ ▶ ▶

NOTICE: **Being a vampire is a fly-by-night occupation.**

◀ ◀ ◀ ◀ ◀ ◀ ◀ ◀ ◀ ◀ ◀ ◀ ◀ ◀ ◀ ◀

Knock! Knock!
Who's there?
Welcome.
Welcome who?
Welcome to your rescue if vampires attack.

▶ ▶ ▶ ▶ ▶ ▶ ▶ ▶ ▶ ▶ ▶

What happened when the clock saw a vampire bat?
It became alarmed.

◀ ◀ ◀ ◀ ◀ ◀ ◀ ◀ ◀ ◀ ◀

What do you get if you cross a vampire with soda pop?
Count Dracola.

Knock! Knock!
Who's there?
Wheelbarrow.
Wheelbarrow who?
Wheelbarrow your bloodhounds to track down Dracula.

▶ ▶ ▶ ▶ ▶ ▶ ▶ ▶ ▶ ▶ ▶ ▶ ▶ ▶ ▶ ▶ ▶

NOTICE: When it comes to trusting creatures of the night, never stick your neck out for a vampire.

◀ ◀ ◀ ◀ ◀ ◀ ◀ ◀ ◀ ◀ ◀ ◀ ◀ ◀ ◀ ◀ ◀

Knock! Knock!
Who's there?
Achoo.
Achoo who?
Achoo on people's necks, said the vampire.

▶ ▶ ▶ ▶ ▶ ▶ ▶ ▶ ▶ ▶ ▶ ▶ ▶ ▶ ▶ ▶ ▶

What is Santa Vampire's favorite kind of blood?
Type O-O-O.

◀ ◀ ◀ ◀ ◀ ◀ ◀ ◀ ◀ ◀ ◀ ◀ ◀ ◀ ◀ ◀ ◀

Where do chicken vampires live?
In Hensylvania.

▶ ▶ ▶ ▶ ▶ ▶ ▶ ▶ ▶ ▶ ▶ ▶ ▶ ▶ ▶ ▶ ▶

NOTICE: **Hobo vampires have been known to hop on fright trains.**

◀ ◀ ◀ ◀ ◀ ◀ ◀ ◀ ◀ ◀ ◀ ◀ ◀ ◀ ◀ ◀ ◀

What do you get if you cross a large bell with a vampire?
A ding bat.

▶ ▶ ▶ ▶ ▶ ▶ ▶ ▶ ▶ ▶ ▶ ▶ ▶ ▶ ▶ ▶ ▶

What is a baby vampire's favorite game?
Batty-cake.

◀ ◀ ◀ ◀ ◀ ◀ ◀ ◀ ◀ ◀ ◀ ◀ ◀ ◀ ◀ ◀ ◀

Why did the vampire bite a light bulb?
He wanted brighter teeth.

How do you prove a vampire can turn into a bat?
Give it a fly detector test.

Knock! Knock!
Who's there?
Shirley.
Shirley who?
Shirley you're not afraid of vampires.

Why was the young vampire unhappy?
He needed braces.

Why did Dracula go to the hospital lab?
He wanted to get some blood work.

NOTICE: Actors who always play vampires are blood type cast.

Knock! Knock!
Who's there?
Menu.
Menu who?
Menu see Count Dracula, protect your neck.

What did Dracula ask the vampire?
Are you a blood relative?

What do you get if you cross Dracula with a bad boxer?
Count Meout.

Knock! Knock!

Who's there?

Harold.

Harold who?

Harold is Count Dracula? I bet he's at least one hundred years old.

What do you get if you cross Dracula with Sir Lancelot?

A bite in shining armor.

FLASH! Then there was the dumb vampire who cheated on his blood test.

What did Dracula get when he bit the Abominable Snowman?

Frost bite.

Knock! Knock!

Who's there?

Cheese.

Cheese who?

Cheese kind of cute even if she is a vampire.

What's the fastest way to destroy a vampire?

Use a minute stake.

What happened when a vampire bumped into the Abominable Snowman?

Frost bite.

What's the tallest structure in Transylvania?

The Vampire State Building.

Why doesn't Godzilla eat vampires?
They leave a bat taste in his mouth.

Knock! Knock!

Who's there?

Cement.

Cement who?

Cement to scream when she saw Dracula, but she fainted instead.

What do you call a dead pharaoh lying next to a sleeping vampire?
Mummy and Batty.

Why does Count Dracula use mouthwash?

He has bat breath.

Why did the witch divorce her vampire husband?
The magic had gone out of their relationship.

What is a vampire's favorite game?

Batminton.

What happens when vampires visit
New York City?

They take a bite out of the Big Apple.

NOTICE: Count Dracula is a graduate of night school.

Reporter: Do you like playing vampires in every movie you make?

Actor: Yes. Acting's in my blood.

What did the mother vampire tell the baby vampire at meal time?

Take little bites.

NOTICE: Dracula has a bat reputation.

What are the two things Dracula takes with him when he travels light?

His casket and his toothbrush.

Werewolf: I just insured key parts of my body. See this clawed hand. It's insured for a thousand dollars.

Vampire: Wow! So that's your grand paw!

Why did the vampire climb out on the barn roof?

To get to the weather vein.

FLASH! Count Dracula's victim walked off the set of a big horror movie because the director only gave her a bit part.

What do you get if you cross a vampire with a Brontosaurus?
A monster that sleeps in the biggest coffin you ever saw.

....

What's the most dangerous job in Transylvania?
Being Dracula's orthodontist.

....

Why did Dracula pal around with Frankenstein?
He wanted a friend he could look up to.

....

Knock! Knock!
Who's there?
Vein.
Vein who?
Vein you go to Dracula's castle be sure to wear garlic around your neck.

....

Why did Dracula run out of the garden?
He saw sunflowers coming up.

....

Knock! knock!
Who's there?
Doughnut.
Doughnut who?
Doughnut go to
Dracula's castle
after sunset.

....

**What did the
vampire have for
dessert?**
Veinilla ice cream.

What's the difference between a senior citizen and an old vampire?
At night a senior citizen's teeth come out and that's when an old vampires teeth go in.

Where does hypnotist Dracula live?
In Trancelvania.

Why did the vampire join the circus?
He wanted to be a jugular.

What month does Count Dracula like best?
Noveinber.

Zack: Did you hear the joke about Dracula's teeth?
Mack: No.
Zack: Never mind. You wouldn't get the point.

Knock! Knock!
Who's there?
Lena.
Lena who?
Lena little closer. I want to bite your neck.

* COUGH *
* COUGH *

Why is the vampire family so close?
Because blood is thicker than water.

Why did Dracula take cough medicine?
To stop his coffin.

Son: Mom, am I really a vampire?
Mother: We'll talk about that later, son. The sun is rising. Now close your coffin and go to sleep.

What do you get if you cross a giant vampire with a hairy beast?
A big bat wolf.

What kind of soup does a vampire eat?
Alpha-bat soup.

What did Mrs. Vampire say to her son at dinnertime?
Take small bites, son.

Zombies

What's another name for Attila the Zombie?
The Hun-Dead.

Where do zombies go swimming?
In the Dead Sea.

What did one zombie say to the other?
We're a dying breed.

Why did Mrs. Zombie join a monster health club?
She was starting to lose her ghoulish figure.

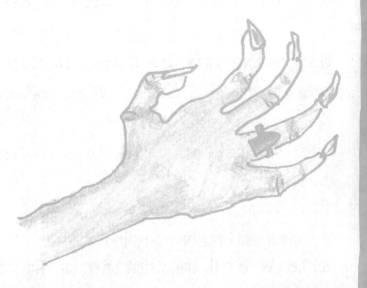

Boris: Does Mrs. Zombie's wedding ring have a diamond in it?
Igor: No. It has a tombstone.

Why was Mr. Zombie so carefree?
He never had to worry about cost-of-living expenses.

What did the boy zombie say to the pretty girl zombie?
I've been dying to go out with you.

What did the zombie say to the funny comedian?
Stop! Your jokes are killing me.

When did the phone turn into a zombie?
After the line went dead.

What's the worst job to have in zombie land?
Selling life insurance.

What did one zombie surfer say to the other zombie surfer?
Get a life, dude!

What do male zombies splash on their faces when they wake up?
After grave lotion.

Zombie #1: **You look exhausted.**
Zombie #2: **I'm so tired I'm dead on my feet.**

What game do zombie kids like to play?
Corpse and robbers.

How did the zombie make his house burglar-proof?
He put deadbolt locks on all the doors.

What's one thing a zombie can never be at a social gathering?

The life of the party.

ATTENTION: Zombie pirate captain needs a skeleton crew to sail his ghost ship.

Boy Zombie: **If you don't go out with me, I'll just die.**

Girl Zombie: **It's a little late for that.**

NOTICE: Zombie appliances don't come with a lifetime guarantee.

Monster Hunter: For your crimes, Mr. Zombie, we plan to rebury you.

Zombie: Humph! Don't think I'm going to accept this punishment lying down.

What position did the zombie play on the football team?

Dead end.

Where did the zombie finish in the Boston marathon?

Dead last.

Where did the zombie family go camping?

In Death Valley.

DEFINITION: Zombie — a person with a bad life-insurance policy.

Why can't a zombie write an autobiography?

He has no life story.

What's one thing you never find in the home of a zombie?

Living-room furniture.

Why did the zombie go to a psychologist?

He had grave problems.

What happens when a zombie graduates from college?

Everyone mourns his passing.

....

When did the watch maker become a zombie?

When his time was up.

....

When did John Deere become a zombie?

When he bought the farm.

....

When did the fisherman become a zombie?

When he reached the end of the line.

....

What do you get if you cross a snail with a zombie?

Slow death.

....

What do you get if you cross zombies with a library.

Dead silence.

....

Where do zombies reside?

On dead end streets.

....

What did the zombie say to the judge at the end of his trial?

Please, your honor, give me a life sentence.

Knock! Knock!

Who's there?

Zombies.

Zombies who?

Zombies gather honey while others guard the hive.

....

NOTICE: Zombie actors refuse to perform in front of a live audience.

....

What did the zombie say when a voodoo witch doctor jumped out of the shadows?

Gosh! You scared the life out of me.

....

When did the hairdresser become a zombie?

After she dyed.

When did the football player become a zombie?
After he kicked off.

When did the frogman become a zombie?
After he croaked.

When did the door maker become a zombie?
After he got knocked off.

When did the quarterback become a zombie?
After he passed.

When did the cowboy become a zombie?
After the last roundup.

When did the jogger become a zombie?
After his final race was run.

When did the desk clerk become a zombie?
After he checked out for the last time.

Ghoul: Are you going to that new horror play?
Zombie: No. I wouldn't be caught dead in the audience.

Artist #1: I'd like to paint a zombie.
Artist #2: Why risk having a brush with death?

Igor: Is that a zombie goose?
Boris: No. It's just a dead duck.

Why couldn't the zombie go for a boat ride?
He refused to wear a life jacket.

Mad Doctor: Is there a law against creating zombies?
Policeman: Yes. And there's a stiff penalty for breaking it.

Actor: I'm playing a zombie in a horror movie.
Actress: Is it a difficult part?
Actor: Most definitely. This part will be the death of me for sure.

Knock! Knock!
Who's there?
Candice.
Candice who?
Candice zombie be brought back to life?

What do you find under the hood of a zombie car?
A very dead battery.

Why did the zombie drummer get kicked out of the band?
He was a dead beat.

What did the angry father zombie say to his teenage son zombie?
You're totally grounded!

When did the warranty become a zombie?
After it expired.

Why did the zombie go to a doctor?
He was as pale as a ghost.

Why didn't the zombie enlist in the military?
He had no life to give for his country.

Who turned Attila into a zombie?

An evil Hundertaker.

▷ ▷ ▷ ▷ ▷ ▷ ▷ ▷ ▷ ▷ ▷ ▷ ▷ ▷ ▷ ▷ ▷ ▷

Why do zombie couples never divorce?

They stay married till death do they part.

◁ ◁ ◁ ◁ ◁ ◁ ◁ ◁ ◁ ◁ ◁ ◁ ◁ ◁ ◁ ◁ ◁ ◁

What did the coach shout to his team of zombies?

Hey! Show a little life on the field.

▷ ▷ ▷ ▷ ▷ ▷ ▷ ▷ ▷ ▷ ▷ ▷ ▷ ▷ ▷ ▷ ▷ ▷

What do you call a band of thankful zombies?

The Grateful Un-dead.

◁ ◁ ◁ ◁ ◁ ◁ ◁ ◁ ◁ ◁ ◁ ◁ ◁ ◁ ◁ ◁ ◁ ◁

Knock! Knock!

Who's there?

It's a waffle.

It's a waffle who?

It's a waffle sight to see zombies walking around.

▷ ▷ ▷ ▷ ▷ ▷ ▷ ▷ ▷ ▷ ▷ ▷ ▷ ▷ ▷ ▷ ▷ ▷

Why was the little person zombie so unhappy?

He had such a short lifespan.

◁ ◁ ◁ ◁ ◁ ◁ ◁ ◁ ◁ ◁ ◁ ◁ ◁ ◁ ◁ ◁ ◁ ◁

What is a zombie's favorite play?

Death of a Salesman.

▷ ▷ ▷ ▷ ▷ ▷ ▷ ▷ ▷ ▷ ▷ ▷ ▷ ▷ ▷ ▷ ▷ ▷

Why don't zombies tell stories?

Because dead men tell no tales.

◁ ◁ ◁ ◁ ◁ ◁ ◁ ◁ ◁ ◁ ◁ ◁ ◁ ◁ ◁ ◁ ◁ ◁

Zombie Desk Clerk: **Monsters live on every floor of this hotel.**

Vampire: **How nice. This place is full of horror stories.**

▷ ▷ ▷ ▷ ▷ ▷ ▷ ▷ ▷ ▷ ▷ ▷ ▷ ▷ ▷ ▷ ▷ ▷

Where did the zombie work at the post office?

In the dead letter department.

Nurse: Should I put this zombie patient on life support?
Doctor: You're joking right?
Nurse: No, I'm dead serious.

Knock! Knock!
Who's there?
I'm Cher.
I'm Cher who?
I'm Cher afraid of zombies.

What is a zombie's favorite sport?
Hearseback riding.

DAFFY DEFINITION:
Zombie Library — a place that is deadly silent.

Who did the zombie invite to his big party?
All of the guests he could dig up.

What did the Wild West zombie say to the cowboy?
Bury me not on the lone prairie.

Why couldn't the zombie keep a secret?
She was dying to tell someone.

What do you call a contest that awards zombies as prizes?
A dead giveaway.

"Psssst"

168

Monster

And Werewolves

What did the surfer say as he watched the werewolf run away?
Hairy back, dude!

....

When do werewolves act silly?
When the fool moon rises.

....

When does a werewolf feel depressed?
Once in a blue moon.

....

How did the Wolfman get to be a CEO?
He clawed his way to the top.

....

SIGN ON A CLOSED WEREWOLF STORE:
Dog gone for the day.

....

How many parents does the Wolfman have?
One maw and four paws.

....

Knock! Knock!
Who's there?
Wendy.
Wendy who?
Wendy full moon rises, werewolves start
to prowl around.

....

What should you use when you change a baby werewolf's diaper?
Flea powder.

Where do you store wolfmen?
In a werehouse.

Knock! Knock!
Who's there?
Obscene.
Obscene who?
Obscene men change into wolves when the full moon rises.

WANTED: Horror writer needed to pen hair-raising tales for bald werewolf.

What do you get if you cross King Kong with a werewolf?
A giant, very hairy beast that goes ape when the full moon rises.

When does the Wolfman turn into a two-bit monster?
When the quarter moon rises.

DAFFY DEFINITION: Werewolf—a haunting dog gone wild.

Knock! Knock!
Who's there?
Voodoo.
Voodoo who?
Voodoo you think is more dangerous, Dracula or Wolfman?

Knock! Knock!
Who's there?
Decry.
Decry who?
Decry of the Wolfman sends shivers down my spine.

Wolfman: Who gave you that bad scratch on your face?

Wolfboy: Nobody gave it to me. I had to fight for it.

Poodle: I turn into a wolf when the full moon rises.

Spaniel: That's just a doggie brag.

ATTENTION: The Wolfman entered a midnight marathon so he could run with the pack.

NOTICE: Werewolves often have hair-brained ideas.

Psychologist: Why are you so depressed, Mr. Zombie?

Mr. Zombie: I have no life.

What do you call a metric werewolf?

The liter of the pack.

What did the shoe salesman say to the Wolfman?

What size do you wear, wolf?

What do you call an athletic werewolf?

A sports cur.

Monster Barber: Why do you always come in for a haircut when the moon is full?

Wolfman: That way I'm sure to get my money's worth.

Dracula: **Tonight there's a full moon. Tomorrow there isn't.**

Wolfman: **Oh well. Hair today. Gone tomorrow.**

What do you get if you cross the Wolfman with Santa Claus?

You get a furry Merry Christmas.

What do you get if you cross a lumberjack with the Wolfman?
A timberwolf.

Who prevents forest fires and attacks campers when the moon is full?
Smokey the Bearwolf.

Knock! Knock!
Who's there?
Defer.
Defer who?
Defer coat of a werewolf is very thick.

NOTICE: A werewolf who squeals on his friends is a pack rat.

Knock! Knock!
Who's there?
Eyelid.
Eyelid who?
Eyelid a secret life as a werewolf.

What do you get if you cross Kris Kringle
with the Wolfman?
Santa Claws.

Knock! Knock!
Who's there?
Dozen.
Dozen who?
Dozen anyone believe I was chased by a werewolf?

Why did the Wolfman wear torn pants and a ripped shirt?
Because he was dressed to kill.

What did Mrs. Werewolf say to Mr. Werewolf during their argument?
Don't snap at me.

Knock! Knock!
Who's there?
Hubie.
Hubie who?
Hubie in before the full moon rises or a werewolf might get you.

What do you call a bunch of funny werewolves?
A pack of real cards.

Show me a wolfman about to be married...and
I'll show you a dog groomer.

NOTICE: The Wolfman moonlights at a second job.

Which werewolf works for the post office?
The Alpha mail carrier.

How do you get 100 werewolves
in a tiny room?
Pack 'em in.

Who chases the Three Little Pigs when
the moon is full?
The Big Bad Werewolf.

What kind of werewolf goes on hikes and does good deeds?
A wolf cub scout.

What do you get if you cross the Wolfman with a lobster?
I don't know, but you should see the claws on that thing.

Title of Transylvanian Fairy Tale: "The Boy Who Cried Werewolf."

Why do werewolves make bad pets?
They always bite the hand that feeds them.

Oh, My!

NOTICE: **Most ghouls work the graveyard shift.**

Mad Dr. Morgon: **My new monster stands ten feet tall. I named the creature "If."**
Gorgon: **Gosh! That's a mighty big If.**

What happened when the angry villagers trapped the monster orange?
They beat it to a pulp!

Invisible Man: Why won't you give me the lead role in your new horror movie?
Director: Sorry, but I just can't see you in the part.

Knock! Knock!
Who's there?
Dragon.
Dragon who?
Dragon your feet will get your shoes dirty.

What do you call a ghost who haunts a hotel?

An Inn spectre.

Knock! Knock!

Who's there?

Clara.

Clara who?

Clara path! Here's comes a monster and I'm out of here!

Knock! Knock!

Who's there?

Teller.

Teller who?

Teller to scream loud if she sees a monster.

What did the monster say to the alphabet?

I come to eat U.

Knock! Knock!

Who's there?

Hour.

Hour who?

Hour we going to destroy that monster?

What's the best way to view a horror movie?

Watch it on a wide-scream TV.

Knock! Knock!

Who's there?

Barn.

Barn who?

Barn down Frankenstein's castle.

Knock! Knock!

Who's there?

Gargoyle.

Gargoyle who?

Gargoyle with mouthwash. You have bat breath.

KOOKY QUESTION: Do witch computers have spell check?

CRAZY QUOTE: Great men are made not born. —Dr. Frankenstein.

"Booo!"

Why did the ghosts go to the baseball game?

To boo the umpire.

What does a yeti ride?

An Abominable Snowmobile.

What do you get if you cross the Ice Age with a witch?

A long cold spell.

What happens if you don't pay your exorcist on time?

You get repossessed.

How did the witch teacher grade her pupils' spelling tests?

She used a magic marker.

What do you get if you cross a witch doctor with morning mist?

Voodew.

Knock! Knock!

Who's there?

Witch Doctor.

Witch Doctor who?

Witch Doctor do you recommend for this operation?

What giant ape writes horror stories?

Stephen King Kong.

Did you hear about the sea monster that had whale-to-whale carpeting in his house?

What do baby ghosts wear on their feet?

Booties.

What do you call a spook who uses public transportation?

A ghost busser.

Who is spooky and haunts Mother Goose Land?

Little Boo Peep.

What happens when a little ghost falls down at the playground?

He gets a boo-boo.

What is a creep's favorite holiday?
April Ghoul's Day.

Knock! knock!
Who's there?
Icy.
Icy who?
Icy a monster hiding in the bushes.

Abominable Snowman: **Who's paying the check for dinner?**
Sasquatch: **Don't worry. I'll foot the bill.**

What did the ghost driver do when the traffic light turned red?
He screeched to a stop.

Who is spooky and lives under the sea?
Sponge Blob Scare Pants.

What do skeleton students do before exams?
They bone up on their studies.

Knock! knock!
Who's there?
Alp!
Alp who?
Alp me. A yeti is after me.

YOU TELL 'EM:
You tell 'em palm reader, I'll give you a hand.
You tell 'em Abominable Snowman and state the cold, hard facts.

Knock! Knock!
Who's there?
Candy.
Candy who?
Candy monster you created breathe fire?

Why did King Kong Bunny fall off of the Empire State Building?
The hare planes got him.

What did the witch say to the people of Salem, Massachusetts?
You folks really burn me up.

What do you find in a haunted green house?
Bootiful flowers.
Unholy ground.
Poison Ivy.
Morning Gory Flowers.
Man-eating plants.
Wolfbane.
Crab Grass.

What colors are the ghost flag of America?
Red, white, and boooo!

What do you call a monster gopher?
A ghoul digger.

What do you call a sloppy Sasquatch?
The messing link.

What do you get if you cross an evil woman who casts magic spells with corroded metal?
The Wicked Witch of the Rust.

What do you call a ghoul protest?
A demon-stration.

Which monster is a pig farmer?
The Frankenslop monster.

What do you get if you cross a ghost and a small purple flower?
A shrieking violet.

Mad Doctor: I made a monster out of an old locomotive. It has a head full of steam.

Igor: Don't forget to attach its engine ears.

Zelda: I know a hexed number.
Nelda: Witch one?
Zelda: That's right.

Detective: Arrest that mummy and bring me his wrap sheet.

Monster Hunter #1: I'm going to follow these Sasquatch tracks.
Monster Hunter #2: Be careful. That's a big step you're taking.

Knock! Knock!
Who's there?
Value.
Value who?
Value stop growling at me already.

What do you get if you cross a dinosaur with a witch's spell?
Tyrannosaurus Hex.

Knock! Knock!
Who's there?
Uriah.
Uriah who?
Uriah is kind of red, Mr. Cyclops.

Knock! Knock!
Who's there?
Thumb.
Thumb who?
Thumb folks like horror movies. I don't.

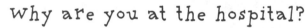

Why are you at the hospital?
Vampire: I need a blood transfusion.
Mr. Zombie: I'm stiff all over.
Mr. Skeleton: I have a fractured bone.
The Invisible Man: I need to clear up my complexion.
Mrs. Devil: I'm having hot flashes.
Abominable Snowman: I have cold feet.
Werewolf: I'm shedding.
Ms. Witch: I'm having fainting spells.

Why is the Frankenstein Monster so well informed?
He's full of current events.

Mad Doctor: **I want to dissect this bee monster.**
Igor: **I'll get the buzz saw.**

What did one invisible man say to the other invisible man?
So long, I won't be seeing you around.

what's scary, hairy and slides down an icy slope real fast?
A yeti on a snowboard.

Igor: Doctor, how's it going?
Dr. Frankenstein: Sew far, sew good.

Robot Space Monster #1: Never invade earth on Sunday. It's too dangerous.
Robot Space Monster #2: Why is that?
Robot Space Monster #1: Because Sunday is a day of rust.

ATTENTION: Bambi the Ghost is a deer haunter.

Vampire: What kind of mouthwash do you use?
Witch: Brand Hex.

How do you unlock a haunted house?
Use a skeleton key.

How did the fortune teller predict the monster's future?
She checked his horrorscope.

What did the Egyptian mummy say to the river?
Nile see you later.

Mad Doctor: Success at last! My apple monster is alive and it's rotten to the core!

Divorce lawyer: Why are you here, Mrs. Frankenstein?

Mrs. Frankenstein: My marriage to the Mad Doctor was an experiment that failed.

High Priest: My mummy is always hungry.

Pharaoh: Maybe it has a tape worm.

Ivan: Want to hear a hangman's joke?

Igor: No. I don't care for gallows humor.

What do you get if you cross Big Foot with a space monster?

Huge star tracks.

Igor: Doctor, you charged this monster with the wrong kind of electricity.

Mad Doctor: What do you mean?

Igor: This creature has a negative attitude.

What happens when Frankenstein owns a butcher shop and has the Wolfman for a customer?

Frankenstein meats the Wolfman.

FLASH: Ms. Godzilla wears fishnet stockings.

What does the Abominable Snowman get when he eats ice cream too fast?

Brain freeze.

Boris: I think the Loch Ness monster is a girl.

Igor: What makes you say that?

Boris: Everyone says it's a she-serpent.

What kind of music do space monsters like?

Moon rock.

....

NOTICE: A space monster from the planet Saturn just landed on earth. Be careful or it'll ring your neck.

....

Where did T-Rex spend his summer vacation?

At the dinoshore.

....

What is the ghost anthem of America?

Three scare for the red, white, and boo.

....

What goes to college in the Midwest and carries a lot of food?

The lunchbag of Notre Dame.

....

THE TWO-HEADED MONSTER ...

... enjoyed talking to himself.
... did a double-take when someone yelled, Head's up!
... was an expert at double-talk.

....

Knock! Knock!

Who's there?

I spider.

I spider who?

I spider sneaking around our secret laboratory.

....

What is T-Rex's favorite game?

Swallow the leader.

....

Why shouldn't a witch on a broomstick lose her temper?

She might fly off the handle.

Who checks haunted houses?
The building in-spectre.

What did the referee say before the monsters' boxing match?
May the best frighter win.

What do you get when a fire-breathing dragon devours a male deer?
Hart burn.

What should you do if a monster breaks down your front door?
Run out the back door.

What did Dr. Frankenstein say to the three-legged monster?
You've grown a foot since I last saw you.

What did Godzilla say when he saw the vegetable garden?
Oh boy! Squash farmers.

What did the friendly geek ghost say?
Don't be afraid of the dork.

Who won the skeleton beauty contest?
No body.

Igor: Is your new girlfriend pretty?
Boris: Well, kind of.
Igor: Is she ugly?
Boris: In a way.
Igor: Then I guess she's pretty ugly.

What do you find on the windows of a haunted house?
Shudders.

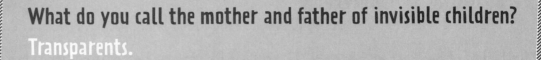

What do you call the mother and father of invisible children?
Transparents.

How do you make a skeleton laugh? Tickle its funny bone.

Why does the headless horseman ride every Halloween?
He's trying to get ahead in life.

What do you find on a haunted safari?
A big game haunter.

Who is the most famous witch detective?
Warlock Holmes.

Where do monsters like to water ski? On Lake Erie.

What is a ghost's favorite month?
Februscary.

Knock! Knock!
Who's there?
Willis.
Willis who?
Willis nightmare ever end?

What do you do with a yellow monster?
Scare the big coward away.

Where do baby monsters stay while their parents work?
At dayscare centers.

Why are skeletons bad baseball players?
They make too many boneheaded plays.

What month was Frankenstein born?
Shocktober.

Igor: Is the Abominable Snowman a mean monster?
Boris: No, but he is a little cold-hearted.

Why did Frankenstein like to hear his Mad Doctor's jokes?
Because they kept him in stitches.

Drac: **Does Mr. Skeleton play the trumpet?**
Wolfie: **No. He plays the trom-bone.**

What do you do with a green monster? Let it ripen.

Boris: I know a monster with one eye called Cyclops.
Igor: What's his other eye called?

What skeleton was a famous music conductor?
Leonard Bonestein.

What do you call a skeleton that refuses to work?
Lazy bones.

What does a witch order while staying in a hotel?
Broom service.

Where do sea monsters sleep?
On waterbeds.

Witch: Why did you give up fortune telling?
Gypsy: I saw no future in it for me.

What monster glows in the dark?
The Frankenshine Monster.

What did the witch say to her broom at bedtime?
Sweep dreams.

Zack: Did you hear the latest monster joke?
Jack: Yes. It's a killer.

What sound does a witch make when she cries?
Brew-hoo! Brew-hoo!

Why was the witch so thirsty?
She just had a dry spell.

What do you call two young witches who share a dorm room?
Broom mates.

How do you make a haunted house more creepy?
Turn on the scare conditioner.

What did the Invisible Man say to his youngsters?
Children should be heard and not seen.

Why did Frankenstein act so goofy after meeting Dracula?
He was scared silly.

What did the evil mummy say after they wrapped him in aluminum?
Curses! Foiled again!

What's a cold evil candle called?
The Wicked Wick of the North.

What do you call a short play about witchcraft?
A magic act.

Why did the Mummy take a vacation?
He needed to unwind.

What did the little girl ghost get for her birthday?
A haunted dollhouse.

Why did the tidy witch put her broom in the washing machine?
She wanted to make a clean sweep.

What did the Mad Doctor say to his new monster?
You can be frank with me.

Why won't a witch wear a flat hat?
Because it's pointless.

▶ ▶ ▶ ▶ ▶ ▶ ▶ ▶ ▶ ▶ ▶ ▶ ▶ ▶

Why did the Hobbit have to stay after school?
He forgot to do his gnome work.

◀ ◀ ◀ ◀ ◀ ◀ ◀ ◀ ◀ ◀ ◀ ◀ ◀ ◀

What do you find at the top of Ghost Mountain?
Peak-a-boo.

▶ ▶ ▶ ▶ ▶ ▶ ▶ ▶ ▶ ▶ ▶ ▶ ▶ ▶

What kinds of football games do monsters like the best?
Ones that end in sudden-death overtime.

◀ ◀ ◀ ◀ ◀ ◀ ◀ ◀ ◀ ◀ ◀ ◀ ◀ ◀

Ghoul: did you like the horror movie?
Zombie: No. It bored me to death.

▶ ▶ ▶ ▶ ▶ ▶ ▶ ▶ ▶ ▶ ▶ ▶ ▶ ▶

Why do witches wear nametags at the Spelling Convention?
So they know which witch is which.

◀ ◀ ◀ ◀ ◀ ◀ ◀ ◀ ◀ ◀ ◀ ◀ ◀ ◀

Who does all of the talking at a ghost press conference?
The spooksperson.

▶ ▶ ▶ ▶ ▶ ▶ ▶ ▶ ▶ ▶ ▶

What is spookier than the outside of a haunted house?
The inside.

◀ ◀ ◀ ◀ ◀ ◀ ◀ ◀ ◀ ◀ ◀

What did the ghost order at the haunted Italian restaurant?
Spookgetti.

▶ ▶ ▶ ▶ ▶ ▶ ▶ ▶ ▶ ▶ ▶

What do you do with a blue monster?
Cheer it up.

CHAPTER 4

THE WACKY WORKING WORLD

What did Attila the Barbarian do after he lost his job?

He collected hunemployment.

....

Knock! Knock!

Who's there?

Len.

Len who?

Len me ten bucks until payday.

....

Why did you quit your job at the coffee shop?

They didn't offer me enough perks.

....

Mr. Smith: I invest in skyscrapers.

Mr. Jones: You must have a lot of high-interest accounts.

....

Knock! Knock!

Who's there?

Olive.

Olive who?

Olive our job openings are filled.

....

What do you get if you cross a Catholic Sister with your accountant?

Nun of your business.

....

DAFFY DEFINITION:

ATM — A real money market.

....

NOTICE: Buy Acme camera phones — just picture yourself owning one.

....

WANTED: Person to plan charity events. Plenty of benefits.

....

SIGN ON A BUNGEE CORD COMPANY: Even when our sales are down, we always bounce back.

Knock! Knock!
Who's there?
Alana.
Alana who?
Alana Georgia is where my factory is located.

....

SILLY SALES PITCH:

Acme Footwear: Wouldn't you like to be in our shoes?

....

What did one wacky gold prospector say to the other?
Catch me if Yukon.

....

WANTED: Scientist to work on secret glue formula. Must be bonded.

....

Knock! Knock!
Who's there?
Mystery.
Mystery who?
Mystery argue over your bonus every year?

....

Show me a real hip dude who works below
ground ... and I'll show you a cool miner.

....

Harry: **Should I quit my job at the glue factory?**
Barry: **I suggest you stick with it.**

....

Mr. Chubb: **I gained twenty pounds of belly fat
since I became a rich businessman.**
Mr. Slim: **Just think of it as industrial waist.**

....

ATTENTION: **Abe Lincoln was a union leader.**

Harry: When it comes to cash, I'm like the banker on the great Ark.
Barry: What do you mean?
Harry: I have Noah money.

What do you call the owner of a flower shop who's frozen stiff and can't move a muscle?
The petrified florist.

Mr. Brown: **Why did you buy a bottled water company?**
Mr. Green: **I believe in having liquid assets.**

SILLY SALES PITCH:
Acme Scuba Diving Tanks: Our business is a breath of fresh air.

Knock! Knock!
Who's there?
Toupee.
Toupee who?
Toupee my bills, I had to borrow money.

WANTED: Tree surgeon to operate new branch office.

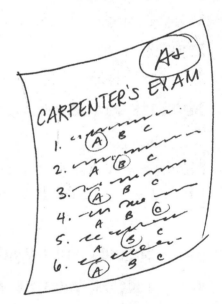

Man: **Why are your baked goods so expensive?**
Baker: **Blame it on the rising cost of dough.**

Matt: **How did you do on your carpenter's exam?**
Pat: **I nailed it!**

DAFFY DEFINITION:
Mining expert — a person with a coal, calculating mind.

Builder: **I don't have enough money to pay for the bridge supports.**
Foreman: **Why don't you start a truss fund?**

WANT ODDS

WANTED: Contortionist needed to teach yoga class. Flexible hours.

WANTED: Person to fill salt and pepper shakers at restaurant. Seasonal work.

WANTED: Cowboy to lasso steers. Must know the ropes and have lots of pull.

WANTED: Person to work in rearview mirror factory. Excellent hindsight a plus.

WANTED: Person to build playground equipment. Swing shifts.

WANTED: Person to mop floors and dust ceilings. Must be willing to start from the bottom up.

WANTED: Assistant to archaeologist. Applicant must love the good old days.

WANTED: Person to work in burlap bag factory. No sack guarantee.

WANTED: Straight man to team with very funny comedian. No kidding around.

WANTED: Person to inflate balloons. The ideal candidate knows how to blow things out of proportion.

WANTED: Riding instructor with a sense of humor needed at equestrian school. We want someone who will horse around with our students.

WANTED: Kennel needs pet exercisers willing to work until they're dog tired.

WANTED: Workers for sheep farm. We offer a profit-shearing plan.

WANTED: Workers for dairy farm. Learn to milk our cash cows.

WANTED: Gardeners needed to raise plants. Pay as you grow.

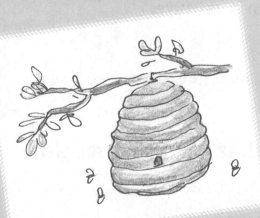

WANTED: People to brush horses. Cash and curry business.

WANTED: Workers for cannery plant. A top tin company.

WANTED: Mechanics needed to design tires for economy cars. Job leads to promotion to big wheels.

WANTED: People needed to tend beehives. Our buzz word is success.

WANTED: Night watchman. If you're looking for security, this is the job for you.

Two lumberjacks were standing in front of a tall tree and they were having a heated argument. "Back off," said one lumberjack to the other. "I saw it first."

▶ ▶

How do you learn the mattress business?
Go to spring training.

◀ ◀

WANTED: Electrician needed for light construction work. Must have current references.

▶ ▶

Knock! Knock!
Who's there?
I Cher.
I Cher who?
I Cher would like to work here.

▶ ▶

Knock! Knock!
Who's there?
Daryl.
Daryl who?
Daryl be a bonus in this deal for you.

◀ ◀

SIGN IN A WATCH SHOP: Someone will help you in a minute.

▶ ▶

ANOTHER SIGN IN A WATCH SHOP: Check out our hourly rates.

◀ ◀

STILL ANOTHER SIGN IN A WATCH SHOP: Our repairs may take some time to complete.

▶ ▶

Why do people who clean fireplaces like winter so much?
Business is always good during flue season.

What did the cast say to the bone?
Don't bother me now. I'm on my break.

▸ ▸ ▸ ▸ ▸ ▸ ▸ ▸ ▸ ▸ ▸ ▸ ▸ ▸ ▸ ▸

Knock! Knock!
Who's there?
Foreman.
Foreman who?
Foreman get more work done than three men.

◂ ◂ ◂ ◂ ◂ ◂ ◂ ◂ ◂ ◂ ◂ ◂ ◂ ◂ ◂ ◂

Tim: I plant shrubs for a living.
Jim: Now that's a bush-league job.

▸ ▸ ▸ ▸ ▸ ▸ ▸ ▸ ▸ ▸ ▸ ▸ ▸ ▸ ▸ ▸

Lester: Did you take a job working in the mine?
Chester: No. I got coal feet.

◂ ◂ ◂ ◂ ◂ ◂ ◂ ◂ ◂ ◂ ◂ ◂ ◂ ◂ ◂ ◂

Millie: Do you like selling pillows for a living?
Tillie: Yes. It's a soft job.

▸ ▸ ▸ ▸ ▸ ▸ ▸ ▸ ▸ ▸ ▸ ▸ ▸ ▸ ▸ ▸

Who collects taxes owed to the Devil?
The Inferno Revenue Service.

◂ ◂ ◂ ◂ ◂ ◂ ◂ ◂ ◂ ◂ ◂ ◂ ◂ ◂ ◂ ◂

ATTENTION: Real Estate Agents are home schooled.

▸ ▸ ▸ ▸ ▸ ▸ ▸ ▸ ▸ ▸

What do you call a Munchkin who prepares fast, easy meals in a diner?
A really short order cook.

Knock! Knock!
Who's there?
Euell.
Euell who?
Euell be sorry if you don't hire me.

....

WANTED: Assistant barber needed. Part-time hours.

....

What do you call a person who makes miniature alarm clocks?

A small-time operator.

....

The Oil Man's Motto: We want to fuel everyone.

....

Why was the middle-class zombie so sad?

Because he'd worked all of his life and he was still working after it ended.

....

NOTICE! New plumbers needed. We'll make your pipe dreams come true.

....

NOTICE! Tailors needed. Come in for an interview so we can size you up.

....

NOTICE! Person needed to sell front doors. Entry level position.

....

What do you call a zombie who has two jobs?

A working stiff.

How did the plumber fix the leaky pipe?

He gave it a good wrench.

....

Knock! Knock!
Who's there?
Dakota.
Dakota who?
Dakota paint you put on my house is starting to peel.

....

What runs on a train track and goes Puff! Puff! Puff!?

A late commuter trying to catch his train.

....

What group do working cowboys belong to?

Western Union.

....

Why did Davy Jones hire a music teacher?

Because he wanted to tuna fish.

....

Why was the new locksmith so successful on his first job?

Beginner's lock.

....

Why is not working so tiring?
Because you can't stop and rest.

....

What did the tired tree say to its boss?
I need a leaf of absence.

SILLY SLOGANS:

ACE PICTURE FRAMERS — Let us hang around your house.

ACE CORN FARMS — Try our product and you'll smile from ear to ear.

ACE YOGA CLASS — We're your local limber yard.

ACE SHOELACES — Tie us. You'll like us.

ACE SPORTS TARPS — We cover all the bases.

ACE BELTS — Let us hold up you.

ACE BOUNTY HUNTERS — We reward our employees for good work.

....

Sal: Do you like working as an exterminator?

Hal: No. It bugs me.

....

WANTED: Space Explorers needed. The pay is out of this world!

....

Why didn't the watchdog show up for guard duty?

He took a sic day.

....

DAFFY DEFINITIONS:

Dating Service — a meet marketplace.

Levee Builders — a banking business.

Knock! Knock!
Who's there?
Event.
Event who?
Event home sick from work.

....

Why are movie directors like fishermen?

Because they both like a perfect cast.

....

What's the best way to sell math problems to students?

Hire someone to run an add campaign.

Knock! Knock!
Who's there?
Musk.
Musk who?
Musk you work late every single night?

How does a person become a lumberjack?
First you have to pass an axe-am.

What did the cowboy do in the Senate?
He was a member of the steering committee.

What did the bullhorn do in Congress?
It was the Speaker of the House.

what did the frog foreman say to his workers?
Let's get hopping, people.

What did the alligator foreman say to his workers?
Let's snap to it, men.

What did the dog foreman say to his crew?
Bark to work, fellas.

what did the centipede foreman say to his workers?
On your feet, feet, feet guys.

Bart: **I got a job gathering hens' eggs.**
Art: **Is it hard?**
Bart: **No. But I often have to work around the cluck.**

What did the nervous elephant say to the lumberjacks?
Back away from my trunk.

Mr. Big: **I'm the president of a lumber company.**
Mr. Small: **I bet you attend a lot of board meetings.**

Lumberjack #1: Can I chop down that old tree?
Lumberjack #2: Hey! I axed first!

What did the butcher say to the tough steak?

I'll tender you later.

Knock! Knock!
Who's there?
Sy.
Sy who?
Sy-los are good places to store grain.

What did the calendar say to its boss?

I need a day off.

What do you get if you cross an auto mechanic and thunder?
Greased lightning.

Then there was the sad tale of the lumberjack who got axed from his job.

Why did the hungry man go into the lamp store?
He was looking for a light snack.

Knock! Knock!
Who's there?
Sofa.
Sofa who?
Sofa we have two good applicants for the job.

NOTICE: Work for Acme Canine Trainers. When you retire from our company we give you a watchdog.

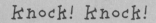

knock! knock!
Who's there?
Higher.
Higher who?
Higher the man in the pinstripe suit.

What does a baker do when he wants to sleep late?
He puts up a donut disturb sign.

MORE SILLY SLOGANS:

ACME LIBRARY BOOKS – Check us out on the net.

ACME SOLARED VEHICLES – We're the hottest new car company under the sun.

ACME LONG-LASTING BALLPOINT PENS – Our motto is write on and on and on.

ACME CUSTOM FURNITURE – Let us chair for you.

ACME MUSIC STORE – Stop by at play time.

ACME STAIR COMPANY – Step up to a better life.

ACME CAR IGNITIONS – We start every day right.

ACME WATCH SELLERS – Our time should be your time.

ACME TAXI COMPANY – If you're feeling run down, let us pick you up.

ACME BATTERY COMPANY – We charge a little to charge you a lot.

How did the first barber come to the United States?
He arrived on a clipper ship.

Zack: I answered an ad that said surefire opportunity.

Mack: Did you get the job?

Zack: Yes. And then I got fired.

Why did the firemen rush to the forest?
Someone reported a tree-alarm fire.

NOTICE: Casino seeks card dealers. It's a wise bet for your future.

Publisher: So you wrote a book about a Scottish musical instrument?

Author: Yes. It's the story of my fife.

What did the trumpet player say to the musician next to him?

I need to make a call. Can I use your sax-a-phone?

ACME CANNON COMPANY – Join our team while business is booming. We never fire our employees.

ACME CLOTHESLINE COMPANY – Come in and we'll teach you the ropes.

ACME SOLAR PANELS – You'll have a bright future working with us.

DAFFY DEFINITION:
Lumberjacks — tree wise men.

What do you get if you cross an athlete with a road construction worker?
A jock hammer.

What do you call a mean guy who chops down trees?
A lumberjerk.

WACKY WANTEDS:

Movie actors needed for small roles. Bit part-time work.

Vegetable pickers needed. Peas Corps volunteers welcome. Bring your own iPods.

Balloon inflators wanted. We welcome people who are full of hot air.

People needed to peddle barbells. Strong sales skills required.

Artist models needed. Become part of the big picture.

What's very quiet and cleans streets?
A mime sweeper.

Why did the farmer play his guitar in the cornfield.
It was music to his ears.

What do disc jockey surfers ride?
Radio waves.

How did the circus animal trainer get squashed?
He was teaching his elephant to lie down and roll over.

DAFFY DEFINITIONS:

Yacht Owners — successful sailsmen.

Fishing Gear Vendors — reel estate agents.

Do parsons and ministers get prayed vacations?

When do lumberjacks kick back and relax?
On tree-day weekends.

What do you get if you cross a rock and an employee?
A hard worker.

NOTICE: Sir Lancelot works the knight shift.

Rick: **I produce calendars for a living.**
Nick: **Oh! So you're a day worker.**

Knock! Knock!
Who's there?
Comma.
Comma who?
Comma in for a job interview.

Boy: **I work in costumes at Disney World.**
Girl: **What do you do?**
Boy: **I have a Mickey Mouse job.**

Randy: Minnie finally got a job.
Sandy: Good for her. Now she's a working min.

Why did the fisherman go to the Anglers' Conference?
To do some networking.

LUGGAGE MAKER — A case worker.

MIME – A person who is lost for words.

A young man was applying for a job as a magician with a circus. "What's your best trick?" asked the owner of the show. "It's sawing a woman in half," boasted the young performer. "Isn't that a difficult trick?" asked the owner. "Not really," answered the magician. "I first started performing it on my sisters." "Do you come from a large family," asked the circus owner. The magician smiled. "I have six half sisters."

What did the lumberjack use after Saw A and Saw B?
He used his C-saw.

What did the cheerleaders do when they saw the Rolling Stones?
They did a rockin' cheer.

Why did the teller stand next to the bank vault?
She wanted to be on the safe side.

How does an acrobat read a magazine?
He flips through the pages.

What do you call a necktie salesman who earns a million dollars?
A tycoon.

What did the clock maker say to the revolutionary soldier?
Give me a minute, man.

what did the unhappy workers at the fence factory do?
They formed a picket line.

Why was the conductor crying?
His train was on a wailroad track.

What's the best way to avoid taxes?
Take a quick right at New Mexico.

What is a truck driver's favorite paint?
Semi-gloss.

Zack: What do you do at the clock factory?
Mack: I make faces.

What did the sailor say when Carly gave him an order?
Aye Carly.

What do train conductors wear with a suit?
A railroad tie.

Then there was the politician who fired his writers and ended up speechless.

What do you get if you cross boulders and musicians?
Rock concerts.

What do you get if you cross a hip-hop singer with a traveling salesman?
Someone who raps at your front door.

Who is in charge of Santa's workshop?
The C.E. HO! HO! HO!

SIGN ON AN ANTIQUE STORE: Stop in and see our new old stuff.

How's your job at the compost plant?
It's rotten work and the hours stink.

How's your job at the tire factory?
Wheel good, but tiring.

How's your job at the clothesline factory?
It leaves me fit to be tied.

How's your job at the bread crumb plant?
It's getting stale fast.

How's your job in the propaganda office?
You won't believe it if I tell you, but then again, maybe you will.

How's your job at the fantasy game company?
It's unreal.

How's your job at the travel agency?
It's going nowhere.

How's your job at the window plant?
It panes me to talk about it.

How's your job at the U.S. mint?
I'm not making any money.

How's your job at the prune juice factory?
The pay is regular.

How's your job at the clock company?
I'm getting paid time and a half.

How's your job at the power plant?
I don't have the energy to talk about it.

How's your job at the beef jerky factory?
I bit off more than I could chew.

How's your job at the firearms plant?
My nerves are shot.

How's your job at the peanut plant?
The work is driving me nuts.

How's your job at the fan factory?
It's a breeze.

How's your job at the school textbook company?
I'm getting promoted.

How's your job at the steak knife plant?
They're cutting back my hours.

How's your job at the baby diaper company?
I'm in need of a change.

How's your job at the crystal ball factory?
It's hard to predict my future there.

◀ ◀

Company President: We had three outstanding applicants for the vice president position. However, in my opinion Mr. Morgan is most deserving of promotion, so he will be our new vice president. Is there anything you'd like to say, Mr. Morgan?

Mr. Morgan: Yes, sir! Thanks a lot, Dad.

▶ ▶

What kind of education do you need to work as a store greeter?

Just a "Hi" school diploma.

◀ ◀ ◀ ◀ ◀ ◀ ◀ ◀ ◀

What did the boss match say to the employee match?

You're fired.

▶ ▶ ▶ ▶ ▶ ▶ ▶ ▶ ▶ ▶ ▶

What did one match investor say to the other?

I've got a hot tip for you.

SIGN ON A MATCH-MAKING COMPANY: Employees on strike!

▶ ▶ ▶ ▶ ▶ ▶ ▶ ▶ ▶ ▶ ▶ ▶ ▶ ▶ ▶ ▶ ▶ ▶

WANTED: Scientist needed to develop new explosives. Dynamite opportunity.

◀ ◀ ◀ ◀ ◀ ◀ ◀ ◀ ◀ ◀ ◀ ◀ ◀ ◀ ◀ ◀ ◀ ◀

ATTENTION: An unemployed ghost looking for work is a job haunter.

▶ ▶ ▶ ▶ ▶ ▶ ▶ ▶ ▶ ▶ ▶ ▶ ▶ ▶ ▶ ▶ ▶ ▶

Who makes cruise ships?
Factories with assembly liners.

▶ ▶ ▶ ▶ ▶ ▶ ▶ ▶ ▶ ▶ ▶ ▶ ▶ ▶ ▶ ▶ ▶ ▶

Knock! Knock!
Who's there?
A bonus.
A bonus who?
A bonus what a dog likes to chew.

◀ ◀ ◀ ◀ ◀ ◀ ◀ ◀ ◀ ◀ ◀ ◀ ◀ ◀ ◀ ◀ ◀ ◀

When do lumberjacks harvest pine trees?
During the Christmas chopping season.

▶ ▶ ▶ ▶ ▶ ▶ ▶ ▶ ▶ ▶ ▶ ▶ ▶ ▶ ▶ ▶ ▶ ▶

SIGN IN A BUSY BARBER SHOP: Watch out for falling locks.

◀ ◀ ◀ ◀ ◀ ◀ ◀ ◀ ◀ ◀ ◀ ◀ ◀ ◀ ◀ ◀ ◀ ◀

SIGN ON A COAL COMPANY: There's no fuel like an old fuel.

▶ ▶ ▶ ▶ ▶ ▶ ▶

Sal: I used to work in the circus as a trapeze artist.
Al: What happened?
Sal: I was let go.

◀ ◀ ◀ ◀ ◀ ◀ ◀ ◀ ◀ ◀ ◀ ◀ ◀ ◀ ◀ ◀ ◀ ◀

SIGN ON A CALENDAR COMPANY: **We offer our employees a free dating service.**

Businessman's son: My father owns a factory.

Farmer's son: My father owns so many plants I can't count them.

▷ ▷ ▷ ▷ ▷ ▷ ▷ ▷ ▷ ▷ ▷ ▷ ▷ ▷ ▷ ▷ ▷ ▷ ▷ ▷

Then there was the owner of a dry-cleaning store who held a press conference to announce his grand opening.

◁ ◁ ◁ ◁ ◁ ◁ ◁ ◁ ◁ ◁ ◁ ◁ ◁ ◁ ◁ ◁ ◁ ◁ ◁ ◁

Jimmy: I used to be a racecar driver. Now I'm unemployed.

Zimmy: What happened?

Jimmy: There was a stock car market crash.

▷ ▷ ▷ ▷ ▷ ▷ ▷ ▷ ▷ ▷ ▷ ▷ ▷ ▷ ▷ ▷ ▷ ▷ ▷ ▷

Man: I'd like to work in men's clothing.

Personal director: Well, I have a job that may suit you.

◁ ◁ ◁ ◁ ◁ ◁ ◁ ◁ ◁ ◁ ◁ ◁ ◁ ◁ ◁ ◁ ◁ ◁ ◁ ◁

Knock! Knock!

Who's there?

Aisle.

Aisle who?

Aisle call you when I get to the mall.

▷ ▷ ▷ ▷ ▷ ▷ ▷ ▷ ▷ ▷ ▷ ▷ ▷ ▷ ▷ ▷ ▷ ▷ ▷ ▷

What happens when a steamship gets angry?

It blows its stack.

◁ ◁ ◁ ◁ ◁ ◁ ◁ ◁ ◁

Knock! Knock!

Who's there?

Yule.

Yule who?

Yule be glad you hired me.

Boss: Why are you late for work, Mr. Broom?

Mr. Broom: I overswept.

....

Joe: Yesterday I went to apply for a job and fell face first in wet cement.

Moe: Well at least you made a good impression.

....

Zack: I have a great job.

Mack: What do you do?

Zack: I'm the team dentist for a pro hockey team.

....

KOOKY QUESTION: **Do plumbers have pipe dreams?**

....

How do you mail a message for a fisherman?

Post it on the net.

....

What did the sailor say at his wedding ceremony?

Aye Aye Do.

....

What do girls call a very handsome sailor?

Aye candy.

what did the sick shoe say to the cobbler?

Please heel me.

....

Knock! Knock!
Who's there?
A maid.
A maid who?
A maid you look!

....

Show me a fisherman named Harry Potter ... and I'll show you a boy who knows how to cast spells.

....

What do plumbers in Scotland fix?

Leaky bagpipes.

....

A local TV weatherman was wrong so often his predictions made him a laughing stock with viewers. They sent him tons of emails ridiculing his forecasts. Finally, the weatherman asked the station manager to transfer him to an affiliate clear across the country. The station manager was concerned. "Why do you want to relocate?" he asked his employee. "Because," replied the weatherman, "the climate here doesn't agree with me."

....

Andy: Yahoo! Yippee! I got a job installing new sidewalks.

Randy: Great, but please curb your enthusiasm.

Loony Law & Order

Lawyer #1: Mr. Rabbit, will you please tell the court what Mrs. Bunny said to you.

Lawyer #2: Objection, your honor. Haresay.

. . . .

Then there was the mob dentist who took care of patients with crooked teeth.

. . . .

Annette: How's your job at the law office?

Jeannette: Every day it's a test of wills.

. . . .

NOTICE: A who-done-it play has lots of crime scenes.

. . . .

Accused: I plead insanity, your honor.

Judge: You're out of your mind.

Accused: Thanks for allowing my defense, Judge.

. . . .

Knock! Knock!
Who's there?
We flounder.
We flounder who?
We flounder innocent of all charges.

Judge: Counselor, where is your client?

Magician's lawyer: I expect him to appear before you any second now.

. . . .

How do you contact a convict in jail?
Call him on his cell phone.

. . . .

Who proofreads all manuscripts written by jailhouse authors?
The corrections officer.

What did the detective say when he arrested a mime?

You have the right to remain silent.

Why is a judge like a reserve baseball player?
They both spend a lot of time on the bench.

Which police squad does a lot of camping?
The criminal in tent unit.

Zack: Did you apply to the police academy?
Mack: No. I copped out.

Lawyer: Whenever I stand up in court to speak to the judge, I suddenly feel ill. What's wrong with me?
Doctor: It sounds like motion sickness to me.

What did the chief say when Attila joined the police force?
Now he's Hun the job.

Robber: My son's a snitch. Do you think he'll get over it?
Crook: There's no telling.

Reporter #1: Did the cops catch the crooked train conductor?
Reporter #2: Yes. They have him down at the station.

You're under arrest!

Cop: I just saw a kid fishing from a railroad bridge over the river.
Detective: Arrest him. Off track baiting is illegal in this state.

Why did the lawyer bring a mattress to court?
He was about to rest his case.

NOTICE: A civil court is a tennis court open to the general public.

DAFFY DEFINITION:
American Robbers, Inc. – a U.S. steel company.

What did the sheep thief do after the robbery?
She took it on the lamb.

What did the detective say to his shirt?
You're under a vest!

Why did the cop give the hog a ticket?
Because he went through a slop sign.

What do you get if you cross a werewolf with a legal agreement.
Claws in the contract.

What do you get if you cross a yellow vegetable with a policeman?
Corn on the cop.

Can a detective roast a chicken?
No. But he can grill a canary.

What fruit is a famous attorney?
Berry Mason.

What do you call a bunch of crooks playing musical instruments?
A robber band.

What happened to the ripe tomato robber?
He got caught red handed.

 Lady: The man who runs our church has disappeared. What should I do?
Cop: File a missing parson report.

ATTENTION: Sponge Bob Robber is on the F.B.I.'s Moist Wanted List.

NUTTY LEGAL NAMES

Mr. Scott Free
Mr. Carl D. Witness
Mr. Al Stan Trial
Mr. Otto Order
Ms. I.M. Innocent
Mr. Mike A. Motion
Mr. Ken Hugh Postbale
Mr. Howe Dewey Plead

Then there was the jailhouse spoon who went stir crazy.

Teacher: I work at an elementary school. My favorite part of the day is recess.
Attorney: I'm a trial lawyer. That's my favorite part of the day, too.

Lawyer: Your honor, my client is accused of stealing a dead car battery.
Judge: In that case I guess they'll be no charges.

 Crook: Hi Judge. How are you?
Judge: Fine! One hundred dollars. Pay the clerk.

Court Clerk: Do you swear to tell the whole truth and nothing but the truth?

Woman: I do.

Court Clerk: State your age.

Woman: Well, which do you want? The whole truth and nothing but the truth or my age?

Singer: I did a benefit show at the prison.

Reporter: How was the crowd?

Singer: They were a captive audience.

Then there was the crooked India rubber man who did a long stretch at the state prison.

Who is the head of the Expresso Crime Family?
The Capo Coffee.

The economy is making things tough even for the rich. The other day a mugger held me up while his butler pointed a gun at me.

Then there was the dumb crook who pointed his finger at a victim and said, "Stick 'em up! I need money to buy a gun."

What do you find on the front of a gangster's limo?
A hood ornament.

What do you get when a messy crook spreads dirt everywhere?
A grime scene.

▶ ▶ ▶ ▶ ▶ ▶ ▶ ▶ ▶ ▶ ▶ ▶ ▶ ▶ ▶ ▶ ▶

Knock! Knock!
Who's there?
Abby.
Abby who?
Abby up for parole soon.

◀ ◀ ◀ ◀ ◀ ◀ ◀ ◀ ◀ ◀ ◀ ◀ ◀ ◀ ◀ ◀ ◀

Knock! Knock!
Who's there?
Denny.
Denny who?
Denny took the money and ran.

▶ ▶ ▶ ▶ ▶ ▶ ▶ ▶ ▶ ▶ ▶ ▶ ▶ ▶ ▶ ▶ ▶

Knock! Knock!
Who's there?
The parson.
The parson who?
The parson I saw commit the crime is getting away.

▶ ▶ ▶ ▶ ▶ ▶ ▶ ▶ ▶ ▶ ▶ ▶ ▶ ▶ ▶ ▶ ▶

Knock! Knock!
Who's there?
Veer.
Veer who?
Veer were you Friday night at ten o'clock?

◀ ◀ ◀ ◀ ◀ ◀ ◀ ◀ ◀ ◀ ◀ ◀ ◀ ◀ ◀ ◀ ◀

Why did the Energizer Bunny spend a night in jail?
It was a case of battery.

When is it illegal for a cat to fall asleep?
When it's a case of kit napping.

> > > > > > > > > > > > > > > > >

Why did the octopus go to prison?
It was guilty of armed, armed robbery.

< < < < < < < < < < < < < < < < <

Why do gophers make dangerous convicts?
They always try to tunnel out of prison.

> > > > > > > > > > > > > > > > >

Knock! Knock!
Who's there?
Pear.
Pear who?
Pear-jury is a serious offense.

< < < < < < < < < < < < < < < < <

What did the poker player say to the District Attorney?
Give me a good deal.

> > > > > > > > > > > > > > > > >

Why did the judge climb Mt. Everest?
He wanted to preside over the highest court in the land.

< < < < < < < < < < < < < < < < <

Why did the lawyer yell in court?
He wanted to make sure his case was heard.

> > > > > > > > > > > > > > > > >

Knock! Knock!
Who's there?
Hy.
Hy who?
Hy object, your honor.

Knock! Knock!
Who's there?
Phew.
Phew who?
Phew have the right to an attorney.

Knock! Knock!
Who's there?
Eye.
Eye who?
Eye swear to tell the whole truth, judge.

Which birds help clients who can't afford to hire lawyers?
The eagle aid society.

Why did the judge fine lawyer skunk?
He was out of odor.

SIGN ON AN EMPTY POLICE CAR: **Cop Out.**

Detective: You're a dirty crook.
Robber: Hey! Don't blame me if I'm a member of a notorious grime family.

Why did the jail inmate put a clock in the stew?
Because the warden ordered him to serve time in the prison kitchen.

Why do you seldom see crooks in church?
Because crime doesn't pray.

What is Detective Polar Bear great at solving?
Cold cases.

Knock! Knock!

Who's there?

Invest.

Invest who?

Invest-igate all of the suspects.

SIGN IN A POLICE STATION: Join our tennis club. Become a member of the police racket squad.

Then there was the hay farmer who had a second job as a bail bondsman.

Police Chief: Did you arrest the banana thief?

Detective: No. He gave me the slip.

Desk Sergeant: Why are you so upset because someone stole your new pair of shoes?

Victim: They were my sole support.

Knock! Knock!

Who's there?

Police.

Police who?

Police don't arrest me. I didn't do anything.

CRAZY QUESTION: Do Egyptian lawyers handle mummy cases?

Victim: A crime has been committed. Quick. Call 9-1-1!

Dumb Witness: Okay. What's the number?

What did the pork chop shout at the police barbecue?

Please don't grill me, coppers!

What did the meter maid give the pig?

A porking ticket.

. . . .

Did you hear about the pro wrestler who became a judge?

He threw a lot of cases out of court.

. . . .

What game do Detective Angel and Detective Devil play when they interrogate a suspect?

Good Cop — Bad Cop.

. . . .

Why did the detective give the crime boss an ant farm?

He wanted to bug his office.

. . . .

Why is it difficult for a detective in a tee shirt to arrest crooks?

He has no cuffs.

. . . .

What did Mr. Bartlett shout in court?

I want to be judged by a jury of my pears.

. . . .

How do you safeguard a dumb informant?

Put him in the witless protection program.

. . . .

DAFFY DEFINITIONS:

Forger – a check by phony.

Convict – a pen name.

. . . .

Then there was the loudmouth robber the cops arrested who chose not to remain silent.

. . . .

A well-dressed lawyer wears a Brooks Brother law suit.

Knock! Knock!

Who's there?

Hiam.

Hiam who?

Hiam totally innocent.

Knock! Knock!

Who's there?

Karma.

Karma who?

Karma out with your hands up.

Knock! Knock!

Who's there?

Year.

Year who?

Year honor is being unfair to my client.

What did the house say to the crooked carpenters?

I don't want you guys to frame me.

What kind of a weapon does a gangster tuck in his belt?

A tummy gun.

Knock! Knock!

Who's there?

Tess.

Tess who?

Tess-tify as to what you saw.

Lawyer: Aren't you known as Mr. Groundhog. Is Mr. Groundhog your real name?

Attorney: I object, your honor. Counsel is badgering the witness.

....

What happened to the crooked librarian?

The judge threw the book at her.

....

Then there was the antelope convict whose hotshot lawyer got him a gnu trial.

....

CRAZY QUESTION: Do postal police follow the letter of the law?

....

Knock! Knock!

Who's there?

Sybil.

Sybil who?

Sybil court is different than criminal court.

....

DAFFY DEFINITIONS:

Suspenders — Hold-ups.

K-9 Unit — police curs on patrol.

Criminal Lawyer — a rap master.

....

Why did Mr. Nose get convicted?

A witness picked him out of a lineup.

What do you get if you cross an attorney and a creek?

A law brook.

....

What did the tape measure say to the lawyers?

I'll give you my ruling tomorrow.

How did the jury find the defendant?

They went looking for him.

....

What did the detective shout to the gangster duck when he arrested him?

Get down on the ground.

....

What do you get if you cross an IRS agent and a state policeman from Dallas?

A taxes ranger.

Knock! Knock!

Who's there?

Hugh.

Hugh who?

Hugh can't beat City Hall.

....

CIA Boss: Quick! Get all of that information off the computer screen.

CIA Agent: But why?

CIA Boss: No questions. This is erase against time.

....

What did the judge say to Lawyer Crow?

Caw your next witness.

....

What's the most difficult part of being a policeman at a nudist camp?

Finding a place to pin on your badge.

Why does it take a convict so long to write a book?

Because sometimes they take ten years to complete a single sentence.

....

A robber ran into a diner and said to the cashier. "Give me all of your money."

The cashier replied, "Yes, sir. Will you count it here or is this an order to go?"

....

Which number is dishonest?

Two bad.

....

What wolf comes out at night and is in charge of the forest mob?

Big Howl Capone.

....

Who lives in a henhouse and organized a crime syndicate?

Clucky Luciano.

....

What birdbrain was a hit man for Davy Jones?

Bugsy Seagull.

....

Nicky: Did you go to the Gangsters' Convention in Atlantic City?

Mickey: Yeah. It was a real mob scene.

Little Sal: I knew a wise guy who tried to make a new hybrid type car. He took wheels from a BMW, a motor from a Cadillac, seats from a Jaguar, and so on.

Big Al: And what did he get?

Little Sal: Ten years for Grand Theft Auto.

What happened to the funny gangster?
He got riddled with bullets.

How can you tell when you're unwanted?
They'll take down your picture at the post office.

Who mugged the Three Wise Men on their way to Bethlehem?
The three Wise Guys.

Gino: My uncle is in jail because he made big money.

Dino: How big?

Gino: About a quarter of an inch too big.

Why did the little gangster goat get arrested?
He was a kidnapper.

Did you ear about the convicts who dug a fantastic tunnel under the prison wall. It was so popular they put a tollbooth at the end of it.

Auto Mechanic: Gulp! What do you want from me?

Robber: About a $1,000 and that's just an estimate.

Crook: Freeze! Give me fifty bucks or else.

Rich Guy: I'm sorry, but I don't have fifty bucks. Can you break a $100 bill?

What happened to the fleet-footed purse snatcher who always outran the police?
He went to reform school on a track scholarship.

Why did the illiterate crook become a bank robber?
He wanted to be a kidnapper, but he didn't know how to write a ransom note.

Then there was the crook that was so rich he hired a Hollywood movie actor to play him in a police lineup.

▸▸▸▸▸▸▸▸▸▸▸▸▸▸▸▸▸▸▸▸▸▸▸▸▸▸▸▸▸▸▸▸▸▸▸▸

Convict: **What did you study in prison biology?**
Inmate: **Cell division.**

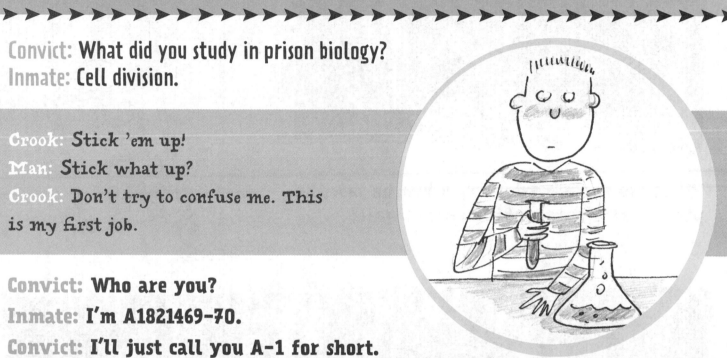

Crook: Stick 'em up!
Man: Stick what up?
Crook: Don't try to confuse me. This
is my first job.

Convict: **Who are you?**
Inmate: **I'm A1821469-70.**
Convict: **I'll just call you A-1 for short.**

Then there was the bank robber who was so rich he hired a Pulitzer Prize winner to write his holdup notes.

These days crime is so bad the safest place to live is in a prison cell.

McCoy: My father is a criminal lawyer.
Lenny: Aren't they all?

Two new convicts were led into their prison cell. "When do you get out?" Big Al asked his cellmate. "I get released in 2020," said Baby Face. "I don't get out until 2022," replied Big Al, "so you take the bunk nearest the door."

"Stick 'em down," yelled the robber. "Don't you mean stick 'em up?" asked the victim. "Ah-ha!" replied the robber. "Now I know what I've been doing wrong."

ATTENTION BURGLARS: The family in this house has the measles. Break in and you'll break out.

Knock! Knock!
Who's there?
Aye, Aye.
Aye, Aye who?
Aye, Aye was robbed, robbed.

What did the gangster say when he saw the picture of a bank robber on the wall?
It's crooked.

what did the girl say after the gangster flirted with her?
I've been hoodwinked.

What do you call a bump on a crook's head?
A hoodlump.

Knock! Knock!
Who's there?
Enos.
Enos who?
Enos I'm not guilty.

226 • The Biggest Joke Book Ever

What do you get if you cross a policeman with a clock?
A crime watch.

Show me a vocalist at the policeman's ball...and
I'll show you a person who sings to the cops.

What do you call a robber who lives next door?   The neighbor-hood.

Girl: What are you watching?
Boy: A reality show about a couple of crooks.
Girl: What's it called?
Boy: Two Bad.

Robber: Is that a Rolex watch?
Man: Y-Yes.
Robber: Well, let me take some time off your hands.

What do you call a crook who steals pigs?   A hamburglar.

What did the cop shout when he saw a police duck?
An officer is down!

What does a polite convict say to everyone?   Please pardon me.

Which law officers have great vision?   Federal officers with the F.B.Eyes.

Show me a convict who swallows a bar of soap ... and I'll show you a prisoner who comes clean when questioned by the warden.

Judge: Have you ever been up before me?
Prisoner: I don't know, your honor. What time do you get up?

Buster: Crime is really bad in my neighborhood. On Christmas Eve Santa Claus comes down the chimney wearing a red suit and a matching ski mask.
Lester: Crime is so bad in my neighborhood a bank robber was mugged racing to his getaway car.

Wacky Waiters

Knock! Knock!
Who's there?
Menu.
Menu who?
Menu wish upon a star.

Knock! Knock!
Who's there?
Pasta.
Pasta who?
Pasta salt and pepper.

What do you get if you cross a waiter with a soldier?
A person who knows how to take and follow orders.

Customer: I'm so hungry I could eat a horse.
Waiter: Well, sir, you certainly came to the right place.

Customer: I'm in the mood for a tasty meal. What would you recommend?

Waiter: I recommend you try another restaurant.

Customer: Ugh! This is the worst meal I've had in two weeks.

Waiter: Where did you eat two weeks ago, sir?

Customer: Right here!

Knock! Knock!

Who's there?

Peas Pasta

Peas Pasta who?

Peas Pasta grated cheese. Thank you.

SIGN ON A TRUCK STOP: We fill your tank and your tummy with gas.

Knock! Knock!

Who's there?

Hal.

Hal who?

Hal have the blue plate special.

Chef: Why are you running?

Waiter: The big guy at table four wants rushin' dressing.

Customer: Waiter, is the fish on this plate fresh?

Waiter: If it were any fresher sir, it would be swimming in your water glass.

Customer: Why do they call this place the canoe diner?

Waiter: There's no tipping allowed.

Customer: I'd like to have a pork chop, and make it lean.
Waiter: Yes, sir. In which direction?

▶ ▶ ▶ ▶ ▶ ▶ ▶ ▶ ▶ ▶ ▶ ▶ ▶ ▶ ▶ ▶ ▶ ▶ ▶ ▶

Where do tennis players go for lunch?

To a food court.

◀ ◀ ◀ ◀ ◀ ◀ ◀ ◀ ◀ ◀ ◀ ◀ ◀ ◀ ◀ ◀ ◀ ◀ ◀ ◀

What did Peter order at the Neverland Italian Restaurant?
Pan Pizza.

▶ ▶ ▶ ▶ ▶ ▶ ▶ ▶ ▶ ▶ ▶ ▶ ▶ ▶ ▶ ▶ ▶ ▶ ▶ ▶

Customer #1: How's the service in this diner?

Customer #2: Terrible. It takes them an hour to serve a minute steak.

▶ ▶ ▶ ▶ ▶ ▶ ▶ ▶ ▶ ▶ ▶ ▶ ▶ ▶ ▶ ▶ ▶ ▶ ▶ ▶

Customer: Why is this place called the Underwater Diner?
Waiter: Sub sandwiches are our specialty.

◀ ◀ ◀ ◀ ◀ ◀ ◀ ◀ ◀ ◀ ◀ ◀ ◀ ◀ ◀ ◀ ◀ ◀ ◀ ◀

What did the waiter shout when John went into the Mexican food restaurant?

Table for Juan!

▶ ▶ ▶ ▶ ▶ ▶ ▶ ▶ ▶ ▶ ▶ ▶ ▶ ▶ ▶ ▶ ▶ ▶ ▶ ▶

SIGN IN A DINER: Early Bird Special: Roast Spring Chicken.

◀ ◀ ◀ ◀ ◀ ◀ ◀ ◀ ◀ ◀ ◀ ◀

Customer: Hey waiter! I've been waiting an

hour for the turtle soup I ordered.

Waiter: I'm sorry, sir, but you know how
slow turtles are.

▶ ▶ ▶ ▶ ▶ ▶ ▶ ▶ ▶ ▶ ▶ ▶

French waiter: Would you like to try
some snails?

American Customer: No thanks. I prefer
fast food.

Knock! Knock!
Who's there?
Aspect?
Aspect who?
Aspect to get free bread with my meal.

Customer: I see you have tomato soup on your menu.
Waiter: Yes, sir. Is that what you'd like to have?
Customer: No. I'd like to have a clean menu.

Knock! Knock!
Who's there?
Sid.
Sid who?
Sid down and a waiter will take your order.

Customer: **Waiter, this apple pie tastes fishy.**
Waiter: **That's impossible, sir. It's crabapple pie.**

Customer: How do you make your famous gold soup?
Waiter: We start out by putting in 14 carrots.

Waiter: Would you like to try our porterhorse steak special?
Customer: Don't you mean porterhouse steak?
Waiter: If you say so, sir.

SIGN IN A DINER: Try our heavenly Devil's Food cake.

Daffy Doctors & Nutty Nurses

What does a psychiatrist like to eat on a picnic?
Southern Freud Chicken.

....

Patient: Doctor, I have an inferiority complex.
Doctor: That's ridiculous. You're too smart for that.
Patient: Oh no I'm not.

....

Doctor: **How long have you had amnesia?**
Patient: **How long have I had what?**

....

Lady: **Doctor, my son thinks he's a submarine.**
Doctor: **Uh oh! He's in deep trouble.**

....

Lady: **Doctor, my husband makes me boiling mad.**
Doctor: **Just simmer down now.**

....

Lady: Doctor, my daughter thinks she's a rubber band.
Doctor: Relax, she'll snap out of it.

....

Lady: **Doctor, my nephew is very sick. He thinks he's a basketball.**
Doctor: **Calm down. He'll bounce back.**

....

What's the name of the psychologists' union?
The United Mind Workers of America.

....

Then there was the baseball umpire who had outpatient surgery.

Lady Patient: Doctor, I feel faint.
Doctor: If you fee faint now, just wait until you get my bill.

Knock! Knock!
Who's there?
Decode.
Decode who?
Decode in my nose is getting worse.

Knock! Knock!
Who's there?
Breed.
Breed who?
Breed deep and say "aah."

What do you get if you cross a Mexican jumping bean and a drug store?
Medicine you don't have to shake before taking it.

What do you get if you cross health pills with nasty druggists?
Vitameanies.

Where does a rabbit go to fix a broken bone?
To a hare setter.

What kind of vitamin did the doctor recommend for the sick spider?
Vitamin Bee.

Who is the most musical of all doctors?
The choir-practor.

Why did the door go to a psychologist?
Because it was all keyed up.

Where does a doctor keep his funny pills?
In his medicine jest.

Why don't chiropractors gamble?
Because they only bet on sore things.

What did Dr. Crow say to say to his patient?
Take two aspirins and caw me in the morning.

If you're feeling sick and run down, sometimes visiting the doctor can prove to be a real shot in the arm.

What did Dr. Oz say to the Tin Man?
Drink lots of fluids and get plenty of bed rust.

SIGN ABOVE A DOCTOR'S SCALE: **Weighting Room.**

Knock! Knock!
Who's there?
Debby.
Debby who?
Debby no charge for your physical exam.

They're a perfect match. She's a family doctor ... and he makes everyone sick.

Did you hear about the girl with the split personality? She went wacky always trying to have the last word.

Zack: **Why did you go to an eye doctor?**
Mack: **I was see sick.**

What advice did the doctor give to the man who lived in a desert?
Get well soon.

You tell 'em, Doc ... give them a dose of their own medicine.

Patient: **Doctor, what's the quickest way to cure double vision?**
Doctor: **Shut one eye.**

Father: My daughter needs braces.

Dentist: Well you'll have to put your money where her mouth is.

....

Patient: What's this prescription for?

Doctor: Tranquilizers.

Patient: When should I take them?

Doctor: Just before you look at my bill.

....

Mr. Jones: Why is your wife jumping rope?

Mr. Smith: Because the doctor told her to take two pills a day for a week and then skip a day.

....

Young Man: Doc, I don't dance, go to amusement parks, eat sweet desserts, or play video games. Do you think I'll live to be 100?

Doctor: You might if you don't die from boredom first.

....

DAFFY DEFINITION

Plastic Surgeon - A doctor who cures people who are sick of their faces.

....

NOTICE: When it comes to the flu, it's always better to give than to receive.

....

DAFFY DEFINITION:

Dentist's Office - a filling station.

Man: What's up, Doc?

Doctor: My malpractice insurance rates.

....

Medical Student #1: I have an anatomy exam tomorrow!

Medical Student #2: Then you'd better bone up on your studies tonight.

....

What kind of seafood does a psychiatrist like?

Freud Fish.

....

What does a doctor use to examine a lumberjack?

An axe-ray machine.

....

What do you get if you cross a cobbler and a doctor?

Someone who heels sick people.

....

Knock! Knock!

Who's there?

Tamara.

Tamara who?

Tamara you'll feel better.

....

Knock! Knock!

Who's there?

Ally.

Ally who?

Alley did was check my temperature and it cost me fifty bucks.

What do you get if you cross a patient with a wheel?
Someone who is sick and tired.

Doctor: So, what's wrong with you?
Patient: That's what I'm paying you to tell me.

Who takes care of sick little fish?
The school nurse shark.

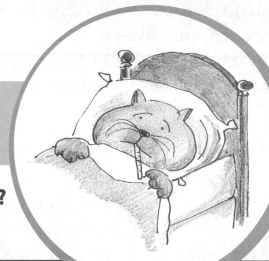

Girl: How can I make my sick cat feel better?
Vet: Fill this purrscription.

What did the dentist say to the duck?
Bite down hard.

ATTENTION: **Bambi has a hart condition.**

What do you get if you cross a saint and a pharmacologist?
A miracle drug.

Nurse: How is the little boy who swallowed the $100 bill?
Doctor: No change yet.

Lady: Doctor, my daughter thinks she's a stick of margarine.
Doctor: What do you want me to do?
Lady: Can you make her butter?

Ann: I work in a hospital during the day and clean houses at night.
Fran: I guess that makes you a nurse maid.

Knock! Knock!
Who's there?
Effie.
Effie who?
Effie feels better, give him some chicken soup.

HOW DO YOU FEEL?

"I need to have my head examined," said Mr. Lettuce.

"I mashed my toes," said Mr. Potato.

"I feel run down," said Mr. Beet.

"I can't concentrate," said Ms. Orange.

Patient: Doc, I have insomnia. What should I do?
Doctor: Try getting a little sleep.

Penny: I don't feel well. I need a doctor's opinion.
Denny: Okay, but you're sure to be ill advised.

What do you get if you cross a hospital with a perfume factory?
A medical scenter.

How does a mentally unstable person find his way home?
He follows the psycho-path.

Man: Doctor, I have amnesia. What should I do?
Doctor: Just forget about it.

Why did the math teacher go to a psychologist?
He had a lot of problems he couldn't figure out on his own.

DOPEY DOCTORS' NAMES

Dr. Euell B. Fine
Dr. Noah Payne
Dr. Hope N. Wide
Dr. Ivanna Secondopinion
Nurse Dee Patients
Nurse Anita Doctor

What did one stethoscope say to the other stethoscope?
Let's have a heart-to-heart talk.

When is a corn farmer like a doctor? When the doctor is an ear specialist.

Nurse: Take this concentrated lemon pill.
Patient: Why?
Nurse: It'll make you feel bitter.

Girl: **Doctors are nice people.**
Boy: **What do you mean?**
Girl: **They don't get mad if you stick your tongue out at them.**

Show me a trained hypnotist ... and I'll show you a stare master.

What do you call a doctor who lives in Egypt?
A Cairo-practor.

Nurse: You have a small fever.
Patient: I've always been a little hot-headed.

What do you need if you skip class at medical school?
A doctor's excuse.

Doctor: **What's wrong with you?**
Patient: **I swallowed a bone.**
Doctor: **Are you choking?**
Patient: **No doctor, I'm serious.**

Knock! knock!
Who's there?
Shirley.
Shirley who?
Shirley you must know what's wrong with me.

Knock! Knock!
Who's there?
Sizzle.
Sizzle who?
Sizzle hurt you more than it hurts me.

Man: **When I get to my job I feel dizzy and sad.**
Doctor: **It's just a case of working daze blues.**

What did the cross-eyed teacher say to the eye doctor?
My pupils are out of control.

Did you hear about the psychiatrist who had an auto mechanic for a patient?
Instead of getting on the doctor's couch, he crawled under it.

Convict #1: My doctor prescribed a placebo for my illness.

Convict #2: A placebo is fake medicine.

Convict #1: That's okay. I paid him with counterfeit money.

▶ ▶ ▶ ▶ ▶ ▶ ▶ ▶ ▶ ▶ ▶ ▶ ▶ ▶ ▶ ▶ ▶ ▶ ▶

Show me a doctor who sets broken bones...and I'll show you a marrow minded person.

◀ ◀ ◀ ◀ ◀ ◀ ◀ ◀ ◀ ◀ ◀ ◀ ◀ ◀ ◀ ◀ ◀

Girl: **Who is the most famous baby doctor?**

Boy: **Who are you kidding, babies can't be doctors.**

▶ ▶ ▶ ▶ ▶ ▶ ▶ ▶ ▶ ▶ ▶ ▶ ▶ ▶ ▶

What is a podiatrist's favorite song?

There's no business like toe business.

◀ ◀ ◀ ◀ ◀ ◀ ◀ ◀ ◀ ◀ ◀ ◀ ◀ ◀ ◀

What did the doctor say to the sick shoe?

Stick out your tongue.

▶ ▶ ▶ ▶ ▶ ▶ ▶ ▶ ▶ ▶ ▶ ▶ ▶ ▶ ▶ ▶ ▶ ▶

Man: My psychologist is a real wise guy. He encourages me to speak freely and then he charges me for listening.

◀ ◀ ◀ ◀ ◀ ◀ ◀ ◀ ◀ ◀ ◀ ◀ ◀ ◀ ◀ ◀ ◀ ◀

A hypochondriac told his doctor he was certain he had a fatal disease. "Nonsense," scolded the doctor. "You wouldn't know if you had that. With that particular disease there's no discomfort of any kind." "Oh no!" gasped the patient. "Those are my symptoms exactly!"

▶ ▶ ▶ ▶ ▶ ▶ ▶ ▶ ▶ ▶ ▶ ▶ ▶ ▶ ▶ ▶ ▶

Patient: Doctor, my chickenpox really itch.

Doctor: Show me the trouble spots.

◀ ◀ ◀ ◀ ◀ ◀ ◀ ◀ ◀ ◀ ◀ ◀ ◀ ◀ ◀ ◀ ◀ ◀

Doctor: The check you gave me last week came back.

Patient: So did the pain in my back you treated me for.

The Merry Military

What did the big octopus soldier say to the little octopus soldier?
You're a small arms expert, aren't you?

▶ ▶ ▶ ▶ ▶ ▶ ▶ ▶ ▶ ▶ ▶ ▶ ▶ ▶ ▶ ▶

Knock! Knock!
Who's there?
Navy.
Navy who?
Navy we'll meet again someday.

◀ ◀ ◀ ◀ ◀ ◀ ◀ ◀ ◀ ◀ ◀ ◀ ◀ ◀ ◀ ◀

ATTENTION: The U.S. Army seeks cleaning personnel for mop-up operations.

▶ ▶ ▶ ▶ ▶ ▶ ▶ ▶ ▶ ▶ ▶ ▶ ▶ ▶ ▶ ▶

Where does a smart general hide his armies?
In his sleevies.

◀ ◀ ◀ ◀ ◀ ◀ ◀ ◀ ◀ ◀ ◀ ◀ ◀ ◀ ◀ ◀

Why did the dentist join the Marines?
He wanted to be a drill sergeant.

▶ ▶ ▶ ▶ ▶ ▶ ▶ ▶ ▶ ▶ ▶ ▶ ▶ ▶ ▶ ▶

WANTED: **Ex-sailors needed to work as shipping clerks.**

◀ ◀ ◀ ◀ ◀ ◀ ◀ ◀ ◀ ◀ ◀ ◀ ◀ ◀ ◀ ◀

Knock! Knock!
Who's there?
Army.
Army who?
Army and my friends invited to your party?

▶ ▶ ▶ ▶ ▶ ▶ ▶ ▶ ▶ ▶ ▶ ▶ ▶ ▶ ▶ ▶

How do ordinary soldiers fly from coast to coast?
They take private jets.

What is a soldier's least favorite month?
March.

What did Captain Skunk say to his soldiers?
Follow my odors, men.

What makes a soldier's foot hurt?
Boot cramp.

What did the soldier say to his Army blanket?
Cover me, pal.

Why do vampires hate all Marines?
Because they're tough leathernecks.

Knock! Knock!
Who's there?
Carrie.
Carrie who?
Carrie on Sergeant.

Knock! Knock!
Who's there?
Haul.
Haul who?
Haul hands on deck.

Admiral: **What does a sailor sit on, Swabby?**
Sailor: **His rear, Admiral.**

What do you get if you cross hurricanes and Marines?
Something that storms a lot of beaches.

Knock! Knock!
Who's there?
Zeke.
Zeke who?
Zeke out and destroy all enemy outposts.

Why do Boy Scouts make good soldiers?
They enjoy taking hikes.

What do carrier pilots play cards with?
A flight deck.

Captain: Would you like me to give your outfit some armored vehicles?
Soldier: Yes, sir. A million tanks!

Mack: Do you fly a jet fighter?
Zack: No, I bailed out of pilot school.

What did the soldier say to the football quarterback?
Can I have a weekend pass.

Why did the soldier become a waiter?
Because he still wanted to serve the public.

Mother: Is that the cafeteria where you have your meals?
Soldier: Yes, mom, but it's a mess.
Mother: Well, someone should clean it up.

Sarge: My troop has been drilling in the hot sun for hours.
Captain: I can tell. They have marching odors.

Knock! Knock!
Who's there?
I, Major.
I, Major who?
I, Major bed for you.

....

Sarge: **Shoulder arms!**
Soldier: **Is this a drill or an anatomy lesson?**

....

How does a chicken join the Army?
She signs henlistment papers.

....

What did the Marine singer record?
A service record.

....

Knock! Knock!
Who's there?
Ann.
Ann who?
Ann-chors away, my boys.

....

Knock! Knock!
Who's there?
Huff.
Huff who?
Huff we go into the wild blue yonder.

....

Knock! Knock!
Who's there?
A Moe.
A Moe who?
A Moe is what a gun shoots.

Why did the crow join the Marines?
He answered the caw of duty.

What do you call volunteers for the Munchkin Armed Forces?
Army weecruits.

NOTICE: **The Army band performed for the Queen of England at a command performance.**

What did the paratrooper say to the parachute maker?
Please. Just chute me.

What do you get when a lumberjack joins the Air Force?
A chopper pilot.

What did the brave baby soldier get?
A goo conduct medal.

ATTENTION ON DECK: **Admirals are fleet-footed soldiers.**

Where does a pilot keep his flying suit?
On a plain hanger.

What do you get if you cross a fast ship with a pair of sharp scissors?
A Coast Guard cutter.

What did the balding drill
sergeant say to his hair?
Fall out!

FALL OUT!

What do soldiers hum?
Pla-tunes.

Why are pilots like real estate agents?

They're both land experts.

Why are landing crews like football fans?

They're always happy when they see a touchdown.

Knock! Knock!

Who's there?

A band.

A band who?

A band on ship men. We're sinking!

Why did the orange become a sailor?

He wanted to be in a navel battle.

Why were there so many fingerprints on the battleship?

Because someone yelled all hands on deck.

What do you get when Army blankets burst into flames?

Cover fire.

Why is a ship's captain like a golfer?

They both want to stay on the right course.

How did the sailor get knocked out?

Someone decked him.

What large reptile do you find on a Navy ship?

The navi-gator.

Where did Soldier Santa take cover?

In a fox ho ho-ho!

Why did the soldiers shoot into the burning building?

They were taught to fight fire with fire.

Why did the pooch train to become a pilot?

He wanted to have some aerial dogfights.

Sergeant: Remember soldier, your rifle is your best friend.

Soldier: Gosh Sarge, I could never fire my best friend.

What do rabbit pilots fly?

Hare combat missions.

....

What does a soldier caddy carry?

Officers clubs.

....

Did you hear about the dumb Navy cook who transferred to the submarine services because he wanted to make sandwiches.

....

Why did Bambi join the Army?

He wanted to be a buck private.

....

What do you get if you cross combat soldiers with a church choir?

Battle hymns.

....

What do you get if you cross a razor and a rifle?

A sharp shooter.

....

Knock! Knock!

Who's there?

Tour.

Tour who?

Tour-pedoes are fired from submarines.

....

What did the Green Giant wear after he joined the Navy?

A pea coat.

Man #1: **I'm an Army doctor.**

Man #2: **Do you treat officers?**

Man #1: **No. I have a private practice.**

....

Why do Navy seals make bad sailors?

They have no sea legs.

....

What did the sergeant say after his soldiers jumped into their bunks?

Cover yourselves, men!

....

Girl: **Were you in the Vietnam War?**

Grandfather: **Yes. I put up a good fight, but they drafted me anyway.**

Where do machine guns hatch their babies?

In machine gun nests.

What did Corporal Stickem win?
A glue conduct medal.

What do you get if you cross shoppers and soldiers?
Customer service.

Why do pilots like Kansas and Oklahoma?
They're great planes states.

What do you get if you cross soldiers and locomotive engineers?
Army training.

Where will you find soldiers and sailors in a retail store?
Check the service desk.

Clerk: Why are you hiring so many ex-military men?
Manager: I'm expecting a price war.

Why couldn't the Army Captain go to the show?
It was general admission only.

LISTEN UP!
You tell 'em, General ... we'll all pay attention.
You tell 'em, Sarge ... and put us at ease.
You tell 'em, Captain ... this isn't a private conversation.

Knock! Knock!
Who's there?
G.I.
G.I. who?
G.I. don't really care.

Soldier: Should I wrap the bandolier of bullets around my belly, Sarge.
Sarge: No solider. Don't waist your ammo.

Money Matters

What kind of books does a banker like to read?
Check books.

. . . .

What do you get if you cross a mortgage company and a songwriter?
Bank notes.

. . . .

How did the bankrupt hay farmers survive?
The government baled them out.

. . . .

KOOKY QUESTION: Do lifeguards have savings accounts?

. . . .

Where does a bad taxi driver keep his money?
In a crash register.

. . . .

Mr. Brown: My restaurant went bankrupt because my customers didn't like my home-cooked meals.

Mr. Green: Oh well. I guess you didn't have the right recipes for success.

. . . .

When do pop singers go bankrupt?
When they hit rock bottom.

. . . .

What is a kangaroo check?
It's one that bounces at the bank.

. . . .

Why was the apple grower happy at harvest time?
His company was in the red ... and that's good.

What did the chicken do at the bank?
She hendorsed her paycheck.

Then there was the art gallery that got into financial trouble because its account was overdrawn.

Terry: I know an investment banker who married a math teacher.
Larry: How did the union work out?
Terry: Not too good. They ended up with a lot of money problems.

How do you pay a lumberyard owner for the boards you ordered?
Write him a plank check.

Knock! Knock!
Who's there?
Iowa.
Iowa who?
Iowa lot of money to my creditors.

Why did the investor throw his money into the river?
He wanted to check his cash flow.

What does a minister get every four weeks?
A monthly pray check.

Bill: Do you like being a professional field-goal kicker?
Will: It helps me foot my bills.

What do you get if you cross a ten-dollar bill with a parrot?
Money that talks.

How can you tell if a whale is bankrupt?
He'll be belly up.

Knock! Knock!
Who's there?
Toucan.
Toucan who?
Toucan no longer live as cheaply as one.

What do you get if you cross talking birds with an ATM?
Parrots with $100 bills.

Why did the little bug pay the dog a dollar?
It was a rental flea.

ATTENTION: Moses had an excellent prophet-sharing plan.

Knock! Knock!
Who's there?
Refund.
Refund who?
Refund two charity events every year.

STUPID STOCK TIP: Use your disposable income to invest in garbage trucks.

How was the Big Bad Wolf able to retire early?
He always earned time and a huff.

YOUR ATTENTION PLEASE:

Yard Sale — buy this lot!

Garage Sale — parked cars not included.

Moving Sale — items are going fast.

Block Sale — square deals.

How did the beekeeper get started selling honey?

He got a buzzness loan from the bank.

How much money does a Bronco rider make?
About twenty bucks an hour.

Mike: I sell diet books.

Spike: Oh. So you make fast money.

Bob: Why should I put my money into Acme vaults?

Rob: It's a safe investment.

Bob: Why should I purchase airline stock?

Rob: It's a high yield investment.

FOR SALE – Topsoil at hole-sale prices.

Why did all of the stockholders have to hang from the ceiling?

Because the Chairman had the floor.

What's the difference between an accountant and a librarian?

Not much. They both keep books.

Jack: I produce charcoal for a living.
Mack: How's business?
Jack: It's always in the black.

Tino: I flip pizzas for a living and the pay is good.
Gino: But isn't that a kind of a pie-in-the sky job?

Gary: How's your job at the bank?
Larry: Good. I'm really cleaning up.
Gary: Are you a loan officer?
Larry: No. I'm a maintenance man.

Why is an accountant like the judge of a beauty pageant?
They both check out all the figures.

Knock! Knock!
Who's there?
Alone.
Alone who?
Alone from a bank is what you need to buy a house.

NOTICES:

Invest in our school for mimes. Silent partners are most welcome.
Invest in a poultry farm. We have a layaway program.
Invest in rare, old comic books. We are not a collection agency.

NOTICE: Money doesn't grow on trees ... unless you're in the lumber business.

Knock! Knock!

Who's there?

Account.

Account who?

Account is just as important as a duke or a baron.

Mr. Good: I sell religious songbooks.

Mr. Sims: Is there a big market for your product?

Mr. Good: Yes. We have a lot of hymn-pulse buyers.

Ike: I sell barbells and weights.

Spike: How's business?

Ike: Sales have been weak.

Mr. Jones: Why did you demolish that structure?

Worker: I thought the building deserved a raze.

Bill: I'm a refrigeration expert.

Will: That sounds like cool work.

Bill: Not really. We're having a pay freeze.

Man: Are there any job openings?

Unemployment Agency: I'm sorry, but the job market is currently flooded.

Man: Yahoo! That's good news. I'm a plumber.

What do you get if you cross a swimming pool with a mortgage company?

Dive-through banking.

What did the pier say to the ship that arrived late in port?

Now I'll have to dock your pay.

Knock! Knock!

Who's there?

Welfare.

Welfare who?

Welfare crying out loud, I need government assistance.

NOTICE: **Invest in Universal Shipbuilding, Inc. You'll be glad you came onboard.**

What do you get if you cross an acrobat with a bargain storeowner?

Someone who rolls back prices.

Where did the gardener keep his money?

In a savings and lawn company.

SALE. Today only. Goose feather vests marked down.

What do you get if you cross a mortgage with morning mist?

Monthly rent that's always dew.

SIGN IN A FISH MARKET: School Sale Today!

Knock! Knock!

Who's there?

Eel.

Eel who?

Eel show you where the sale items are.

ATTENTION: Used boats at sail prices.

▶▶▶▶▶▶▶▶▶▶▶▶▶▶▶▶

Customer: **Why are your wristwatches so expensive?**
Clerk: **Time is money.**

◀◀◀◀◀◀◀◀◀◀◀◀◀◀◀◀

Knock! Knock!
Who's there?
Minny.
Minny who?
Minny mum wage is low pay.

▶▶▶▶▶▶▶▶▶▶▶▶▶▶▶▶

Broker: **Would you like to buy some junk bonds?**
Investor: **Knock off the trash talking.**

◀◀◀◀◀◀◀◀◀◀◀◀◀◀◀◀

Why did the store manager take a sword to work?
He was going to slash some prices.

▶▶▶▶▶▶▶▶▶▶▶▶▶▶▶▶

Knock! Knock!
Who's there?
Urn.
Urn who?
Urn a living or you'll starve.

◀◀◀◀◀◀◀◀◀◀◀◀◀◀◀◀

KOOKY QUESTION:
Does Moby Dick have a lot of credit cods?

Knock! Knock!

Who's there?

Seldom.

Seldom who?

Seldom some common stock.

► ►

Billy: **Having a lot of money isn't everything.**

Tillie: **No, but it can buy everything.**

◄ ◄ ◄ ◄ ◄ ◄ ◄ ◄ ◄ ◄ ◄ ◄ ◄ ◄ ◄ ◄ ◄

Pirate #1: How much did you pay for your earrings?

Pirate #2: A buccaneer.

► ► ► ► ► ► ► ► ► ► ► ► ► ► ► ► ► ► ► ►

What do you sign when you borrow money from an owl?

An I.O.U. Who.

◄ ◄ ◄ ◄ ◄ ◄ ◄ ◄ ◄ ◄ ◄ ◄ ◄ ◄ ◄ ◄

CHAPTER 5

FUNNY FOLKS

What cartoon character lives in a marsh in Scotland?
Sponge Bog Square Pants.

What cartoon character keeps a diary on the internet?
Sponge Blog Square Pants.

Who makes sure Sir Lancelot and his friends do not break curfew?
The knight watchman.

What do you get if you smear jam on a pirate flag?
The Jelly Roger.

Knock! Knock!
Who's there?
Alma.
Alma who?
Alma treasure is buried on a desert island.

Who sails the ocean blue and has fleas?
The Old Sea Dog.

Pirate: How much is your corn?
Farmer: A buck an ear.

Where does Blackbeard keep his gym shoes?
In Davy Jones' locker.

Which pirate is a great fisherman?
Captain Hook.

What do you get if you cross a lion with a mast?
A mane sail.

....

What weapon does a pirate calf carry?

A veal cutlass.

....

By what other name is Bambi the Buccaneer known?
Buckbeard the Pirate.

....

What do you get if you cross a boy who lives in Neverland with a skillet?

Peter Frying Pan.

....

Which lizard was the first treasurer of the United States?
Salamander Hamilton.

....

what did Peter order from the Neverland I-Hop?

Peter pancakes.

....

Who was Michael Jackson Soda Bottle?
The king of pop.

....

When does Tarzan stop swinging through the trees?

When he reaches the finish vine.

....

Who lives in Neverland and tells silly jokes?
Peter Pun.

....

who's the smartest fairy in Neverland?

Thinkerbell.

Who's in charge of the Neverland Fire Department?
Captain Hook and Ladder.

Why didn't Noah do any fishing on the Ark?
Because he only had two worms.

Which member of the Round Table was a famous writer?
King Author.

Who keeps Robin Hood's castle neat and tidy?
Maid Marian.

Why did Robin Hood's men hate living in the woods?
Sherwood Forest only had one little john.

Why did Robin Hood look odd in a tuxedo?
He didn't wear a bow tie.

What do you get if you cross a championship archer with a sweatshirt?
A Robin Hoodie.

Who was the first girl to sit at the Round Table?
Knight Ann Gale.

What lumberjack was an All-Star player for the Atlanta Braves?
Woodchipper Jones.

Who weighs two tons and went to the ball in glass slippers?
Cinderelephant.

Who eats spinach and sews sailor suits?
Popeye the Tailor Man.

what do you call a big lumberjack with sore feet?
Paul Bunion.

What does Robin Hood Elephant shoot?
A dumbow.

What did the Joker say to Bruce, the Secret Crime Fighter?
Wayne, Wayne go away.

Why did the pirate join a health club?
He wanted to be shipshape.

Why did Sir Lancelot remove his heavy armor?
He wanted to be a knight light.

Who was the most famous sports rooter in China?
Cheerman Mao.

Where should you keep your Disney mouse memorabilia?
Put it on your mickey mantelpiece.

Who is geeky and pulls Santa's sled?
Rudork the red-nosed reindeer.

Where does Mickey Mouse's pet sleep when they camp out?
In a Pluto pup tent.

Who carves wooden figures and lives under the sea.
The Whittle Mermaid.

What caped crime fighter has a huge ego?
Bruce Vain.

What cartoon character is a senior citizen?
Don Old Duck.

What's green and pecks on trees?
Woody Woodpickle.

What did Henry VIII say while playing checkers?
King me.

Why does Uncle Sam wear red, white, and blue suspenders?
To keep his pants from falling down.

What did Mickey Mouse say to his girlfriend on her birthday?
Minnie Happy Returns.

What did Bugs Bunny say to his girlfriend on her birthday?
Many hoppy returns.

What frog hero died at the Alamo?
Davy Croakett.

Which one of Robin Hood's merry men was a pilot?
Flyer Tuck.

What monk lives with Ronald McDonald and the Hamburglar?
The French Friar.

What do you get if you cross the Grand Canyon with American's first president?
Gorge Washington.

Why did Robin Hood take his bow and arrow shopping?
He was going to Target.

What did Bugs Bunny say to the geek gopher?
What's up dork?

What kind of vehicle does Mickey Mouse's girlfriend drive?
A Minnie van.

Teacher: Who is your favorite author?
Boy: SpongeBob.
Teacher: SpongeBob is a cartoon character.
He never wrote any books.
Boy: That's why he's my favorite.

What did the Sasquatch eat for lunch?
A big foot long sandwich.

King Arthur: Mount your steed. We're going to kill an evil dragon.
Sir Mordred: Yahoo! A slay ride.

What do you get if you cross a zombie and Sir Lancelot?
The Dead of Knight.

What did Santa shout when he ran in the big race?
On your mark! Get set! Ho-Ho-Ho!

Which dog was famous for his debating skills?
Spaniel Webster.

What do you get if you cross a boy from Neverland and a dork with Yogi Bear?
A panduh! bear.

▷ ▷ ▷ ▷ ▷ ▷ ▷ ▷ ▷ ▷ ▷ ▷ ▷ ▷ ▷ ▷ ▷ ▷ ▷

Pirate #1: How did you get that new ship?
Pirate #2: We found it on sale.

◁ ◁ ◁ ◁ ◁ ◁ ◁ ◁ ◁ ◁ ◁ ◁ ◁ ◁ ◁ ◁ ◁ ◁ ◁

Knock! Knock!
Who's there?
Scooby Doo.
Scooby Doo who?
Scooby Doo your homework right now.

▷ ▷ ▷ ▷ ▷ ▷ ▷ ▷ ▷ ▷ ▷ ▷ ▷ ▷ ▷ ▷ ▷ ▷ ▷

What do you get if you cross Scooby Doo with a library?
Lots of dog-eared books.

◁ ◁ ◁ ◁ ◁ ◁ ◁ ◁ ◁ ◁ ◁ ◁ ◁ ◁ ◁ ◁ ◁ ◁ ◁

Minnie: Did you pass your mouse exam?
Mickey: Yes. I just squeaked by.

▷ ▷ ▷ ▷ ▷ ▷ ▷ ▷ ▷ ▷ ▷ ▷ ▷ ▷ ▷ ▷ ▷ ▷ ▷

Porky Pig took karate lessons. He's a ham-to-ham combat expert. His pork chops are deadly blows that leave opponents bacon for mercy.

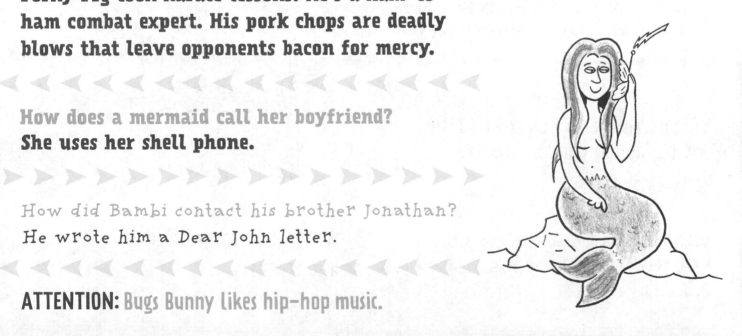

◁ ◁ ◁ ◁ ◁ ◁ ◁ ◁ ◁ ◁ ◁ ◁ ◁ ◁ ◁ ◁ ◁ ◁ ◁

How does a mermaid call her boyfriend?
She uses her shell phone.

▷ ▷ ▷ ▷ ▷ ▷ ▷ ▷ ▷ ▷ ▷ ▷ ▷ ▷ ▷ ▷ ▷ ▷ ▷

How did Bambi contact his brother Jonathan?
He wrote him a Dear John letter.

◁ ◁ ◁ ◁ ◁ ◁ ◁ ◁ ◁ ◁ ◁ ◁ ◁ ◁ ◁ ◁ ◁ ◁ ◁

ATTENTION: Bugs Bunny likes hip-hop music.

What did Cinderella Seal wear to the ball?

Glass flippers.

What did Mickey do when Minnie fainted?

He gave her mouse-to-mouse resuscitation.

Ed: Did Donald leave the party early?
Fred: Yes. He ducked out.

What do Smokey the Bear and Alexander the Great have in common?

They both have the same middle name.

What did Bugs Bunny say to the pier?

What's up, dock?

Who do you get if you cross a hero of the Alamo with an alligator?

Davy Crocodile.

Who do you get if you cross a feline with a famous frontier scout?

Kitty Carson.

What do you get if you cross Sir Lancelot and a bird of prey?

A knight hawk.

Which dog was a space hero?
Bark Rogers.

What is Teddy Roosevelt Skunk's motto?

Walk softly and carry a big stink.

What happened when Tarzan saw Jane?

He went ape over her.

ATTENTION: Tarzan was a swinging bachelor until he met Jane.

Does Tarzan do business in his tree house?

No. He has a branch office.

Where does Tarzan work out?
At a jungle gym.

Knock! Knock!

Who's there?

Tarzan.

Tarzan who?

Tarzan stripes are on the American flag.

....

What does Tarzan the Dairy Farmer swing on?

A bo-vine.

....

How did Tarzan learn the monkeys were unhappy with his leadership?

He heard it through the grapevine.

....

What did Tarzan say to the monkey mime?

Don't try to ape me.

....

NOTICE: Tarzan works a swing shift in the jungle.

....

Do you have to knock on Tarzan's front door?

No. Use the door buzzard.

....

Why was Tarzan mad at his adopted family?

They tried to make a monkey out of him.

Jane: I heard that swimming helps you keep a slim figure.

Tarzan: I don't believe it. Hippos spend most of their time in the water and look at them!

....

Where did Tarzan and Jane reside in California?

They lived on Hollywood and Vine.

....

Who do you get if you cross Bambi, Porky Pig, and a famous American patriot?

Alexandeer Ham-ilton.

....

Which pig was an American president?

George Washingham.

....

Which stuffed bear was an American president?

Teddy Roosevelt.

....

Which U.S. president hit a lot of home runs?

Babe Lincoln.

Where does Robin Hood's sheep live?
Shearwood Forest.

What's purple, lives in the jungle, and likes to eat small, thin pancakes?
Tarzan the Crepe Man.

Who was the devoted sidekick of the prehistoric Lone Ranger?
Tontosaurus.

Which creepy movie stars a mouse and a flying squirrel?
The Bullwinkle and Rocky Horror Picture Show.

What do you get when King Kong steps on the Lone Ranger?
A mashed man.

What did King Midas get when he retired?
A gold watch.

Where does King Midas go for drinks?
To gold bars.

SIGN IN KING MIDAS' LIBRARY: **Silence is golden.**

Why did King Midas call a doctor?
He had gold fever.

What did King Kong wear to the formal dance?
A monkey suit.

KOOKY QUESTION: Did Shakespeare marry an Avon lady?

What does King Midas get when people call his cell phone?

Rings of gold.

What is Smokey's constitutional right?

He has the right to bear arms.

What do you get when Santa goes up in a hot air balloon?

A high ho ho ho!

What is Tinker Bell's favorite flower?

The Peter Pansy.

Mrs. Munchkin: Where are you going?
Mr. Munchkin: I'm taking a short walk.

What did Sailor Santa shout from the crow's nest?

Land Ho Ho Ho!

What did the Munchkin say to the cashier of Oz?

Hey! You short-changed me.

What is a Munchkin scarecrow's favorite dessert?

Strawberry shortcake.

What did Scooby Dog's master say when he took him for a walk?

Scooby Doo pooh.

Why are mimes so polite?
They never talk back to anyone.

Why did the Munchkin go out for his college football team?
He wanted to be a big man on campus.

Dorothy: Tell me all about the Munchkins.
Witch Glenda: Sorry, I don't have time for small talk.

What do you get if you cross Superman and bakery rolls? Buns of steel.

Girl to mime boyfriend: We need to talk.

Knock! Knock!
Who's there?
Mercedes Benz.
Mercedes Benz who?
Mercedes Benz steel in her
bare hands. She's a super girl.

What hobo lives in Neverland? Peter Panhandler.

Who is Santa's favorite comedian?
Bill Murray Christmas.

What does Mother Nature write on during the fall?
Loose-leaf paper.

What did Peter Pan say when he saw the tornado?
Look. It's Windy.

How many ears does Davy Crocket have?
Three. A right ear. A Left ear. And a frontier.

How does the preamble to the Munchkin Bill of Rights begin?
Wee the People.

What did the nasty kid say to Sponge Bob?
Go home and soak your head.

Why didn't Sponge Judy date Sponge Bill?
She thought he was too drippy.

What sheep was the leader of the Forty Thieves?
Ali Baa Baa.

ATTENTION: They crossed George Washington with a person who does everything twice ... and got a general who double-crossed the Delaware.

What does an angel say when it answers its cell phone? Halo.

What do you get if you cross Robin Hood with an old cowboy?

A bow-legged archer.

....

Who leads a Barbarian horde and is made of tin?

Genghis Can.

....

Boy #1: I heard Cupid almost got you last week.

Boy #2: Yes. I had an arrow escape.

....

ATTENTION: Atlas was the world's greatest crook. He held up the entire world.

....

What do you get if you cross the superhero named Flash with a cell phone?

A very fast speed dial.

....

Why did Robin Hood let people chop down trees in his forest?

It was Share-wood Forest.

....

Who is the best athlete in Mother Goose Land?

Jock be nimble. Jock be quick.

....

What knight outlived all the other members of the Round Table?

Sir Viver.

....

What does an envelope say when you lick it?

It just shuts up and says nothing.

....

What did the Lone Ranger say as he set the table?

Hi ho silverware.

What do you call a sad singing cowboy?

Blue Gene Autry.

Jim: **Wow! A super fast superhero just ran past us.**
Tim: **I didn't see him.**
Jim: **That's because he has blinding speed.**

What did the girl wear to Granny's crib?

A little red riding hoodie.

What do you call a petrified Neverland fairy?

Tink hard.

What kind of bread does Santa Claus like?

Ho-Ho-Wheat.

Who is the clumsiest dork in heaven?

Clod Almighty.

What did Captain Gretel shout to her crew?

All Hans on deck!

Who carries a basket to Grandma's house and pens best sellers?

Little Red Writing Hood.

What does Pirate Santa yell when he wants to raise the anchor?

Heave Ho Ho Ho!

How does Tarzan know exactly how long each vine is?
Because Tarzan is the ruler of the jungle.

What famous English sea captain had feathers?
Sir Francis Drake.

Why did Soldier Tarzan take orders from the zebra?
Because the zebras had sergeant's stripes.

Why did Tarzan dump his mate?
She was a plain Jane.

What did Tarzan give his son for his birthday?
A swing set.

Does Tarzan like rock and roll?
No. He's crazy about old time swing music.

When does St. Patrick like reciting the alphabet?
When Irish I's are smiling.

What did the tired auctioneer say?
I'm going back to bid.

What's an empty gun hairdo?
No bangs.

What did the bad golfer say when he went into the pizza place?
I'll have my usual slice.

What do you say when you meet an angel?
Halo.

What is Mr. Jam's favorite song?
For He's a Jelly Good Fellow.

Why did the old lady who lived in the shoe get evicted from Mother Goose Land?
She couldn't foot her bills.

What did Paul Revere Octopus shout during his midnight ride?
Two arms! Four arms! Six arms! Eight arms!

What did the Tin Man say when he was caught in a cloudburst?
This is very rustful.

Beautician: **Would you like a truth hairstyle?**
Girl: **What's that?**
Beautician: **I'll let you have it straight.**

Lady: **Why did you contact our online dating service, sir?**
Guy: **I'd like some miss information.**

What did the NASCAR driver say when he had trouble steering his car?
I'm in wheel trouble.

What kind of weight exercises do beauticians do?
They curl barbells.

Two businessmen met for dinner. One was a ship builder. The other was a peanut butter manufacturer. During the meal the conversation went from sloop to nuts.

What do you get if you cross a Viking and a lumberjack?
A person who uses a battleaxe.

▶ ▶ ▶ ▶ ▶ ▶ ▶ ▶ ▶ ▶ ▶ ▶

Fran: What do you call Judge Cobra?
Dan: Hiss honor.

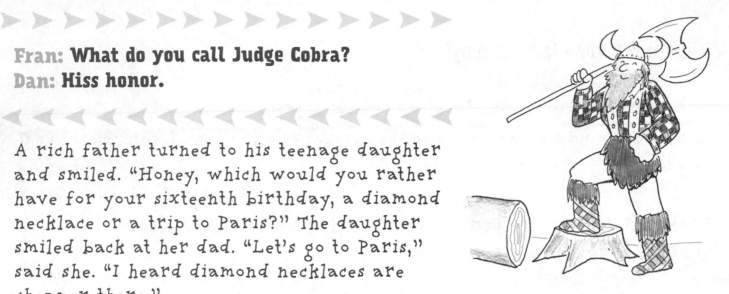

◀ ◀ ◀ ◀ ◀ ◀ ◀ ◀ ◀ ◀ ◀ ◀

A rich father turned to his teenage daughter and smiled. "Honey, which would you rather have for your sixteenth birthday, a diamond necklace or a trip to Paris?" The daughter smiled back at her dad. "Let's go to Paris," said she. "I heard diamond necklaces are cheaper there."

▶ ▶ ▶ ▶ ▶ ▶ ▶ ▶ ▶ ▶ ▶ ▶ ▶ ▶

What did the clock maker's son say to his father?
Watch me, Dad.

◀ ◀ ◀ ◀ ◀ ◀ ◀ ◀ ◀ ◀ ◀ ◀ ◀ ◀

What feline discovered America?
Christopurr Columbus.

▶ ▶ ▶ ▶ ▶ ▶ ▶ ▶ ▶ ▶ ▶ ▶ ▶ ▶

How can a fortune teller predict how well a golfer will play?
She reads his tee leaves.

◀ ◀ ◀ ◀ ◀ ◀ ◀ ◀ ◀ ◀ ◀ ◀ ◀ ◀

What do you get if you cross a clock maker with a dance instructor?
Someone who watches your steps.

▶ ▶ ▶ ▶ ▶ ▶ ▶ ▶ ▶ ▶ ▶ ▶ ▶ ▶

What do you get if you cross Clark Kent with a high yield money market account?
A super fund.

◀ ◀ ◀ ◀ ◀ ◀ ◀ ◀ ◀ ◀ ◀ ◀ ◀ ◀

Why did 007 dye his hair yellow?
He wanted to be James Blond.

Why isn't Cinderella a good softball player?
She always runs away from the ball.

▶ ▶ ▶ ▶ ▶ ▶ ▶ ▶ ▶ ▶ ▶ ▶ ▶ ▶ ▶ ▶ ▶

Wife: I'm sending you to a psychologist to be analyzed.
Husband: I won't take this lying down.

◀ ◀ ◀ ◀ ◀ ◀ ◀ ◀ ◀ ◀ ◀ ◀ ◀ ◀ ◀ ◀ ◀

What is the name of a famous pirate fairy tale?
Booty and the Beast.

▶ ▶ ▶ ▶ ▶ ▶ ▶ ▶ ▶ ▶ ▶ ▶ ▶ ▶ ▶ ▶ ▶

Where did Captain Hook get a tattoo?
On his pirate chest.

◀ ◀ ◀ ◀ ◀ ◀ ◀ ◀ ◀ ◀ ◀ ◀ ◀ ◀ ◀ ◀ ◀

Captain Morgan: Do you have a favorite letter of the alphabet, sailor?
Sailor: I, Captain.

▶ ▶ ▶ ▶ ▶ ▶ ▶ ▶ ▶ ▶ ▶

Who takes care of sailors on payday?
The check mate.

◀ ◀ ◀ ◀ ◀ ◀ ◀ ◀ ◀ ◀ ◀ ◀ ◀

Who takes the ship's crew jogging?
The running mate.

▶ ▶ ▶ ▶ ▶ ▶ ▶ ▶ ▶ ▶ ▶ ▶

What did Romeo Crow say to Juliet Crow?
I just cawed to say I love you.

◀ ◀ ◀ ◀ ◀ ◀ ◀ ◀ ◀ ◀ ◀ ◀ ◀ ◀ ◀ ◀

How does Sir Lancelot put money in the bank?
He uses a knight deposit box.

▶ ▶ ▶ ▶ ▶ ▶ ▶ ▶ ▶ ▶ ▶ ▶ ▶ ▶ ▶ ▶ ▶

Why is Robin Hood's watch so happy?
It has a merry band.

When is the best time to outfit a pirate ship?
When there's a half price sale.

WHAT'S IT LIKE TO BE A MOM?

... you spend a lot of time kidding around.

... the job isn't all child's play.

... you have to baby everyone but yourself.

... you work from son up to son down.

... you have to know more than a daughter who knows everything.

... you have to look young, act young and think young while doing the same old things day after day.

What group did Butch Cassidy and the Sundance Kid belong to?
The World Rustling Federation.

Why was the Munchkin sad?
He always got the short end of the stick.

Why doesn't Pinocchio like to smile?
His teeth are chipped.

Why was Pinocchio upset?
He broke a nail.

What is Pinocchio's favorite game?
Stickball.

WHAT IS A DORK?

A person who opens a fortune cookie and finds a blank slip.

Someone who goes to a palm reader and she tells him to wash his filthy hand.

A person who gets fired from a dollar store because he can't remember the prices of the items for sale.

Someone who walks out of an airplane in mid-flight because he doesn't like the movie.

A person with a birth certificate with a question mark on it instead of a name.

Someone who buys a homing pigeon for a pet and when he lets it go it relocates.

What did Geppetto get when he shook hands with Pinocchio?

Splinters.

What did Geppetto say to Pinocchio?
Go out and play in the lumberyard.

What do you call four singing Pinocchios?

A string quartet.

What does Pinocchio spread on his toast?
Log jam.

What tune does Pinocchio play on the piano?
Chopsticks.

How does Pinocchio play poker?
He uses a wood deck.

Why did Pinocchio break up with his girlfriend?

She was stringing him along.

What is Pinocchio's favorite snack food?
String cheese.

What did Pinocchio say to the carpenter?
Please don't bore me.

How did Pinocchio become a real boy?
Whittle by whittle.

Why did Captain Kirk sit on the tree stump?

It was the captain's log.

Silly Superheroes

Which superheroes do you find on a golf course?
The Fantastic Foursome.

Why did the judge order Superman to be held in jail until his case could be heard?

Because he was a flight risk.

Knock! Knock!
Who's there?
Ida.
Ida who?
Ida made a terrific superhero.

What do you get if you cross a superhero with a fish?
A caped cod.

Where does Bruce Wayne wash up?
In his bat tub.

What is Aquaman's part-time job?
He owns a sub shop.

What do you get if you cross superheroes and a forest?
Trees that have limbs of steel.

Knock! Knock!
Who's there?
Dew.
Dew who?
Dew we know his secret identity?

Who do you get if you cross Bruce Wayne with a geek?
Batman, the Dork Knight.

What do you get if you cross a hangman's knot with a very fast superhero?
A noose flash.

Why did the superhero Flash get a ticket?
He got caught in a speed trap.

Which superhero raced a hare?
The Teenage Mutant Ninja Tortoise.

Reporter: Who are you?
Superhero: I'm Captain Spaceman and my powers are out of this world.

What did the Hulk eat for lunch?
A six-foot comic-book-hero sandwich.

What do you call a masked crime fighter who has no personality?
A super zero.

Where did Boy Torch meet Girl Torch?
On match.com.

What is Super Fish's secret identity?
Carp Kent.

What is Barkman's secret identity?
Spruce Wayne.

Why didn't Wolverine get long nails when he first signed on to be a superhero?
There was no clause in his original contract.

Who works with Batman and floats in the ocean.
Robin, the Buoy Wonder.

What happened when the superhero got really, really old?
He couldn't remember his secret identity.

How does a fast superhero take pictures?
He uses a flash camera.

How quick is Super Ox? He's faster than a speeding bullock.

What kind of vehicle does Captain Genius drive?
A think tank.

What do you call a genetically engineered cow?
A moo-tant.

Why was the Super Shadow so weary?
Too much nightlife.

What do you get if you cross the Human Torch with Aquaman? A heat wave.

Knock! Knock!
Who's there?
Ozzie.
Ozzie who?
Ozzie through brick walls
with my X-ray vision.

Knock! Knock!
Who's there?
Wooden.
Wooden who?
Wooden you like to have super strength?

Knock! Knock!
Who's there?
I'm Mighty Thor.
I'm Mighty Thor who?
I'm Mighty Thor and I need a good chiropractor.

What road does Superman's girlfriend live on?
Lois Lane.

Spidey: How do I get these wrinkles out of my superhero costume?
Thor: Iron, man!

What color is Ms. Electric's costume? Shocking Pink.

Why is the superhero Flash never sick very long?
He always has a speedy recovery.

Mack: This big sandwich tastes like paper?
Zack: Maybe it's a comic book hero.

Where did Munchkin Superman grow up?
In Smallville.

What do you get if you cross Superman's pal with two identical former child stars?
The Jimmy Olsen Twins.

Knock! Knock!
Who's there?
Dish.
Dish who?
Dish looks like a job for Superman!

....

What does Spider Guy use to take pictures?
A web cam.

....

ATTENTION: The Super Torch is full of hot air.

....

Villain: Spider Pig, I've discovered your secret identity.
Spider Pig: Please don't squeal on me.

....

Why did Clark Kent become an actor?
He wanted to be a Hollywood super star.

....

Which hero fixes leaky pipes and broken windows?
The Building Super.

....

Who has long, sharp claws and turns into a superhero when the full moon rises?
Were-Wolverine.

....

Knock! Knock!
Who's there?
Allied.
Allied who?
Allied when I said I had super powers.

....

Who is Super Ghost?
He's a crime frighter.

What kind of hero goes out in a snowstorm?

One that has super plowers.

What do you find in the home of a comic-book artist?

Wall-to-wall paneling.

What do you get when you cross a sleek sailing vessel with a person from Krypton?

Slooper Man.

Villainess: **I'm Cat Woman!**

Hero: **Are you kitten me?**

Knock! Knock!

Who's there?

I, Spider.

I, Spider who?

I, Spider sneaking up on us.

What happened to the evil villain Mr. Elastic?

He's doing a ten-year stretch in the state pen.

PUNNY SUPERHEROES

CAPTAIN KANGAROO — He leaps tall buildings in a single bound.

MR. MATH MARVEL — He'll solve the crime even if clues don't add up.

DR. CARDIAC MAN — He knows what evil lurks in the hearts of men.

LOTTERY LASS — Crooks have no chance of winning when she's around.

Who is Torch Man's mortal enemy?

Smokey the Bear.

Who is Captain Reserve?

He's an X-tra Mutant superhero.

Heroine: Stop where you are, crook. I'm the Invisible Girl and I'm arresting you.

Robber: I don't see that happening.

What do you get if you cross a giant bee with Clark Kent?

Buzzaro Superman.

What do you get if you cross snobby teens with Bruce Wayne's vehicle?

The Bratmobile.

What do you get if you cross a comic-book hero with onions and garlic?

Super bad breath.

Where does a villain go to get a knuckle sandwich?

A fist-food restaurant.

Why did Super Girl go out with the Human Torch?

She thought he was hot.

Knock! Knock!

Who's there?

Izzy.

Izzy who?

Izzy a good guy or a bad guy?

Spidey: Dude, should I hit this golf shot with a driver?

Big Hulk: No. Use an iron, man.

How can you tell where a super mutant lives?
X marks the spot.

What crow has super powers?
Captain Americaw.

What would you call Spiderman if he fought for the South during the Civil War?
A Johnny Web.

Who selects which comic book art will be published?
A panel of judges.

MORE PUNNY SUPERHEROES

CAPTAIN BLABBERMOUTH – He's no longer in the superhero business because he told everyone his secret identity.

SUPER SURFER CHICK – She can end a crime wave before it starts.

SUPER CYCLOPS – He keeps an eye out for trouble.

SERGEANT RAZOR BLADE – He always arrives in the knick of time.

THE FANTASTIC EGGMAN – No crook can beat him.

Where does Clark Kent buy his groceries?
At a supermarket.

Which sheep is a mutant superhero?
Woolverine.

What do you call uncanny super cats?
Mewtants.

Knock! Knock!

Who's there?

Thermos.

Thermos who?

Thermos be a way out of this diabolical trap.

▶▶▶▶▶▶▶▶▶▶▶▶▶▶▶▶▶▶

Why did Bruce Wayne go to a chiropractor?

He had lower bat pain.

◀◀◀◀◀◀◀◀◀◀◀◀◀◀◀◀◀◀

Why did the Shadow become a cardiac specialist?

He wanted to learn what evil lurks in the hearts of men.

▶▶▶▶▶▶▶▶▶▶▶▶▶▶▶▶▶▶

Crook: How do you turn Batman into Splatman?

Robber: Knock him out and push him off a tall building.

◀◀◀◀◀◀◀◀◀◀◀◀◀◀◀◀◀◀

What do you get if you cross a NASCAR racer with a superhero named Flash?

A crime fighter who travels wheelie fast.

▶▶▶▶▶▶▶▶▶▶▶▶▶▶▶▶▶▶

Spider Guy: Iron Dude, how did you let that crook escape?

Iron Dude: I've been out of the superhero biz for a while and I guess I'm a bit rusty.

◀◀◀◀◀◀◀◀◀◀◀◀

What sheep is a superhero?

Baaman.

▶▶▶▶▶▶▶▶▶▶▶

Hero #1: I can soar like an eagle.

Hero #2: I have the eyes of a hawk.

Hero #3: Shut up, bird brains.

Knock! Knock!
Who's there?
One deer
One deer who?
One deer woman to the rescue!

▶ ▶ ▶ ▶ ▶ ▶ ▶ ▶ ▶ ▶ ▶ ▶ ▶ ▶ ▶ ▶ ▶

Where do superheroes play baseball?
In the Justice League.

◀ ◀ ◀ ◀ ◀ ◀ ◀ ◀ ◀ ◀ ◀ ◀ ◀ ◀ ◀ ◀ ◀

What do you get if you cross witches with super mutants?
The Hex-Men.

▶ ▶ ▶ ▶ ▶ ▶ ▶ ▶ ▶ ▶ ▶ ▶ ▶ ▶ ▶ ▶ ▶

What happened when Batman's partner turned to a life of crime?
He changed his name to Robin Hood.

◀ ◀ ◀ ◀ ◀ ◀ ◀ ◀ ◀ ◀ ◀ ◀ ◀ ◀ ◀ ◀ ◀

What did Robin say to Bruce Wayne at bath time?
Can I borrow your bat robe?

▶ ▶ ▶ ▶ ▶ ▶ ▶ ▶ ▶ ▶

Why did the masked crime fighter roll
after the escaping villain?
Because he was a marble superhero.

◀ ◀ ◀ ◀ ◀ ◀ ◀ ◀ ◀ ◀ ◀

What did Batman eat for lunch?
A superhero sandwich and it was
mighty good.

▶ ▶ ▶ ▶ ▶ ▶ ▶ ▶ ▶ ▶ ▶ ▶ ▶ ▶ ▶ ▶ ▶

Which team of gag writers pens the best
superhero puns?
The Joker and the Riddler.

Which superhero battles evil chicken thieves?

The Eggs Men.

Which superhero crime fighter enjoys making bad jokes?

The Pun-isher.

What do you call a person who shows you around Asgard, the home of the Norse thunder god?

A Thor guide.

Why did the boy invite Batman to his midday meal?

He wanted to have a hero for lunch.

What has four wheels, flies, and has amazing powers?

Super Van.

Why did Superman run super fast from one place to another?

He was in a no fly zone.

Which super swift hero is a has-been?

The one who's a flash in the pan.

What do Spider Dude and Iron Guy like to eat for dessert?

Marvel cake.

What is the favorite city of Superman and Batman?

Washington, D.C.

What do you call a group of superheroes who are bodybuilders?

The Flex Men.

Silly Santa & His Holiday Ha Ha's

What goes whoosh! Ho! Ho! Yeow!?

Santa sliding down a chimney with a fire in it.

What nationality is Santa Claus?

North Polish.

Man: You called for a substitute store Santa so I rushed right over here.

Owner: Phew! You arrived in the St. Nick of time.

....

DAFFY DEFINITION:
Mistletoe — a kiss miss plant.

....

What does Cool Santa sing during the holidays?

Gift Rap Songs.

....

What does Santa put in his salad?

Iceberg lettuce.

....

Who shouts Ho! Ho! Whoa?

Santa Cowboy.

....

HOLIDAY SIGN IN A JEWELRY STORE: Ring your Christmas Bell.

....

When does Santa Dork deliver Christmas gifts?

December 26th.

....

What did Santa's dog get for the holidays?

A Christmas flea.

....

Why does Santa Claus wear a red suit?

Because his blue suit makes him look fat.

Millie: Is Santa Claus a talented guy?

Tillie: Yes. He's a very gifted individual.

....

What do Santa and his elves do at sporting events?

They give a little Christmas cheer!

....

Jack: Does Santa Claus have a buzzer on his front door?

Zack: No. He has a sleigh bell.

....

Why did Mrs. Rudolph go to the powder room?

Because her nose was shiny.

....

Who is Santa's smartest reindeer?

Rudolph. He's very bright.

What did Santa shout when he got into his sleigh and found one reindeer was missing?
"No Comet!"

What does Santa do if he meets a dragon during his midnight ride?
He sleighs him.

Why did Santa Claus take his reindeer to a dentist?
Because they all had buck teeth.

Why does Santa's sled get good mileage?
Because it has long-distance runners on it.

What does baby Santa Claus play with?
Blocks of ice.

Why did Santa like his rich aunt so much?
Because she put a Claus in her will.

What does Santa Claus wear on his feet?
Snow shoes.

Who delivers Christmas gifts to little fish in the ocean?
Lobster Claus.

What do you get if you cross jam and Santa Claus?
Jelly Ol' St. Nick.

Why didn't the dork elf join a Christmas club?
He didn't have the time to attend the meetings.

What do Santa Claus and Paul Revere have in common?
They're both famous for their midnight rides.

Why did the dork go to the bank the day after Christmas?
Someone gave him money as a gift and he wanted to exchange it.

What does Santa say when he stubs his toe?
Oh! Oh! Oh!

What does Santa use to play poker with his elves?
Christmas cards.

What does cool Santa say?
Yo! Yo! Yo!

What do you get if you drop a safe on a frozen snowman?
Crushed ice.

Why did Santa go to the zoo?
He needed some Christmas seals.

What brings you season's greetings and has sharp teeth?
A Christmas Card Shark.

What did the jam say to the grape at Christmas?
Tis the season to be jelly.

Whose house is always sloppy during the holidays?
Mary Chris Mess.

Why wouldn't Scrooge make a good baker?
He'd refuse to part with any of his dough.

Knock! Knock!
Who's there?
I Santa.
I Santa who?
I Santa Christmas card to you.
Did you get it?

Why did Scrooge wear a hat made of dollar bills?
Because he liked to keep money on his mind.

How does Scrooge send his Christmas list to Santa?
C.O.D.

HOLIDAY GREETINGS FROM:
A FROG – "Hoppy holidays!"
A CELL PHONE – "Let's ring in the new year together."
THE GREEN GIANT – "Peas on earth."
A TAX AGENT – "Many happy returns."
AN ITALIAN CHEF – "Pizza on earth."
A DATING SERVICE – "Marry Christmas".
A SPICE MERCHANT – "Seasons Greetings."
A SCHOOL PEP CLUB – "Have a cheerful holiday."
A TORNADO CHASER – "Joy to the whirl."
A GROOVY DUDE – "Hippie Hanukkah"

Why doesn't Scrooge mind getting coal for Christmas?
It helps reduce his winter heating bill.

What is Scrooge's Christmas motto? It's better to receive than give.

What did Scrooge find in his stockings on Christmas morning?
His feet. He sleeps with his socks on.

Why did Frosty the Snowman go to the doctor?
He had a cold sore.

Donner: What did Scrooge say to the insect who didn't know the words to any Christmas carols?
Blitzen: Hum bug!

Rudolph: Did you hear about the guy who got arrested for doing his Christmas shopping too early?

Comet: How could anyone get arrested for that?

Rudolph: He did it three hours before the store opened.

Why did Scrooge plant dimes in his garden?
He wanted to raise some cash.

What is Scrooge's favorite gymnastics stunt? The bank vault.

What is Scrooge's favorite kind of bread?
A roll of dollar bills.

Pam: Did Mr. Scrooge charge the Snowman in his front yard rent?

Sam: Yes. He made him pay cold hard cash.

HOLIDAY HINKY PINKYS

What do you call the place where Santa's helpers keep their books?
An elf shelf.

What do you call an inexpensive Christmas present?
A thrift gift.

What do you call a catchy little song about Santa?
A Kringle Jingle.

What do you call little rodents that live at the North Pole?
Ice mice.

What do you call a frozen pickle?
A chill dill.

....

What is Mr. Scrooge's favorite candy?
Mints.

....

What does Santa ride while working in his garden?
A John Deer tractor.

....

What rides with Santa on Christmas Eve and goes woof woof!
Santa's sled dog.

....

Who is the North Pole's most famous celebrity after Santa Claus?
Frosty the Showman.

....

Mrs. Claus: Do you expect snow tomorrow, honey?
Mr. Claus: No rain, dear.

....

How does Santa Claus keep warm during a blizzard?
He covers himself with a blanket of snow.

Why was Frosty the Snowman so sad?

His girlfriend gave him the cold shoulder.

What does Frosty the Snowman like to snack on?

Ice chips and frozen pizza.

Why was the bankrupt buck so sad?

He had no doe.

What do you get if you cross Rudolph and a field of corn?

Buck and ears.

What do you have when Rudolph and Bambi meet?

A couple of bucks.

What does Mrs. Claus plant in her flower garden?

Christmas bulbs.

Why did Frosty the Snowman use a dandruff shampoo?

He had flakes on his shoulders.

What does Santa put in his coffee?

Cold cream.

What did Santa policeman shout to robber Snowman?

Freeze!

What is Santa's favorite breakfast cereal?

Frosted Flakes.

Why was Mrs. Claus mad at the North Pole Bank?
They froze her assets.

NORTH POLE DEFINITIONS:
Snowman – a guy with ice in his veins.
Popsicle – the father of little icicle.
Snow – cloud dandruff.
Igloo – an Eskimo icebox.

What did Santa say to his nervous elf before they took off?
Chill out.

What is the biggest problem athletes at the North Pole have?
Ice water on the knee.

Where do you put an outlaw snowman?
In the cooler.

What do you get if you cross Frosty the Snowman and the Human Torch?
Freezer burn.

Why did the witch move to the North Pole?
She wanted to cast a cold spell.

Knock! Knock!
Who's there?
We fish.
We fish who?
We fish you a Merry Christmas.

Which one of Santa's reindeer is the fastest?
Dasher.

Knock! Knock!
Who's there?
Doughnut.
Doughnut who?
Doughnut open till Christmas.

Knock! Knock!
Who's there?
Oliver.
Oliver who?
Oliver Christmas gifts are wrapped and labeled.

Which one of Santa's reindeer loves Valentine's Day?
Cupid.

Why was Mrs. Rudolph so proud of her daughter?
She was a perfect little deer.

Why don't elves like to go jogging?
Because they're always short of breath.

Chris: Did you read that book of elf tales?
Cringle: Yes. There are some great short stories in it.

Why do elves always get where they're going fast?
They know all of the shortcuts.

Rudolph: Santa just crossed Christmas gifts with homing pigeons.
Cupid: What did he get?
Rudolph: Presents that return themselves to the store if you don't like them.

Cris: What did Santa shout to his toys on Christmas Eve?
Cringle: Okay everyone, it's sack time.

▶ ▶

ATTENTION: Rudolph is a light-hearted reindeer.

◀ ◀

Knock! Knock!
Who's there?
Don.
Don who?
Don we now our gay apparel.

▶ ▶

Knock! Knock!
Who's there?
Doc.
Doc who?
Doc the halls with boughs of holly.

◀ ◀

Knock! Knock!
Who's there?
Candy.
Candy who?
Candy canes are yummy.

▶ ▶

Then there was the elf who turned to a life of crime and became a small-time crook.

◀ ◀

How does an elf grow to adulthood?
Little by little.

Where did the crooked snowman keep his money?

In a slush fund.

▶ ▶ ▶ ▶ ▶ ▶ ▶ ▶ ▶ ▶ ▶ ▶ ▶ ▶ ▶ ▶ ▶

Knock! Knock!

Who's there?

Bitter.

Bitter who?

Bitter watch out. Bitter not cry. Bitter not pout. I'm telling you why. Santa Claus is coming to town.

◀ ◀ ◀ ◀ ◀ ◀ ◀ ◀ ◀ ◀ ◀ ◀ ◀ ◀ ◀ ◀ ◀

Knock! Knock!

Who's there?

Say.

Say who?

Say bells ring, are you listening?

▶ ▶ ▶ ▶ ▶ ▶ ▶ ▶ ▶ ▶ ▶ ▶ ▶ ▶ ▶ ▶ ▶

Knock! Knock!

Who's there?

A Vera Murray.

A Vera Murray who?

A Vera Murray Christmas to you.

◀ ◀ ◀ ◀ ◀ ◀ ◀ ◀ ◀ ◀ ◀ ◀ ◀ ◀ ◀ ◀ ◀

What's the worst job at the North Pole?

Keeping Santa's sidewalk shoveled.

▶ ▶ ▶ ▶ ▶ ▶ ▶ ▶ ▶ ▶

What do you call a North Pole hobo?

A snow drifter.

◀ ◀ ◀ ◀ ◀ ◀ ◀ ◀ ◀ ◀

What does Frosty the Snowman sleep on?

A sheet of ice.

What does Santa magician carry?

A bag of tricks.

How does a dirty snowman get clean?

He takes a cold shower.

What is Frosty the Snowman's best pitch?

A slider.

What is the favorite game of snow children?

Freeze tag.

What does Santa put on his food?

Holiday seasoning.

How does Frosty the Snowman enter his house?

He slides into home.

Knock! Knock!
Who's there?
Elf S.
Elf S. who?
Elf S. Presley.

Why do school kids like to live at the North Pole?

Because every day is a snow day.

Why did the mugger run off with Santa's sack of presents?

He thought it was his grab bag gift.

Why do a lot of people leave home for the holidays?

Because Christmas season is a time for good buys.

Why is the ocean so merry at Christmas?

It's the yuletide.

Is Santa Claus a Republican or a Democrat?

Neither. He belongs to the Christmas Party.

Girl: You're standing under the mistletoe.
Boy: Well plant a kiss on my tulips.

What does Santa Pooch carry pet presents in?

His doggie bag.

Ditzes & Dorks

How do you write a letter to a dork?

Use the geek alphabet.

Mork: Did the doctor measure your brain waves?

Dork: He couldn't. The tide was too low.

Mork: I was born in a hospital.

Dork: Why? Were you a sickly baby?

Why did the dork feed his cows money?

He wanted them to give rich milk.

Why did the dork name his son Cannon?

He wanted him to grow up to be a big shot.

Bill: My name should be "Door."

Jill: Why?

Bill: You're always knocking me.

Why did the dork pour chicken broth on his car?

He wanted to soup up the motor.

Then there was the sick dork that thought he was a jock just because the doctor told him he had athlete's foot.

Reporter: Do you think women should have children after forty?

Dork: Heck no. Forty children are enough.

Joe: I'm glad I wasn't born in Germany.

Moe: Why?

Joe: I don't speak a word of German.

Mork: Do you remember your college days?

Dork: Sure. All ten of them.

Why did the dork put his bed in the fireplace?

He wanted to sleep like a log.

Al: The judge sentenced me to 200 years in jail.

Sal: Whew! You're lucky he didn't give you a life sentence.

Why did the dork buy a farm three miles long and three inches wide?

He planned to raise spaghetti.

What did the dork say when he saw identical twins?

They're as alike as toupees in a pod.

Why did the dork go around in the revolving door for three hours?

Because he couldn't remember if he was coming or going.

What do you get if you cross a dork with a wristwatch?

A slow clock.

Then there was the dork scientist who thought he'd get rich by inventing an egg with an unbreakable shell.

Why did the dork couple take French lessons?

Because they adopted a French baby and wanted to understand what she said when she began to talk.

Football Coach: Why is it important not to lose your head in a close game?

Dork Player: Because then I'd have no place to put my helmet.

Mr. Ugly: Doc, every morning when I wake up I look in the mirror and get sick to my stomach. What's wrong with me?

Doctor: I don't know, but your eyesight's perfect.

Mr. Ugly: Doc, did you check out my family tree?

Doctor: Yes. You're the sap.

Mr. Ugly: I know I'm not handsome. My profile is posted on Ugly Facebook.

Mr. Ugly: I know I'm not handsome. A poison control center uses photos of my face to induce vomiting.

Mr. Ugly: I know I'm not handsome. A Halloween mask company wanted to trademark my face.

Mr. Ugly: I went to a plastic surgeon. He told me there was no hope for me. I was terminally ugly.

Tino: Dad! Gino called me stupid.
Dad: Gino. Tell your brother you're sorry.
Gino: I'm sorry you're stupid, Tino.

Zack: I went to see the play you wrote and it had a wonderful effect on me.
Mack: Really?
Zack: Yes. It completely cured my insomnia.

Why did the dork tattoo watches on his palms?
Because he wanted to have free time on his hands.

Why did the dork poultry farmer go broke?
The roosters he bought didn't lay any eggs.

Why did the dork put a hole in her umbrella?
So she could see when it stopped raining.

What do dork helicopters have for pilots that no other helicopters have?
Ejection seats.

How does a dork cheat on an oral exam?
He sits behind the smartest kid in class so he can copy.

Why did the five dorks fall off a cliff?
They were playing follow the leader.

What did the dork athlete say when a pro team offered him a contract for zero pay?
Triple your offer and you've got a deal.

What game do dorks like to play? Hide and geek.

What game do baby dorks like to play?
Geek-a-boo.

Why did the dork park his car in front of the stop sign?
He was waiting for it to change to go.

What did the girl say when she saw a geek at her front door?
Gee, it's dork outside.

How does a dork back up a car?
He looks behind him, puts the car in drive and steps on the gas pedal.

How did the dork hurt himself making a bungee jump?

He tied his 200-foot elastic cord to a 150-foot high bridge.

What's the difference between a dork using a handkerchief and a dork using a napkin?

After a dork blows his nose in a handkerchief, it goes back in his pocket. After he blows his nose in a napkin, it goes back on the table.

How did the dork plan to travel from California to Hawaii without spending any money?

He was going to hitchhike all the way.

How does a dork cook spaghetti? He throws it on the barbecue.

How does a dork make his mark in the world?
He writes graffiti on a globe.

Why did the dork stay up all night studying history?

She had an English exam in the morning.

Do most geeks have blond hair?
No. They have dork hair.

Chester: Have I told you the joke about the deaf man and the dork?
Lester: No. Tell it.
Chester: Huh? What did you say?

How does a dork score in a soccer game?
She picks up the ball and runs over the goal line.

....

What do you get when you clone a dork?
Double dips.

....

Girl: **Why do you have bruises on the sides of your face?**
Dork: **I've been teaching myself to play piano by ear.**

....

When did the dork learn the difference between bowling and soccer?
When he tried to kick a bowling ball.

....

What do you call a dork lizard?
A Geeko.

....

How many dorks does it take to shoot a basketball?
Two. One to toss the ball in the air and one to fire the shotgun.

....

How did the dork sink his canoe?
He cut a hole in the bottom so he could watch the fish.

....

Where does a dork jogger go to run in the Boston Marathon?
New York City.

....

Why did the dork shower in his clothing?
Because the tags read "wash and wear."

....

How does a geek soldier check a field for land mines?
He uses a sledgehammer.

Man: You have your shoes on the wrong feet.
Dork: But these are the only feet I have.

What do you call a geek on a pier?
The dork of the bay.

How did the dork sink his submarine?
He opened a window to let in some fresh air while submerged.

Girl: You're a vegetable dork.
Boy: What does that mean?
Girl: You have a bean brain.

When does a dork go to bed?
When he's nincompooped.

Tillie: Why are you standing in front of a mirror with your eyes shut?
Millie: I want to see what I look like when I'm asleep.

Chester: I just bought a suit that came with two pairs of pants, but I don't like it.

Lester: Why not?

Chester: It gets hot wearing two pairs of pants.

Who is the world's dumbest detective?
Dork Tracy.

TWO WAY
WRIST
YO-YO

Tina: You should start saving money now.
Gina: Why?
Tina: It might be worth something someday.

Why did the dork bury pictures of his relatives?
He wanted to grow a family tree.

Why did the dork put a duck under his mattress?
So it could swim in the Spring.

What do geeks wear to see better?
Dork glasses.

Why did the dork put burned bread in the blender?
He wanted to drink a toast.

Zingers & Stingers

Where do you dig up the girls you date, in a cemetery?

Girls don't close their eyes when they kiss you. You have to blindfold them.

You and I make a great pair. You're the most beautiful girl in the world and I'm the biggest liar in the world.

If looks could kill, a glance at your face would be fatal.

I bet you go to the dentist twice a year. Once for each tooth.

I see you have wavy hair. Too bad it's waving goodbye.

Does your barber charge you for cutting your hair or for searching for it?

You have a big heart and a stomach to match.

You act like a big shot, but your mind is a blank.

There's something heavenly about you. People look at your face and shout, "Oh, God!"

He has such a big head that he has to go through the Lincoln Tunnel sideways.

His hair is so greasy, lice only visit his head when they want to go skiing.

He has so much dandruff, the fleas live on his head in blizzard conditions.

We'd like a breath of fresh air, so do us a favor and hold yours.

She's so boring she couldn't be the life of the party at a zombie convention.

**He's such a blockhead he doesn't get dandruff.
He gets sawdust.**

Is it true elephants never forget or do you
have trouble remembering certain things?

You're in a bad mood today. What did
you do? Get up on the wrong side of
your cage this morning?

**A stork didn't deliver you to the maternity
ward. It was a vulture.**

Okay tough guy. I admit that you're stronger than I am. But bad breath isn't everything.

▶ ▶

Your grandfather is so old he remembers when Adam's picture was on a dollar bill.

◀ ◀

Your uncle is so old he sold Noah flood insurance.

▶ ▶

Your grandfather is so old he used to play catch with Abner Doubleday in the backyard.

◀ ◀ ◀ ◀ ◀ ◀ ◀ ◀ ◀ ◀ ◀ ◀ ◀ ◀

Your grandfather is so old he knew Hercules when he was a 98-pound weakling.

▶ ▶ ▶ ▶ ▶ ▶ ▶ ▶ ▶ ▶ ▶

Your grandpappy is so old he had a snowball fight with George Washington at Valley Forge.

◀ ◀ ◀ ◀ ◀ ◀ ◀ ◀ ◀ ◀ ◀ ◀

Your grandpappy is so old he knew Moses when there were only five commandments.

▶ ▶

Your grandpappy is so old he played harmonica while Nero fiddled.

◀ ◀

Your grandparents are so old they visited Stonehenge when it was only a rock garden.

▶ ▶

Your grandparents are so old they jumped across the Grand Canyon when it was only a muddy ditch.

◀ ◀

Your grandparents are so old they traveled through the forest when the Giant Redwoods were just saplings.

You're such an animal your birth certificate is recorded at the public zoo.

In your case, looks aren't everything. In fact, they're nothing to speak of.

Oh, by the way. Sasquatch called, he wants his feet back.

You have a sympathetic face. Everyone who sees it feels sorry for you.

You have a cheery disposition, but your looks are the pits.

A lot of exercise is good for a person. Your tongue must be in great shape.

There's only one problem with your face: it shows.

She's so homely, she had a coming-out party and then they made her go back in again.

If Dr. Frankenstein removed your brain, he could carry it home in a thimble.

When you were born, people came from miles around to see you. And everyone asked the same question. What is it?

You look like a million—every year of it.

She has to go to the beauty parlor two days in a row. The first day is to get an estimate.

She has a baby face and an infantile brain.

Last week she had a song running through her head. There was nothing in the middle to stop it.

He wanted to be a football player, but he couldn't figure out the plays. He couldn't tell an X from an O.

His brain cells are filled with inmates convicted of criminal stupidity.

I finally figured out why you always have that stupid grin on your face. You're just naturally stupid.

When she sends out brainwaves, they're microwaves.

A fortuneteller read her mind. It was a very short story.

If you were a house, the attic would be filled with cobwebs, dust, and useless junk.

He's a guy who is rock solid, especially his head.

You should become a bone specialist. You've got the head for it.

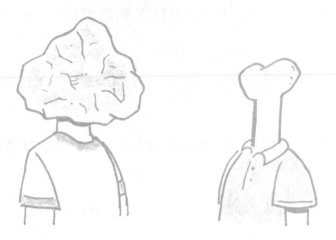

No one can drive him out of his mind. All it takes is a little putt.

He has a one-track mind ... driven by locomotives.

Your stomach may be rumbling, but it's your brain that's out to lunch.

She's like the statue of Venus de Milo—beautiful, but not all there.

He's living proof of reincarnation. No one could get that dumb in a single lifetime.

She has a pretty little head and a brain that's pretty little too.

He has a soft heart and a head to match.

Everyone is rooting for him to get ahead. The one he already has is useless.

He hasn't seen his twin brother in so long; he's forgotten what he looks like.

Your brain is like a lost roll of film. It was never developed.

She's so dumb she brought a bar of soap to a bridal shower.

He had a headache so he went to a doctor to have his brain examined. The doctor found nothing.

She's so stupid she thinks you have to stand on your head to bake an upside-down cake.

He's so dumb he thinks the Kentucky Derby is a hat.

He had his brain checked out when he was young, and it never checked back in.

My doctor told me to exercise with dumb-bells so I came by to invite you and your brother to jog with me.

He's getting a B.A. degree. He finally mastered the first two letters of the alphabet even though he got them backwards.

If he played poker in a casino, they'd arrest him for being a dope dealer.

Otto is his name. He's smart enough to spell it frontward, but too dumb to spell it backwards.

If your I.Q. were ten points higher you'd be a rock.

If he has a chip on his shoulder, it's a splinter from that block of wood above it.

He's so dumb he thinks hotdogs can have puppies.

If ignorance is bliss, he's the world's happiest guy.

She had a brain operation; it was microsurgery.

He's so dumb he needs a GPS to find his way from his bedroom to the bathroom.

I have a pet guppy that has twice the brains you have.

An intelligent thought doesn't last long in his brain. It can't stand the solitary confinement.

He's so dumb someone told him to call 911 and he started shouting, "9-1-1! 9-1-1!"

He needs to exercise his brain more. Maybe then he wouldn't be such a fathead.

It's no wonder you're the teacher's pet. **With a face like that you belong on a leash.**

You went to beauty school and got expelled for ugliness.

Your face is so ugly it doesn't just make people sick; it causes an epidemic.

Your doctor diagnosed your problem as terminal ugliness.

If you met Albert Einstein your face would scare the wits out of him.

When you joined the Army, the drill sergeant yelled, "About face ... yours is too ugly to look at."

Help keep America beautiful. Don't show your face in public.

Aren't you a famous movie actor? Didn't you star in *Toy Story* as Mr. Potato Head?

You're so ugly when someone asks your parents which one of them you resemble, they flip a coin and the loser says "me."

You have a strange growth on your neck. I think it's your head.

You're so ugly; you could never be a hypnotist. People couldn't stand to look you in the eye.

You're so ugly, the last mosquito that tried to bite your face died of a heart attack.

With a face like yours, you must be a lot of laughs to be around.

His family urged him to pursue a life of crime ... just so he'd wear a mask over his face.

Your schnoz is so big, when they created your nose, the department had to work overtime.

She has a beautiful figure. It reminds me of a warped toothpick.

Your smile reminds me of the Old West ... lots of wide-open spaces.

You're a brave man. It takes a lot of guts to walk around in public with a face like that.

She's so ugly; she made an electric eye blink in pain.

I might have a face that could stop a clock, but your face gave Father Time a heart attack.

Your eyes remind me of two cool pools of water ... polluted water.

Did you come by your looks naturally or did a doctor prescribe ugly pills for you as a child?

You're the only person I know who can make funny faces without even trying.

You're so ugly that if they made your life story into a movie, it would be a horror flick.

Every time I look at your face I get the feeling you're about to say trick or treat.

With a face like yours, you should be thankful mirrors don't come with an automatic laugh track.

If ugliness were a crime, your face would be a felony.

Is that your head or did someone find a way to grow hair on a meatball?

If Moses had seen your face there'd be an Eleventh Commandment against ugliness.

You don't need a gun to go hunting. You just walk through the woods and your face scares wild animals to death.

Talk about ugly. I've seen better heads on pimples.

They looked up his family tree and found that his head is petrified wood.

He's so unpopular. Yesterday at breakfast his talking cereal called him a dirty name.

What's the name of the perfume you're wearing, ode de skunk?

He's a man of few words. Trouble is, he keeps repeating them.

You're really dumb. The last time you had a brainstorm it was nothing but a drizzle.

I dreamed about you last night. My mother warned me if I ate a snack before bedtime I'd have nightmares.

Is that your head or are you carrying a pumpkin on your shoulders?

Your I.Q. is so low you misspelled I.Q.

Big Foot just called for you. He wants his feet back.

If you were a house, the attic would be empty except for cobwebs.

I'd try to read your mind if the print wasn't so tiny.

He's the kind of guy you'd really like to run into sometime—when he's walking and you're driving a car!

What are you doing here? Was there a jailbreak at the zoo?

Does your mother know you're out here without your leash?

Help beautify America! Don't show your face in public.

The American Medical Association should give you a yearly bonus. Your face makes people sick.

Look up "dumb" in the dictionary and your name is listed in the explanation.

When you took your Army I.Q. test, you qualified for training in the K-9 Corps.

Your face is as pretty as a flower ... a cauliflower.

Did I hear you singing or was someone torturing a cat?

I have nothing to compare you to. That's because you're a complete zero.

I heard you had to go in for a checkup. What did the vet have to say?

Your life has been a real trip, and it looks like you fell on your face.

Normally I don't like it when people turn their back on me. But please do. I can't stand looking at your face.

Your brother is so dumb that he saw the word "race" on his job application and ran out of the room.

Your grandparents are so old they studied ancient history when it was called current events.

Where do you dig up your dates? In a cemetery?

Is that your nose or are you eating a banana?

Do you want to prove how brave you are? Look in a mirror and keep your eyes wide open.

Money means nothing to him. When you ask him for money, you get nothing.

You're so old you knew the Garden of Eden when it was a seed farm.

I heard your parents adopted you from an animal shelter.

You're so dumb that when you take a test you have to write your name on your hand in order to get it right on the exam.

If I were married to your aunt, I'd be a monkey's uncle.

Guys like you don't grow on trees. They swing from them.

You should visit the zoo more often. I'm sure your relatives would be glad to see you.

Everyone thought you were a marvel of science until they discovered you were a boy instead of a talking chimp.

Some people have a face that could stop a clock. You've been banned from England for having a face that could break Big Ben.

I've seen better bodies on cars in a demolition derby.

Some tough guy you are. You're so weak you couldn't whip cream.

The last time he went to the zoo, the monkeys threw peanuts to him.

You'd better hide quick! Here comes the dogcatcher.

The circus just came to town. Why don't you see if you can get a job? I heard they're hiring elephants.

You may have muscles of steel, but your brain is corroded.

His cologne isn't exactly appealing to people. Yesterday a skunk followed him home!

I heard you had a walk-on part in the *Lord of the Rings* movies. Which Orc were you?

The police should arrest you for being criminally ugly.

On a scale of 1 to 10, you're a 2. Too dumb, too silly, and too ugly.

His B.O.is so bad the teacher gave him an automatic A in class participation so he'd never have to raise his hand.

You're so dumb the only time you have something on your mind is when you wear a hat.

A movie producer wants to buy the rights to your life story. It's going to make a great horror flick.

What did Santa bring you for Christmas last year? A flea collar and a box of dog treats.

You're so dumb your parents tattooed your name on your arm so you won't forget who you are.

I can't take anything away from your I.Q. How can you subtract from zero?

He's so lazy that waking up in the morning makes him tired.

She's very useful at picnics. She keeps the flies away from the food.

I was in the post office yesterday and saw your face on an unwanted poster.

If stupidity were gold, you'd be Fort Knox.

She had to stop talking to her plants. Her breath was so bad it made them wilt.

▶ ▶ ▶ ▶ ▶ ▶ ▶ ▶ ▶ ▶ ▶ ▶

He's so out of shape that they paid him not to donate his body to science.

◀ ◀ ◀ ◀ ◀ ◀ ◀ ◀ ◀ ◀ ◀

He's such a blockhead his parents took out termite insurance on his brain.

▶ ▶ ▶ ▶ ▶ ▶ ▶ ▶ ▶ ▶ ▶ ▶ ▶ ▶ ▶

He has a lot of blind dates. The only girls who will go out with him are one who can't see his face.

◀ ◀ ◀ ◀ ◀ ◀ ◀ ◀ ◀ ◀ ◀ ◀ ◀ ◀ ◀

They looked up his family tree and discovered he's nothing but dead wood.

▶ ▶ ▶ ▶ ▶ ▶ ▶ ▶ ▶ ▶ ▶ ▶ ▶ ▶

Nobody likes her. Even her talking breakfast cereal gives her the silent treatment.

◀ ◀ ◀ ◀ ◀ ◀ ◀ ◀ ◀ ◀ ◀ ◀ ◀ ◀

You're such a pizza face. Your first name should be pepperoni.

▶ ▶ ▶ ▶ ▶ ▶ ▶ ▶ ▶ ▶ ▶ ▶ ▶

In high school you were voted the face most likely to be laughed at.

◀ ◀ ◀ ◀ ◀ ◀ ◀ ◀ ◀ ◀ ◀ ◀ ◀ ◀

Your mom is a great cook. She's the only person I know who can burn ice cream.

▶ ▶ ▶ ▶ ▶ ▶ ▶ ▶ ▶ ▶ ▶ ▶ ▶

He talks tough. That's because his breath is real bad.

◀ ◀ ◀ ◀ ◀ ◀ ◀ ◀ ◀ ◀ ◀ ◀ ◀ ◀

Everyone runs when he puts up his fists. That's because his pits smell so bad.

▶ ▶ ▶ ▶ ▶ ▶ ▶ ▶ ▶ ▶ ▶ ▶ ▶

Do us all a favor. Fight air pollution. Gargle with mouthwash.

He's so dumb his head is the original dead end.

▶ ▶ ▶ ▶ ▶ ▶ ▶ ▶ ▶ ▶ ▶ ▶ ▶ ▶ ▶ ▶ ▶ ▶

If your shoes were two sizes smaller, you'd be Big Foot's twin.

◀ ◀ ◀ ◀ ◀ ◀ ◀ ◀ ◀ ◀ ◀ ◀ ◀ ◀ ◀ ◀ ◀ ◀

I've seen nicer hairstyles on old mops.

▶ ▶ ▶ ▶ ▶ ▶ ▶ ▶ ▶ ▶

When they were handing out noses, you thought they said roses and asked for a big red one.

◀ ◀ ◀ ◀ ◀ ◀ ◀ ◀ ◀ ◀ ◀

Hey! Make a funny face. Never mind. It comes natural to you.

▶ ▶ ▶ ▶ ▶ ▶ ▶ ▶ ▶ ▶ ▶ ▶ ▶ ▶

I hear you got banned from the zoo. Your face scares all of the animals.

◀ ◀ ◀ ◀ ◀ ◀ ◀ ◀ ◀ ◀ ◀ ◀ ◀ ◀ ◀ ◀ ◀

I heard the Dieters' Club wants to market a picture of you as a health aid. Looking at your face makes hungry people lose their appetites.

▶ ▶ ▶ ▶ ▶ ▶ ▶ ▶ ▶ ▶ ▶ ▶ ▶ ▶

She went to beauty school and got an "F" for looks.

◀ ◀ ◀ ◀ ◀ ◀ ◀ ◀ ◀ ◀ ◀ ◀ ◀ ◀ ◀ ◀ ◀

Shouldn't you be hanging around a leaky faucet, you big drip.

▶ ▶ ▶ ▶ ▶ ▶ ▶ ▶ ▶ ▶ ▶ ▶ ▶ ▶ ▶ ▶

I admit it. You're stronger than I am, but breath isn't everything.

◀ ◀ ◀ ◀ ◀ ◀ ◀ ◀ ◀ ◀ ◀ ◀ ◀ ◀ ◀ ◀ ◀

What are you doing here? I thought all dodos were extinct?

▶ ▶ ▶ ▶ ▶ ▶ ▶ ▶ ▶ ▶ ▶ ▶ ▶ ▶ ▶ ▶

Is that your hair or did someone dump a bowl of spaghetti on your head?

I bet that nose of yours is the envy of a lot of elephants.

You're such a blockhead that when you scratch your scalp you get splinters.

You're so dumb, when you got a job as a babysitter you thought you had to sit on a baby.

Noah couldn't have taken you along on the Ark. He couldn't find anyone half as ugly to pair you up with.

You're so dumb you failed your SATs because you didn't know how to make a dot.

Did you come by your looks naturally or did your mom feed you ugly baby formula when you were an infant?

Is that your head or did someone find a way to grow hair on a watermelon?

You've always been ugly. When you were born the doctor slapped your parents.

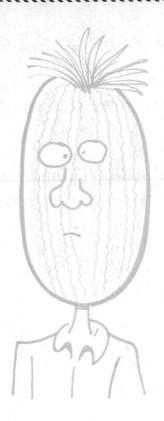

Oh you're a bad dude all right. Bad Breath. Bad Odor. And bad looking.

There's one positive factor to your B.O. Mosquitoes won't come near you.

He's so dumb he thinks Buffalo wings come from flying buffalos.

You're a haunting beauty. You have a face people boo.

He's so bowlegged he can ride a team of horses at the same time.

He's so lazy he sets an alarm clock so he'll know when it's time to stop taking a nap and time to go to bed.

He's so bald, when he visited a poultry farm the hens all tried to hatch his head.

His breath is so bad he takes garlic pills to improve it.

She's so boring people with insomnia invite her over to put them to sleep.

They call her Moon Face because her skin is full of craters.

I heard a mean wizard put a spell on your face. And what he spelled is U.G.L.Y.

Hey guess what? I saw clowns at a circus last night and somebody stole your face.

Your boyfriend is a three-letter man in school. Y.U.K.!

I'd go out with you, but it's against my religion to date chimpanzees.

Your feet are so big you have to wear suitcases for shoes.

Your feet are so large you gave Big Foot an inferiority complex.

He has one of those mighty minds— mighty empty.

His clothes are so filthy people think he's a compost pile with legs.

She's so dumb she can't recite the alphabet unless you give her a hint at what letter it starts with.

I'm not saying you're a turkey, but how do you manage to survive every Thanksgiving.

The last time I saw ears as big as yours they were on a cornstalk.

Her hair is so frizzy the hairdresser doesn't cut it ... she prunes it.

I heard you went to a comic book convention and won a prize for having the best monster costume. Next year why don't you dress up?

He lost his dog, but he won't put an ad in the newspaper. He says it's no use—his dog can't read.

I heard you had plastic surgery to improve your looks. How's the malpractice suit going?

You're so weak you couldn't bend licorice.

Why don't you join your boyfriend for dinner tonight? Feeding time at the zoo is at 6:00.

Hey, Halloween is over. Take off your mask.

I thought I saw your boyfriend at the shore last week until I found out it was a beached whale.

A face and body like yours is almost positive proof that some humans evolved from apes.

If you had a body to match your face, you could run in the Kentucky Derby.

Millie: Lola has a Supreme Court figure.
Tillie: Yeah, no appeal.

Boyfriend: Did you like the birthday gift I gave you?

Girlfriend: Yes. I can't wait to exchange it.

Lady: I have the face of an eighteen-year-old girl.

Man: Give it back. You're getting it all wrinkled.

Waldo ran up to confront Chumley. "What's the big idea of telling everyone I'm a complete jerk and I smell like an old skunk?" Waldo roared. "Calm down, Waldo," Chumley replied softly. "You've got it all wrong." "Really?" Waldo replied as his temper began to cool. "Yes," continued Chumley. "What I said is you're a total moron and you smell like a dirty pig."

He has a nice head on his shoulders. But it would look better on a neck!

Zack: Spell Imbecile.

Mack: Y.O.U.

Zack: That's incorrect.

Mack: That's what you think.

Grandfather: When I was your age I could name all of the U.S Presidents in order.

Boy: Big deal! How hard is it to remember George Washington, John Adams and Thomas Jefferson?

The last time he walked through a circus sideshow the freaks gave him a standing ovation.

Millie: I just spent two hours in front of a mirror admiring my beauty. Is that vanity?

Tillie: No. Imagination.

Millie: I know something that does the work of ten men?
Tillie: What?
Millie: Five women.

Rudy: My uncle has a memory like an elephant.
Judy: And a body to match.

Grandmother: When I was growing up everybody was a gentleman.
Granddaughter: You mean you were the only woman on earth, Granny?

Wife: Golf! Golf! Golf! I think if you spent one whole weekend at home, I'd drop dead.

Husband: Don't say that, dear. You know you can't bribe me.

That woman is a living saint. People look at her and exclaim, "Holy Cow!"

Ben: Do you want to see me do a magic trick?
Jen: Only if you promise to disappear.

Lady: Do you call that hideous thing modern art?
Artist: No. I call it a mirror.

Writer: Do you think I should put more fire into my new novel?

Agent: No. I think you should put your new novel into the fire.

Aunt Bertha: How much do you weigh, Joey?

Joey: About a hundred pounds.

Aunt Bertha: I remember when I weighed a hundred pounds.

Joey: Gosh, you have a good memory.

RHYME TIME

Roses are red.
Daisies are yellow.
You sure are dumb.
But I'm a smart fellow.

CHAPTER 6

FUNNY THINGS

What did the clock shout on its birthday?

It's party time!

What did the tired rubber band say to the sofa?

I think I'll stretch out on you.

What did the wristwatch say to the lost travel clock?

How did you wind up here?

What do you get if you cross rocks and clocks?

Hard times.

What do you get if you cross a car tire and a poker player?

A wheeler dealer.

What do you call a dumb chunk of coal?

A stupid fuel.

How does a boy car meet a girl truck?

It uses a pickup line.

What do you call a wager between ABC and XYZ?

An alpha-bet.

Why is a piano an expert on locks?

Because it has lots of keys.

What do you get when you cross super glue with a novel?

A book you can't put down.

How do you make a V-6 car go faster?

Give it a V-8.

....

What did one doorknob say to the other?

Wait for your turn.

....

WHAT DO YOU LIKE TO READ?

"Comic books," said the comedian.

"Short stories," said the little person.

"Tall tales," said the basketball center.

"Sci-fry," said the alien cook.

"Books with twist endings," said the bottle cap.

"Hair-raising tales," said the bald man.

"Nun fiction," said Mother Superior of the convent.

....

How do you make an elastic band hurry?

Tell it to snap to it.

....

What gets wetter the more it dries?

A towel.

....

What did the cup say to the sad coffee maker?

Perk up.

....

What did the angry paintbrush say to the floor?

One more wise remark and I'll shellac you.

....

Why did the clock go jogging?

He was running late that day.

What do you get if you cross a car and a garden?

A Ford plant.

What did one compact say to the other?

You always make up stories.

What did the doctor say to the sick pot of glue?

Stick out your tongue.

What do you get if you cross a fast car and a camera?

A zoom-zoom lens.

What do you get when a dollar bill loses its temper?

Mad money.

Why did the oil well make a mess?

It was crude oil.

What did the driller say to the oil well?

Come on. Spill your guts.

What did the pencil say to the paper?

I dot my I's on you.

Dolly: How much does this bottle of glue cost?

Molly: Check the sticker price.

How do you keep a bus from going down the bathtub drain?
Put in a bus stopper.

What did one lipstick say to the other?
Let's kiss and make up.

What happened to the nervous crepe paper?
It became unraveled.

What happened when the glue went to the fruit stand?
It got stuck with a lemon.

What do you call a piano whose children have children?
A grand piano.

How can you change a flat tire with a deck of cards?
Take out the jack.

What do you get if you cross fifty-two cards and a stool?
A deck chair.

What do you get if you cross matches and a car motor?
A fire engine.

What did the cork say to the jug?
Be quiet or I'll plug you.

Knock! Knock!
Who's there?
Attic.
Attic who?
Attic of cards is what you need to play poker.

What's a post wedding?
It's when two poles get married.

Why was the clock so proud?
He started a neighborhood watch group.

Dan: That cruise ship must love the coastline.
Van: What makes you say that?
Dan: It's hugging the shore.

What did the envelope say to the pen?
Were you addressing me?

What did the tennis racket ask the tennis ball?
Do you mind if I court you?

What did the stopwatch say to the grandfather clock after their race?
You lose big time.

What kind of hat makes suds and bubbles?
A soapbox derby.

What has a hundred legs but can't walk?
Fifty pairs of pants.

Why didn't the clock have any friends?

It was two faced.

▶ ▶ ▶ ▶ ▶ ▶ ▶ ▶ ▶ ▶ ▶ ▶ ▶ ▶

What kind of pretty dolls sing in harmony?

A Barbie shop quartet.

◀ ◀ ◀ ◀ ◀ ◀ ◀ ◀ ◀ ◀ ◀ ◀ ◀ ◀

Why was the tornado so proud?

It set a whirl record.

▶ ▶ ▶ ▶ ▶ ▶ ▶ ▶ ▶ ▶ ▶ ▶ ▶ ▶

Why did the newspaper have a mild heart attack?

It had poor circulation.

◀ ◀ ◀ ◀ ◀ ◀ ◀ ◀ ◀ ◀

How do you find a missing book in a hotel lobby?

Get someone to page it.

▶ ▶ ▶ ▶ ▶ ▶ ▶ ▶ ▶

Mrs. Jones: What do you think of paper plates?

Mrs. Smith: They're tearable.

◀ ◀ ◀ ◀ ◀ ◀ ◀ ◀ ◀ ◀ ◀ ◀ ◀ ◀

SIGN ON A DEAD BATTERY – Free, no charge.

▶ ▶ ▶ ▶ ▶ ▶ ▶ ▶ ▶ ▶ ▶ ▶ ▶ ▶

What kind of hat has lots of fingerprints on it?

A felt hat.

◀ ◀ ◀ ◀ ◀ ◀ ◀ ◀ ◀ ◀ ◀ ◀ ◀ ◀

Where does a piece of sod sit?

In a lawn chair.

▶ ▶ ▶ ▶ ▶ ▶ ▶ ▶ ▶ ▶ ▶ ▶ ▶ ▶

What do you call an intelligent crevice?

A wisecrack.

NOTICE: A yacht that needs a lot of repairs is nothing but a big woe boat.

▷ ▷ ▷ ▷ ▷ ▷ ▷ ▷ ▷ ▷ ▷ ▷ ▷ ▷ ▷ ▷ ▷ ▷ ▷

What happens when a shy rock grows up?

It becomes boulder.

◁ ◁ ◁ ◁ ◁ ◁ ◁ ◁ ◁ ◁ ◁ ◁ ◁ ◁ ◁ ◁ ◁ ◁ ◁

Gina: Why are Mr. and Mrs. Three so happy?
Nina: They're going to have a little one.

▷ ▷ ▷ ▷ ▷ ▷ ▷ ▷ ▷ ▷ ▷ ▷ ▷ ▷ ▷ ▷ ▷ ▷ ▷

Why was the little milk container so bad?

His parents spoiled him.

◁ ◁ ◁ ◁ ◁ ◁ ◁ ◁ ◁ ◁ ◁ ◁ ◁ ◁ ◁ ◁ ◁ ◁ ◁

What do you get if you cross glue and a pigskin?

A tackle stickball game.

▷ ▷ ▷ ▷ ▷ ▷ ▷ ▷ ▷ ▷

Why was Mrs. Plate so upset?

She came from a dishfunctional family.

◁ ◁ ◁ ◁ ◁ ◁ ◁ ◁ ◁ ◁

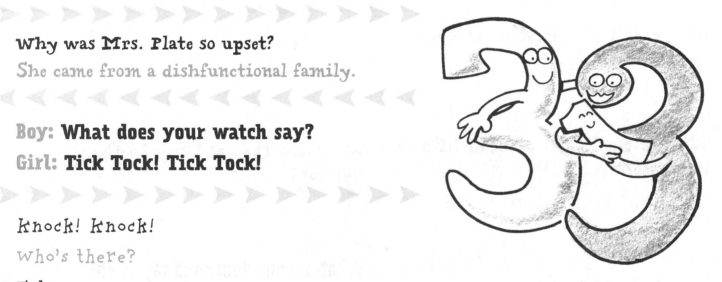

Boy: What does your watch say?
Girl: Tick Tock! Tick Tock!

▷ ▷ ▷ ▷ ▷ ▷ ▷ ▷ ▷ ▷

Knock! Knock!

Who's there?

Esteem.

Esteem who?

Esteem locomotive goes choo, choo!

◁ ◁ ◁ ◁ ◁ ◁ ◁ ◁ ◁ ◁ ◁ ◁ ◁ ◁ ◁ ◁ ◁ ◁ ◁

John: This is my cheesy watch.
Lon: Why do you call it that?
John: Because it's Swiss.

What happens to a crooked grandfather clock?

He winds up in jail.

....

What did the girl clock say to the boy clock?

Takes your hands off of me!

....

ATTENTION: Football clocks love the two-minute drill.

....

How did the clock make the track team?

It ran fast.

....

Why didn't the wristwatch make the track team?

It ran too slow.

....

Why do clocks get a lot of hits in baseball?

Their swings are well timed.

....

Mrs. Paste: Did you make a glue year's resolution?

Mr. Paste: Yes, but I don't think I'll stick to it.

....

What did the trunk say to the broken suitcase?

You need to get a grip on yourself.

When does a wallet get a wedgie?

When money is tight.

....

What's the best way to mail a bird's egg?

Use nest day delivery.

CAN'T KEEP UP WITH THE OLD MAN, EH?

What did the cart say to the vendor?

Stop being so pushy.

....

What did one doorknob say to the other?

Let's play a game and take turns.

....

What do you call a tiny cell phone?

A micro phone.

Why do all clocks hate April 15th?
Because it's tax time.

What kinds of clocks make great wide receivers?
Ones that have good hands.

Why did the man turn the grandfather clock toward the wall?
Because it had an ugly face.

What kind of car does a rich golfer drive?
A Caddylac.

What did the police shade say to the drapes?
Watch out for the curtains, they're carrying a rod.

What kind of shoe talks too much?
One that has a tongue that wags.

What did the teen calendar ask her parents?
Am I old enough to go out on dates alone?

Where does a broom scout nap on a campout?
In a sweeping bag.

What do you try to keep after giving it to someone else?
A promise.

Food for Thought

What did the fruit tree say to the farmer?
Go and pick on someone else.

A patron walked into a coffee house. "I'd like a mug of coffee with no cream," said the patron. "I'm sorry," apologized the waitress. "I can't give you a mug of coffee without cream because we don't have any cream, but I can give you a mug of coffee with no milk."

Why did the fruit become a comedian?
It was berry funny.

What do you get if you cross a lighthouse and a chicken coop?
Beacon and eggs.

An African lion was about to eat a missionary. The lion cornered the man and then suddenly got down on its knees and began to pray. "It's a miracle," the missionary shouted. I'm saved. The lion isn't going to eat me." The hungry lion looked at the missionary and licked his chops. "You've made a big mistake. I'm just saying grace."

Girl: I don't like this cheese with the holes in it.
Mother: Just eat the cheese and leave the holes on your plate.

What do you get if you cross asparagus and horseradish?
Some hot tips.

Bob: Why did you name your dog Waiter?
Rob: Because he never comes when I call him.

Patron: Why is my cake crushed flat?
Waiter: Well, sir, you told me to bring you your dessert and step on it.

Knock! Knock!
Who's there?
Micah.
Micah who?
Micah snack, I'm hungry.

Mom: When my son Barry feels sad, I always bake him a pie.
Aunt: Is it a blue Barry pie?

What do you get if you cross an ice cube and a frankfurter?
A chili dog.

What noise does Rice Chickies cereal make?
Snap! Cackle! Pop!

What do you call a messy cup of coffee?
Sloppy Joe.

How do you make dork doughnuts?
Deep fry nerd dough.

What's chewy and makes up rhymes to music?
A bubblegum rapper.

What does a skater use to slice bread?
A roller blade.

What did one plate say to the other?
Let's break for lunch.

What kind of health food goes down and then come back up?
Yo-yogurt.

Willie: Can you name the greatest bubblegum battle ever fought?
Dilly: World War Chew.

What do snobby vegetables do when they see poor farmers?
They turnip their noses.

NOTICE: High food prices are hard to swallow.

MUST HAVE BEEN ALL THOSE CANDY SPRINKLES!

What is the pickles' marriage vow?
Dill death do we part.

What do you call a dopey steak? Beef jerky.

Which pastry has a flabby mid-section?
The belly doughnut.

what did the coleslaw say to the detectives?
You don't have a shred of evidence against me.

Why was the beef soup giggling? It was made with laughing stock.

How do you fix a broken pizza?
Use tomato paste.

What do you get if you cross a trumpet player
and an orchard with Ben and Jerry?
Tooty Fruity Ice Cream.

What do you get if you cross a McDonald's hamburger with a snail?

Fast food that's slow cooked.

John: I'm so hungry because I've been tracking cattle thieves for two days.

Wayne: Well, let me rustle up some chow.

Salesman #1: What do you sell?

Salesman #2: Pepper.

Salesman #1: Shake, pal.

What do you get if you cross dogs and cheese?

Mutts-a-rella.

What kind of sandwich does an interrogator eat?

Grilled cheese.

What grows on a fruit tree and repairs shoes?

An apple cobbler.

What is the most dangerous vegetable to have on a sailboat?

A leek.

Why was the vegetable farmer so optimistic?

He figured something good would turnip.

....

Pancho: Can I eat that?

Cisco: Not. It's nacho cheese.

....

Boy: There are two things I never eat for breakfast.

Girl: What are they?

Boy: Lunch and dinner.

....

Why is it bad to write a letter on an empty stomach?

Because it's much better to write on paper.

....

What do you get if you cross barley wheat and corn with country music?

The Grain Ol' Opry.

....

Why doesn't the Abominable Snowman celebrate Thanksgiving?

He quit cold turkey.

....

Did you hear about the nasty jogger who got into trouble because he always ran off at the mouth?

....

What do you get when two peas fight?

Black-eyed peas.

....

What did the farmer yell to the field of lettuce at harvest time?

Heads up, everyone!

What do well-dressed corn stalks wear?
Earrings.

Jenny: How about if we have clams for dinner tonight?
Denny: I can dig that.

Knock! Knock!
Who's there?
Seafood.
Seafood who?
Seafood. Eat food. Digest food.

What does a peanut become when it sneezes?
A cashew!

Why was the clam so weak?
It had no mussels.

FAMOUS CHEFS:

I. Noah Recipe	Bern D. Stake
Ken I. Cook	Link Sausage
Hugh Etta Finemeal	Sal Idd
Seth D. Table	Al Mike Moore
Francie Foods	Frank Footer
Dot S. Goode	Will Dunne

Knock! Knock!

Who's there?

I, flounder.

I, flounder who?

I, flounder hiding under the table.

What do you call a twisted path in a cornfield?

A maize.

NOTE FOR A VEGETARIAN TRACK TEAM **– No meat today.**

Which vampire is always on a diet?

Count Calories.

Muskrat: **What did you have for dinner last night?**

Beaver: **A tree course meal.**

What did Mrs. Goat say to her children?

Eat your vegetables. They're good for growing kids.

Knock! Knock!

Who's there?

We zealots.

We zealots who?

We zealots of ice cream in the summer.

Why do bananas make bad soldiers?

They all have yellow streaks.

What do you put on a corny beef sandwich?
A dull pickle.

HOW DO YOU WANT YOUR EGGS?

"Hard boiled," said the detective.

"Scrambled," said the running quarterback.

"Sunnyside up," said the weatherman.

"Raw," said the pro wrestler.

"Poached," said the illegal hunter.

"Runny" said the jogger.

"Over easy," said the pole-vaulter.

"With hot sauce," said the fireman.

SIGN ON A FISH MARKET:
No credit cods.

Mrs. White: **What are you cooking?**

Mrs. Green: **This is my secret recipe for the best dinner in town.**

Mrs. White: **But you're burning everything.**

Mrs. Green: **I know. And when my husband comes home and sees this charred mess, he'll take me out to a fancy restaurant.**

NOTICE: A food scientist discovered how to duplicate dessert and now produces plenty of ice cream clones for everyone.

What do you get if you cross a cornfield and a chicken coop?
Corny yolks.

Knock! Knock!

Who's there?

Gut.

Gut who?

Gut milk? I'm thirsty.

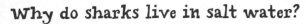

Why do sharks live in salt water?

Because pepper water makes them sneeze.

STAYING ON A DIET IS TOUGH WHEN ...

You win a free turkey in a raffle.

You boyfriend is a gourmet chef.

You have to walk past a sub shop, a pizza parlor and a bakery on your way to the health club.

You have a friend who can eat anything anytime without gaining a pound because he or she has a super metabolism.

Your apartment is above a four star Italian restaurant.

You win a year's supply of snack cakes.

You start your diet the day before Thanksgiving, Christmas, or New Year's Eve.

Your family brings home twenty bags of Halloween candy.

You have lots of friends who constantly invite you out to dinner and always pick up the check.

Your parents own a fast-food place.

Your mom is the all-time, pie-baking champion at the state fair.

Your grandma bakes homemade bread and your grandpa churns real butter.

Jenny: **My mom won a saucepan playing bingo.**

Lenny: **Wow! Talk about pot luck.**

Knock! Knock!
Who's there?
House.
House who?
House about coming over for dinner.

▶ ▶ ▶ ▶ ▶ ▶ ▶ ▶ ▶ ▶ ▶ ▶ ▶ ▶ ▶ ▶ ▶ ▶

Bill: Where did you learn to make such great ice cream desserts?
Jill: I went to Sundae school.

◀ ◀ ◀ ◀ ◀ ◀ ◀ ◀ ◀ ◀ ◀ ◀ ◀ ◀ ◀ ◀ ◀ ◀

Mr. Pear: Why are you going to the doctor?
Mr. Banana: Because I'm not peeling well.

▶ ▶ ▶ ▶ ▶ ▶ ▶ ▶ ▶ ▶ ▶ ▶ ▶ ▶ ▶ ▶ ▶ ▶

The lunch lady likes you and always gives you an extra portion.
Your uncle owns a fleet of ice cream trucks.

◀ ◀ ◀ ◀ ◀ ◀ ◀ ◀ ◀ ◀ ◀ ◀ ◀ ◀ ◀ ◀ ◀ ◀

What do Munchkins use to make sandwiches?
Shortbread.

▶ ▶ ▶ ▶ ▶ ▶ ▶ ▶ ▶ ▶ ▶ ▶ ▶ ▶ ▶ ▶ ▶ ▶

Patron: Waiter, will my pizza be long?
Waiter: No, sir. It will be round.

◀ ◀ ◀ ◀ ◀ ◀ ◀ ◀ ◀ ◀ ◀

Why did the farmer sprinkle salt
and pepper on his field?
It was planting season.

▶ ▶ ▶ ▶ ▶ ▶ ▶ ▶ ▶ ▶

What's the best way to bake perfect buns?
Use a roll model.

What did the corn field say when the farmer asked if it was listening?

I'm all ears.

. . . .

Tim: Do you have breakfast in the morning?

Jim: Of course I do. If I had it in the afternoon, it would be lunch.

. . . .

Knock! Knock!

Who's there?

Mangos.

Mangos who?

Mangos to a restaurant when he's hungry.

. . . .

What does the chef in a Chinese restaurant wear on his feet?

Woking shoes.

. . . .

YOU MAY NEED A DIET IF...

The only books in your house are cookbooks.

You go to sporting events just to grill food in the parking lot and not to watch the game.

You have three-course meals for breakfast, lunch, and dinner.

Eating late-night snacks doesn't give you nightmares. They make you dream about more food.

You order Chinese food not by the item, but by the column.

You don't mind kicking the bucket as long as it's filled with fried chicken.

Your idea of exercise is jogging from the pizza place to the doughnut shop to the ice cream parlor.

. . . .

What do you call a book about squashed oranges?

Pulp fiction.

. . . .

Why did the farmer only plant one type of fruit tree in his orchard?

Because he was plum crazy.

. . . .

Mother: Would you like to help me fix dinner?

Daughter: I'm sorry, Mom, but I think your cooking is beyond repair.

. . . .

Mother: Junior why are you holding a slice of bread over your head at the breakfast table?

Son: I want to propose a toast.

. . . .

Ben: I can make a pumpkin roll.

Jen: Big deal. I can make an apple turnover.

. . . .

How does a giraffe save money on food?

One bite goes a long way.

Uncle Al: My wife went to cooking school and graduated with frying colors.

....

Chef: Are the peas and corn happy?
Cook: No, but the potatoes are chipper.

....

Why did the cookie crumble?

Because its mother had been a wafer so long.

....

What did Mrs. Coffee Pot say to her teenage son?

Perk up your clothes.

....

Why was Ms. Corn so happy?

Her boyfriend finally popped the question.

....

What is the one thing farmers don't want to grow?

Older.

....

SIGN ON AN HERB SHOP: Closed. Out of Season.

....

What do you call a hard-shelled mollusk on a bun?

A clam burger.

How do you win free pancakes for life?

Buy a waffle ticket.

....

Knock! Knock!
Who's there?
Zip.
Zip who?
Zip your zoup quietly.

....

What did Mrs. Swiss Cheese say to her nasty son?
You're a holey terror.

....

Knock! Knock!
Who's there?
Bebe.
Bebe who?
Bebe cakes.

Knock! Knock!

Who's there?

Rice.

Rice who?

Rice you to the breakfast table.

Man: How much are your bananas?

Grocery Clerk: A penny each.

Man: Great. I'll take ten.

Grocery Clerk: That will be ten dollars and ten cents.

Man: Hey! I thought you said bananas were a penny each.

Grocery Clerk: They are. The peels they come in are a dollar each.

What do you get if you cross a lemon with a short letter?
A sour note.

What do you get if you cross two scoops of wet flour with an ostrich egg?
A dough-dough bird.

Knock! Knock!
Who's there?
Fun Al.
Fun Al who?
Fun Al cakes.

What did the melon groom say to the melon bride?
We cantaloupe tonight.

SIGN ON A 24-HOUR CHINESE RESTAURANT: We wok around the clock.

Where were the first chickens fried?

In Greece.

▶▶▶▶▶▶▶▶▶▶▶▶▶▶▶▶▶▶▶▶▶▶▶▶▶▶

Patron: Why is there a fly in my water?
Waiter: I guess he doesn't like our soup.

A friend got some vinegar in his ear, now he suffers from pickled hearing.

Patron: **Waiter, this fish steak isn't as good as the fish steak I had here last week.**
Waiter: **That's odd, sir. It's cut from the same fish.**

What did one potato chip say to the other?

Let's go for a dip.

▶▶▶▶▶▶▶▶▶▶▶▶▶▶▶▶▶▶▶▶▶▶▶▶▶▶

What did the hungry monk say to the hamburger?

Out of the frying pan and into the friar.

SIGN IN A SMALL RESTAURANT: Eat now – pay waiter.

What did the farmer bet in the poker game?

All of his corn chips.

What did the farmer say to the noisy green vegetables?

Peas, be quiet.

Where do they grow old-fashioned French fries?

On Old MacDonald's farm.

Where did the first bakery open?
On the yeast coast of America.

Waiter: You want a turtle steak?
Patron: Yes and make sure it's slow cooked.

What did Cowboy Hotdog
say to City Slicker Frank?
Go wurst young man.

The price of food is so high today gourmet cookbooks are now considered works of fiction for the middle class.

Why do postmen have good digestion?
Because the meal must go through.

What is a rabbit's favorite frozen treat? A hopsicle.

Why do golfers like doughnut makers?
They admire people who can make a hole in one.

How do you lace a vegetable shoe? Use string beans.

Why did the bakery hire a fitness instructor? To firm up their buns.

What did Soldier Potato do during the Korean War?
He served with a Mash Unit.

what do you call a cow that can't produce dairy products? A milk dud.

Why did the short chef cook pork instead of beef?
He could reach the chops, but the steaks were too high.

Lady: How much for a slice of sponge cake?
Baker: It's 66 cents.
Lady: And how much for a slice of upside-down cake?
Baker: 99 cents.

When do pears and apples need to wear helmets?
When they play in a fruit bowl game.

Sal: Is it difficult to bake bread?
Hal: Yes. It's not easy being a loafer.

What did one corn farmer say to the other?
Let's have a plower lunch tomorrow.

Show me a dancing polish ham ... and I'll show you a pig in a polka.

Harry: **What happens when ears of corn get hot under the collar?**
Larry: **They pop off at the mouth.**

What did one cowboy pea say to the other?

Howdy Podner.

What do you get if you cross morning mist with a pastry chef?

Dewnuts.

Patron: Hey! What's the big idea? My corn on the cob is missing lots of kernels.

Waiter: Just calm down and I'll give you a new earful.

When do two soda cans get engaged?

After one pops the question.

What do vegetables yell when the farmer wants to play a game?

Pick me! Pick me!

What is Popeye the Sweet Potato's motto?

I yam what I yam and that's all that I yam.

Show me a cat who falls into a barrel of dill pickles ... and I'll show you a real sour puss.

Waiter: Is something wrong with your meal, gentlemen?

Patron #1: Yes. The food is poison.

Patron #2: And the portions are too small.

Patron: What's the nude salad?

Waiter: It has no dressing on it.

Waiter: Would you like a table, sir?
Patron: No. I came here to eat, not to buy furniture.

What do pumpkin cars do in a demolition derby?

They smash into each other.

What do you call a carved out pumpkin athlete?

A jock o lantern.

What kind of football do pumpkins play?

Smashmouth football.

What do you put on a Jewish pizza?

Matzoh-rella cheese.

RHYME TIME

Mary had a little lamb
Its body plump and round.
Everywhere the Mary went
It followed her around.
They went to the butcher's one day.
That was a very stupid thing to do.
For when Mary sat down to supper that night...
The lamb was in her stew!

How did the rooster win the race?

He beat the eggs.

Mess Sergeant: I want you to make six pounds of mashed potatoes and do the job right.

Cook: And suppose I don't.

Mess Sergeant: Well then you can just lump it.

Jack: **Did you try those new hotdogs?**

Zack: **Yes. They're the wurst ever!**

What happened to the tomato boxer?

He got beat to a pulp.

What dance did the barbecued ribs do?

The char char.

A boy went to see his doctor. He had a string bean in one ear and a cherry in the other. He had a strawberry stuck in one nostril and a pea in the other. "What's wrong with me, Doc," asked the boy. Replied the doctor, "You're not eating right, son."

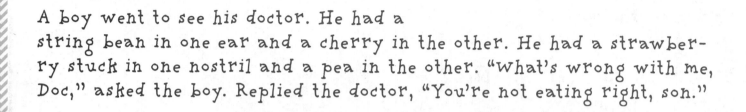

Car-Toons

What kind of cars do Hollywood stars like?

Os-cars.

ATTENTION: **Joggers like cars that run.**

What does a duck use to change a flat tire?

A quacker jack.

Knock! Knock!

Who's there?

Oil.

Oil who?

Oil change that flat tire for you.

What do kangaroos do when their engines won't turn over?
They jump-start their cars.

DAFFY DEFINITION:

Mobile Home Salesman — a wheel estate agent.

Why didn't Mr. Zombie's car start?
It had a dead battery.

What do you get if you cross an elephant with a luxury car?
A vehicle with lots of trunk space.

What does an earthworm use to season its food?
Ground pepper.

Why did the traffic light turn red?
You'd turn red too if you had to change in the middle of the street.

What did the jack say to the flat tire?
Can I give you a lift?

When is a car not a car?
When it turns into a parking lot.

What do all golf carts have?
Fore-wheel drive.

Husband: Your driving is making me crazy.
Wife: Save your sanity. Get out and walk.

What do NASCAR drivers wear on their heads?

Hub caps.

◄ ◄ ◄ ◄ ◄ ◄ ◄ ◄

What does a yeti have on his car?

Snow tires.

► ► ► ► ► ► ► ► ►

What happened to the snow tires the yeti put on his car?

They melted.

◄ ◄ ◄ ◄ ◄ ◄ ◄ ◄ ◄ ◄ ◄ ◄ ◄ ◄ ◄

What do you get if you cross an auto body shop and a farmer?

A bumper crop.

► ► ► ► ► ► ► ►

Mechanic: Your racecar looks to be in good shape.

NASCAR Driver: Yup! It's in first crash condition.

◄ ◄ ◄ ◄ ◄ ◄ ◄ ◄

What did the meter maid say at the end of her shift?

I've done a fine day's work.

► ► ► ► ► ► ► ► ► ► ► ► ► ► ►

What do you get if you cross a car and a thundercloud?

A driving rainstorm.

◄ ◄ ◄ ◄ ◄ ◄ ◄ ◄ ◄ ◄ ◄ ◄ ◄ ◄

How do you make a flower car speed up?

Press down on the gas petal.

ATTENTION: Traffic cops whistle while they work.

▶ ▶ ▶ ▶ ▶ ▶ ▶ ▶ ▶ ▶ ▶ ▶ ▶ ▶ ▶ ▶ ▶ ▶

Quarterback: I hate driving down this road.

Halfback: Why? It's a nice road.

Quarterback: I know, but it's a no passing zone.

◀ ◀ ◀ ◀ ◀ ◀ ◀ ◀ ◀ ◀ ◀ ◀ ◀ ◀ ◀ ◀ ◀ ◀

Why did the baseball player get dragged into traffic court?
It was a case of hit and run.

▶ ▶ ▶ ▶ ▶ ▶ ▶ ▶ ▶ ▶ ▶ ▶ ▶ ▶ ▶ ▶ ▶ ▶

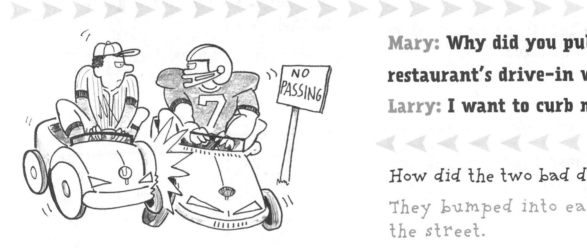

Mary: Why did you pull into that restaurant's drive-in window?
Larry: I want to curb my appetite.

◀ ◀ ◀ ◀ ◀ ◀ ◀ ◀ ◀ ◀ ◀ ◀ ◀ ◀ ◀

How did the two bad drivers meet?
They bumped into each other on the street.

▶ ▶ ▶ ▶ ▶ ▶ ▶ ▶ ▶ ▶ ▶ ▶ ▶ ▶ ▶ ▶ ▶ ▶

What kind of cars do horses drive?
Oatsmobiles.

◀ ◀ ◀ ◀ ◀ ◀ ◀ ◀ ◀ ◀ ◀ ◀ ◀ ◀ ◀ ◀ ◀ ◀

What kind of cars do Woody and Buzz Lightyear drive?
Toyotas.

▶ ▶ ▶ ▶ ▶ ▶ ▶ ▶ ▶ ▶ ▶ ▶ ▶ ▶ ▶ ▶ ▶ ▶

Why did the man leave his car in a burning garage?
He wanted to turn it into a hotrod.

◀ ◀ ◀ ◀ ◀ ◀ ◀ ◀ ◀ ◀ ◀ ◀ ◀ ◀ ◀ ◀ ◀ ◀

What do you get if you cross a car with a vacuum?
A vehicle that has good pickup.

Why was Dracula driving on the freeway?

He was looking for a main artery.

Inventor: This vehicle I invented runs on lawn clippings.

Reporter: Really.

Inventor: Yes. And it gets good grass mileage, too.

What do you get if you cross a flap-jack with a car motor?

An engine that needs to be turned over if it gets too hot.

What's the best thing to put on a cold engine?

An extra muffler.

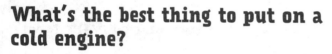

What sickness do racecar drivers get?

Indy-gestion.

Knock! Knock!

Who's there?

Indy Anna.

Indy Anna who?

Indy Anna Jones, the Raider of the Lost Ark.

ATTENTION: Mechanics who work under leaky car engines go to bed oily.

Why did the tow truck go to the NASCAR race?

He wanted to be on hand in case he had to pull a fast one.

SIGN IN AN AUTO BODY REPAIR SHOP: We know the right dents steps.

What kind of hat crashes into other hats?

A demolition derby.

How can you tell if a car is over-weight?

It'll have a spare tire.

....

How do you make a car cry?

Turn on the windshield weepers.

....

what do you get if you brew coffee in your car?

A perking ticket.

Jed: Do you drive a NASCAR?

Ed: Yup! But my pappy's car is even nicer than mine.

....

How do you make a Volkswagen bug go faster?

Step on it.

Garbage disposal mailboxes that automatically shred junk mail and unwanted flyers.

....

Fish tanks that float in the sky for flying fish that need a rest stop.

....

An encyclopedia with blank pages for people who think they know it all.

....

A wristwatch that runs fast on purpose for people who are always late.

Jet packs for penguins so they can fly like other birds do.

....

Shirts that automatically unbutton themselves when you snap your fingers.

Wave machine fish bowls for goldfish that want to get some exercise.

Miniature life preservers for flies that fall into bowls of soup.

Bungee cords for window washers who work on skyscrapers. They make work safer and more fun.

Special books with pages made out of thin bread so readers can digest the plot of the story.

Combination slipper/running shoes for sleepjoggers.

Candy-flavored glue for use on the flaps of envelopes so they taste good when you have to lick them.

A device that, when you clap your hands together, shuts the mouth of a politician.

Shoes with special holes in them that automatically drain sand out when you walk on the beach.

Shopping carts that total up the cost of the food you select as you put items into the basket.

X-ray glasses that passengers at airports can wear so they can inspect the security guards who inspect them. We can never be too safe.

A pair of robot slippers that fetch your pet dog.

A remote control lawnmower that works like a toy car. ◄ ◄ ◄

Special miniature cows that give evaporated milk.

Cell phones in the shape of caps for people who talk through their hats.

Giant toothbrushes for elephants and walruses.

Mountains with escalators—for lazy mountain climbers.

Glue that sticks to everything except your fingers.

Pre-threaded needles for nervous people who like to sew.

A bed that exercises your body while you sleep.

Mouth locks for people on diets who have no willpower.

Forest sprinkler systems that attach to trees to prevent forest fires.

Trumpets that play music with anyone blowing into them; for musicians who are short of breath.

Miniature hot-air balloons for birds that want to go south for the winter, but are too tired to fly.

Wallets with sirens that go off if your pocket is picked.

Bubblegum that chews itself—for really lazy kids.

Giant spaceships that can take elephant astronauts into space.

A talking bathroom scale that lies.

Shoelaces from India that wiggle around and tie themselves when you play a special flute.

A toaster with mechanical arms that butters your toast.

A tea kettle that whistles a jaunty tune of your choice.

Bedposts that glow at night—for kids who are afraid of the dark.

Bubblegum you can form into a bouncing rubber ball when the flavor is chewed out.

Giant bird baths for ostriches.

Shoes with a built-in GPS system, so you can never get lost while taking a walk.

Tomato sauce you can finger paint onto spaghetti so you can play with your food before you eat it.

A talking breakfast cereal that tells you the answers to test questions so you don't have to study the night before an exam.

Shirts with buttons that grow back if the original ones fall off.

Trees that never lose their leaves so we can have shade during the winter.

A cat that barks: for cat lovers who need a watchdog.

Soft cement so you won't get hurt if you fall while rollerblading.

Special rocks that let you hear the sound of bubbling mountain creeks and streams when you hold them to your ear.

CAN YOU MAKE IT 7% INTEREST? I CAN'T COUNT TO TWELVE!

APPLICATION

LOANS

Shoes with built-in socks to save time while dressing.

Trees with built-in ladders that make climbing them easier.

A bank that makes small loans to little kids so they don't have to ask for advances on their allowances.

Special alarm clocks that politely tell your houseguests when it's time to go home.

Bunk beds with attached trampolines so you can bounce up into the upper bunk.

Corn cobs that can be refilled with corn kernels.

A robot belt that snakes its way through the loops in your pants.

Pens and pencils that glow when you write the correct answers to test questions and buzz if you write a wrong answer.

Very tiny false teeth for termites that broke their own gnawing on petrified wood.

A machine that converts polluted water into soda pop.

Talking comic books for little kids just learning to read.

Chewing gum that can be molded into a piece of jewelry after its flavor is gone.

Purses with tiny time bombs that explode if snatched away from their owners.

Scuba gear for tadpoles that have just turned into frogs and need to practice.

A Velcro horse saddle that helps new riders stick to their horses.

Clothing that walks over to the closet and hangs itself up after you take it off and drop it on the floor.

Ice skates for snowshoe rabbits who want to try something different.

Digital cameras that automatically touch up pictures and make ugly people look beautiful.

Martial arts courses for birds so they can defend themselves from cat attacks.

Coward sandwiches for hungry people who don't like heroes.

Trees with windmill-like branches that help generate power to farms.

Fire extinguishers that can be hung on tree trunks in the woods to help prevent forest fires.

Trained canaries that not only sing, but also play tiny guitars.

Hotdogs with mustard inside them so it never spills or drips on the person eating the frank.

Special feline straws for cats so they don't have to lap up milk with their tongues.

Erasable coloring books that young artists can use over and over.

A lawnmower that cuts grass into tiny cubes you can feed to farm or zoo animals.

No-drip soup spoons for sloppy eaters.

Litter boxes for cats that can be flushed.

Air-conditioned work shoes for people with hot feet.

A submarine sandwich that fires a small torpedo sandwich so a parent and a child can enjoy a meal together.

Parrots trained to answer annoying phone calls. They repeat catch phrases like, "This call may be recorded!"

A small economy car that transforms into a briefcase you can carry so drivers never have to worry about finding a parking place in the city at rush hour.

Flags that proudly wave even when the wind isn't blowing.

Special remotes that mute nagging parents, teachers, or spouses.

Snooze alarm collars for tired watchdogs that fall asleep on the job.

Pens filled with jelly ink for people with big mouths who end up eating their own words.

Special parachutes for birds that run out of energy during long migration flights.

Waterproof songbooks for people who like to sing in the shower.

Pizza cartons you can dip in tomato sauce and eat when there's no pizza left.

A bathtub with a timer that shuts off the water just before it overflows.

Skateboards and rollerblades for snakes so they don't have to crawl around on their stomachs all the time.

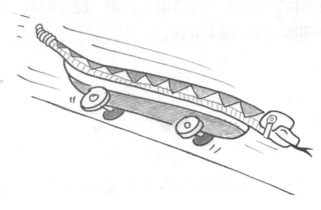

Round hotdogs you can eat on hamburger buns and long hamburgers you can eat on hotdog rolls ... for when someone brings the wrong thing to a barbecue.

Disposable cheap cars you throw away when something goes wrong with them so you never have to pay repair bills.

A boomerang arrow for bad hunters.

A refrigerator with a combination lock on the door ... for dieters with no willpower.

A new car that runs on old pickle juice.

A heated snow shovel that melts snow so you don't have to lift it.

A dill pickle pie to discourage folks on a diet who crave dessert.

Toothpicks made out of steel for beavers that get splinters of wood stuck between their teeth.

One-way windows in houses that let you see out, but keep others from seeing in.

Living room furniture that rearranges itself every few months to keep homeowners from getting bored.

A shower button, that when pressed, automatically adjusts the water stream to the perfect temperature.

Breakfast cereal that tastes just as good when you add water instead of milk.

Miniature pogo sticks for tired grasshoppers.

A rake with no teeth for cleaning up yards in the fall that have no trees.

A magic word that when spoken, opens clams and oyster shells.

An android buddy programmed to do homework and business reports.

No-drip ice cream cones.

Credit cards that self-destruct if lost or stolen.

Liquid peanut butter for nut freaks who don't like to have sticky choppers.

Soap erasers for cleaning paper plates.

A golf cup that expands as the ball rolls toward, it so golfers make more putts.

Tiny motorboats for ducks and geese that are tired of paddling with their feet.

Daffy Definitions

DIETING - the victory of mind over platter.

DIVINE — what de grapes grow on.

FLOOD — a river too big for its bridges.

BOW — a fiddlestick.

BARBED WIRE - a sarcastic telegram.

DUST — mud with the juice squeezed out.

EGG — a bird's hometown.

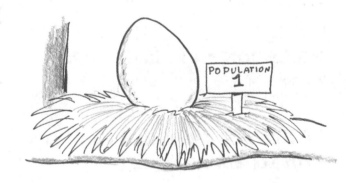

STEAM — hot water that's blowing its top.

SKIING - A fall sport.

SHEPHERD — a person all kids flock to.

EGOTIST — someone who's always me-deep in conversation.

FLASHLIGHT — a case used to carry dead batteries.

GRAND CANYON – the hole of fame.

ENLISTMENT PAPERS – a service contract.

HOG WASH – a pig's laundry.

IDEAL – my turn to shuffle the cards.

PARADOX – a mallard and his mate.

LAUGH – a smile that can't contain its enthusiasm.

TENSION – what the sergeant shouts to his soldiers.

SAUNA BATH – a safe way of getting into hot water.

BREAD – raw toast.

BRAGGART – a person who opens his mouth and puts his foot in it.

BOYCOTT – a small bed for a male child.

GOOSE PIMPLES – duck acne.

LAWSUIT – a policeman's uniform.

CLOUD BANK – a place to save your money for a rainy day.

MINE OWNERS – coal-hearted people.

MIDDLE AGES – knight time.

SNORING – sheet music.

SAUNA BATH – a slimming pool.

SKI JUMP – a soar spot.

DIETING – the victory of mind over platter.

DIVINE – what de grapes grow on.

FLOOD – a river too big for its bridges.

BOW – a fiddlestick.

BARBED WIRE – a sarcastic telegram.

DUST – mud with the juice squeezed out.

EGG – a bird's home town.

STEAM – hot water that's blowing its top.

SKIING – A fall sport.

SHEPHERD – a person all kids flock to.

UNIVERSITY – a mental institution.

ACTRESS – a person who works hard at not being herself.

ANTARCTIC – snowman's land.

BEE – a buzzy busybody.

ILLEGAL – a sick bird of prey.

FLOWER SHOP – a budding business.

FENCING MASTER – a person with a duel personality.

MEDITATION – an inner calm system.

PETRIFIED FOREST – a bunch of trees that came up the hard way.

THIEF – a person who has a habit of finding things before others lose them.

SECRET – something we tell everyone not to tell anyone else.

BACTERIA – the cafeteria's rear annex.

BOASTER – a person with whom it is sooner done than said.

BARBER SHOP – a hairport.

LEOPARD – a dotted lion.

MISS AMERICA CONTEST – the lass roundup.

FEMALE WRESTLER – the belle of the brawl.

RIDING – the art of keeping a horse between you and the ground.

TEARS – remorse code.

TENNIS PRO – a network executive.

SURGEON – the person who was a cut-up at medical school.

FIGHT ARENA – a punch bowl.

HYPOCHONDRIAC – a person with plenty of sham pain.

KLEPTOMANIAC – a person who helps herself because she can't help herself.

GOSSIP — a person with a real sense of rumor. ◄ ◄ ◄ ◄ ◄

NAPKIN – a cloth laptop.

PEACE – the shortest distance between two wars.

TEMPER TANTRUM – call of the riled.

ABSTRACT ARTIST — a person who draws his or her own confusions.

SEAMSTRESS — a material girl.

WITCHES – hexperts.

VAMPIRE – hemogoblin.

FUMIGATION – a smoke-flea environment.

COMPUTER GOSSIP — chat rumors.

PSYCHIATRIST – a person who doesn't have to worry as long as other people do.

ROTISSERIE – a Ferris wheel for food.

WAITRESS – a woman who thinks money grows on trays.

FLU SHOT — an ouch of prevention.

SLOW POKE – the kind of punch a tired boxer throws.

GRAVY – a liquid magically attracted to ties.

SOCKS – gloves for your feet.

Tom Swiftlies

"Don't shoot! I'll throw down my weapon," the criminal cried disarmingly.

"I haven't been bowling well lately," the man groaned gutterly.

"I haven't eaten much in three days," said the dieter hungrily.

"My axe is not dull," remarked the lumberjack sharply.

"We're headed for rough water," yelled the river guide rapidly.

"Hey Troll! I'm crossing your bridge," shouted the Billy Goat gruffly.

"I love to eat hotdogs," admitted the baseball fan frankly.

"The correct answer is eighty-two," replied the student smartly.

"Water! Water! Give me water!" gasped the thirsty man dryly.

"Go to the corner and turn right," said the lady directly.

So, What's a Tom Swiftly, Anyway???

Good question. Tom Swift was the main character in a series of adventure novels for kids first written in the early 1900s. (Sort of like the Hardy Boys and Nancy Drew, but not as well known.) In some of the novels, the authors tried really hard not to use the word "said" without an adverb to go along with it. So instead of writing:

"We must hurry," Tom said.

They'd instead write:

"We must hurry," Tom said swiftly.

It wasn't long before people began creating puns in which the adverb not only described how Tom and others said something but also somehow became a play on words with what was being said. There are hundreds of Tom Swiftlies out there, and after your done reading these, come up with some of your own.

"The mad doctor didn't give me a brain," muttered the sad monster mindlessly.

"Burn the witch!" shouted the mayor of Salem wickedly.

"You've been a bad boy today," said the evil spirit devilishly.

"This lemon-aide is too sour," said the man bitterly.

"I want to be a shepherd when I grow up," admitted the boy sheepishly.

"I'm a mischievous spirit," said the little ghost impishly.

"I don't like frozen yogurt," snapped Jane coldly.

"How do you stop a runaway horse?" shouted the rider woefully.

"This hat cost $1,000," boasted the man grandly.

 "I'm really in love," shouted Mr. Rabbit hoppily.

"I'm not proud of what I did," sighed the crook shamefully.

"I've decided to change your test score, Tom," the teacher remarked.

"Is it time to turn the pancakes?" Tom asked flippantly.

"I hurt my ankle and can hardly walk," said Tom lamely.

"I've been under water for two and a half minutes," said Tom breathlessly.

"This entire story sounds like a tragic fairy tale," said Tom grimly.

"I just cut myself with an electric saw," said Tom offhandedly.

"I'm late for a pressing engagement," said Tom steaming.

"Let's have chicken and lamb chops for dinner," Tom clucked sheepishly.

"Stop cracking your knuckles," Tom popped off.

"Don't skate on that thin ice," Tom cracked.

"It's time for a sweet snack," Tom snickered.

"I want to be a banker," Tom said with interest.

"I smell gas," Tom fumed.

"Keep your dog quiet," Tom barked loudly.

"My baseball team needs a homerun hitter," said Tom ruthlessly.

"I'm making chocolate cake," said Tom devilishly.

"I keep banging my head against the wall," said Tom bashfully.

"Growing vegetables is very relaxing," sighed the Green Giant peas-fully.

"I've been laid off due to the recession," said Tom idly.

"I got the lowest I.Q. score of anyone who took the test," said Tom mindlessly.

"I just can't seem to put thoughts into words," said Tom indescribably.

"This dangerous liquid will eat through walls," said Tom acidly.

"Duh," said Tom stupidly.

"I think archery is an aimless sport," Tom said with a quiver.

"I love mountain music," Tom sang loftily.

"I cut firewood for three hours," Tom said as he lumbered through the door.

"Light the lamp," said Tom wickedly.

"We're out of pumpernickel bread," said the baker wryly.

"I like making furniture," said the carpenter in a crafty tone.

"I'm leaving you all my worldly possessions," said the dying man willingly.

"This is the end of me," Tom concluded.

"Quick! Blow on the fire's embers," Tom bellowed.

"Watch out! That kind of turtle bites," Tom snapped.

"We're having pork tonight," said Tom as he licked his chops.

"Get your hotcakes!" Cook Tom flapped.

Knock Knocks

Knock! Knock!
Who's there?
Tillie.
Tillie who?
Tillie opens the door, I'm staying right here.

Knock! Knock!
Who's there?
I, Noah.
I, Noah who?
I Noah secret so open up.

Knock! Knock!
Who's there?
Tara.
Tara who?
Tara-rah-boom-de
yah!

Knock! Knock!
Who's there?
Attila.
Attila who?
Attila tell you to open the door, keep it closed.

Knock! Knock!

Who's there?

Reed.

Reed who?

Reed some books over summer vacation.

Knock! Knock!

Who's there?

Despair.

Despair who?

Despair of shoes is too tight.

Knock! Knock!

Who's there?

Beehive.

Beehive who?

Beehive when we get to Grandma's house or you'll be sorry.

Knock! Knock!

Who's there?

Icy.

Icy who?

Icy you have a satellite dish.

Knock! Knock!

Who's there?

Rail.

Rail who?

Rail be home late, so don't wait up.

Knock! Knock!

Who's there?

Sy.

Sy who?

Sy-ber space.

Knock! Knock!

Who's there?

Mae.

Mae who?

Mae I sit next to you?

Knock! Knock!

Who's there?

Thelma.

Thelma who?

Thelma I won't be home for dinner.

Knock! Knock!

Who's there?

Jimmy.

Jimmy who?

Jimmy your lunch money, dork!

Knock! Knock!

Who's there?

Madison.

Madison who?

Madison is good to take when you're sick.

Knock! Knock!
Who's there?
Hank.
Hank who?
Don't mention it.

Knock! Knock!
Who's there?
Warren.
Warren who?
Warren you in this same class last year?

Knock! Knock!
Who's there?
Roland.
Roland who?
Roland! Roland! Roland on a river.

Knock! Knock!
Who's there?
Cord.
Cord who?
Cord you please speak a little louder?

Knock! Knock!
Who's there?
Ardor.
Ardor who?
Ardor any chicken wings left?

Knock! Knock!

Who's there?

Stan Stell.

Stan Stell who?

Stan Stell and stop fidgeting.

Knock! Knock!

Who's there?

Fitz.

Fitz who?

Fitz the doorbell and I won't have to knock.

Knock! Knock!

Who's there?

Teller.

Teller who?

Teller a good joke and she'll laugh out loud.

Knock! Knock!

Who's there?

Aaron.

Aaron who?

Aaron away from home and now I miss my folks.

Knock! Knock!

Who's there?

Albie.

Albie who?

Albie a son of a gun.

Knock! Knock!
Who's there?
Checker.
Checker who?
Checker ID at the door.

Knock! Knock!
Who's there?
Norma Lee.
Norma Lee who?
Norma Lee I don't knock on the doors of strangers.

Knock! Knock!
Who's there?
Bill Clinton.
Bill Clinton who?
Bill Clinton for the clothes Hillary bought.

Knock! Knock!
Who's there?
Musk.
Musk who?
Musk you always be so stubborn?

Knock! Knock!
Who's there?
I mist.
I mist who?
I mist you at the party last night.

Knock! Knock!
Who's there?
Wyatt.
Wyatt who?
Wyatt's my old pal Morgan.

Knock! Knock!
Who's there?
A vowel.
A vowel who?
A vowel-in-tine for you.

Knock! Knock!
Who's there?
Effie.
Effie who?
Effie keeps knocking, call the police.

Knock! Knock!
Who's there?
Spine.
Spine who?
Spine on me through the peephole is not very polite.

Knock! Knock!
Who's there?
Nickel.
Nickel who?
Nickel vouch for me. Just ask Nick.

....

Knock! Knock!
Who's there?
Howdy.
Howdy who?
Howdy do that?

....

Knock! Knock!
Who's there?
Christmas.
Christmas who?
Christmas be lost, call Chris on his cell phone.

....

Knock! Knock!
Who's there?
Ribbon.
Ribbon who?
Ribbon looking for your house for hours.

....

Knock! Knock!
Who's there?
Thames.
Thames who?
Thames fightin' words, Englishman!

Knock! Knock!
Who's there?
Dare.
Dare who?
Dare must be some mistake.

....

Knock! Knock!
Who's there?
Huron.
Huron who?
Huron dangerous ground.

....

Knock! Knock!
Who's there?
Dozen.
Dozen who?
Dozen anyone care that I'm out here?

....

Knock! Knock!
Who's there?
Ann Dan.
Ann Dan who?
Ann Dan along came Jones.

....

Knock! Knock!
Who's there?
Lars.
Lars who?
Lars tells a lot of fibs.

Knock! Knock!
Who's there?
Zoom.
Zoom who?
Zoom did you expect?

Knock! Knock!
Who's there?
Cairo.
Cairo who?
Cairo the boat now?

Knock! Knock!
Who's there?
Fiber.
Fiber who?
Fiber get you ten I'm right.

Knock! Knock!
Who's there?
Tailor.
Tailor who?
Tailor Swift.

Knock! Knock!
Who's there?
Omar.
Omar who?
Omar goodness! I'm locked out.

Knock! Knock!
Who's there?
Poison Ally.
Poison Ally who?
Poison Ally I don't care if you open up or not.

Knock! Knock!
Who's there?
Faun knee
Faun knee who?
Faun knee you should ask that question.

Knock! Knock!
Who's there?
Halo.
Halo who?
Halo and good-bye. I'm tired of waiting.

Knock! Knock!
Who's there?
Sedan.
Sedan who?'
Sedan you're rocking the boat.

Knock! Knock!
Who's there?
Pecan.
Pecan who?
Pecan through the window isn't very polite.

Knock! Knock!
Who's there?
Amen.
Amen who?
Amen selling vacuum cleaners.

Knock! Knock!
Who's there?
Harley.
Harley who?
Harley a day goes by when this doesn't happen to me.

Knock! Knock!
Who's there?
Arch.
Arch who?
You'd better take something for that cold.

Knock! Knock!
Who's there?
Howell.
Howell who?
Howell I get in if you don't open up?

Knock! Knock!
Who's there?
Musk.
Musk who?
Musk I knock again?

Knock! Knock!
Who's there?
Bertha.
Bertha who?
Bertha day greetings to you.

Knock! Knock!
Who's there?
Esther.
Esther who?
Esther another door I can go to?

Knock! Knock!
Who's there?
Patty Cake.
Patty Cake who?
Patty Cake! Patty Cake! How many times do I have to tell you?

Knock! Knock!
Who's there?
Manny.
Manny who?
Manny people know me and like me.

Knock! Knock!

Who's there?

Lexie.

Lexie who?

Lexie how long you'll keep me waiting.

. . . .

Knock! Knock!

Who's there?

Avery.

Avery who?

Avery time I come here it's the same old thing.

. . . .

Knock! Knock!

Who's there?

A.C.

A.C. who?

A.C. come A. C. go.

. . . .

Knock! Knock!

Who's there?

Alma.

Alma who?

Alma friends are out here too.

. . . .

Knock! Knock!

Who's there?

Argo.

Argo who?

Argo jump in a lake.

Knock! Knock!

Who's there?

Alp.

Alp who?

Alp! Alp! I'm drowning.

- -

Knock! Knock!

Who's there?

Lurie.

Lurie who?

Lurie Lurie Hallelujah.

- -

Knock! Knock!

Who's there?

Allied.

Allied who?

Allie when I said I'm not mad. Open up!

- -

Knock! Knock!

Who's there?

Unaware.

Unaware who?

Unaware is what you put on first when you get dressed.

- -

Knock! Knock!

Who's there?

Teller.

Teller who?

Teller a good joke and make her laugh.

Knock! Knock!

Who's there?

Socket.

Socket who?

Socket to me.

Knock! Knock!

Who's there?

Albee.

Albee who?

Albee back tomorrow.

Knock! Knock!

Who's there?

Alda.

Alda who?

Alda neighbors let me in their houses.

Knock! Knock!

Who's there?

I Astor.

I Astor who?

I Astor very politely to open the door.

Knock! Knock!

Who's there?

Roland.

Roland who?

Roland down a hill will make you dizzy.

Knock! Knock!

Who's there?

Alex.

Alex who?

Alex you one more time to open up.

~~~~~~

Knock! Knock!

Who's there?

Radio.

Radio who?

Radio not. Here I come.

~~~~~~

Knock! Knock!

Who's there?

Balfour.

Balfour who?

Balfour batter. Take your base.

~~~~~~

Knock! Knock!

Who's there?

Stan Bach.

Stan Bach who?

Stan Bach! I'm breaking down the door.

~~~~~~

Knock! Knock!

Who's there?

Bolivar.

Bolivar who?

Bolivar friends are on their way over here.

Knock! Knock!

Who's there?

It's Cole.

It's Cole who?

It's Cole out here. Let me come in.

Knock! Knock!

Who's there?

Hiram.

Hiram who?

Hiram because he's the right man for the job.

Knock! Knock!

Who's there?

Guido.

Guido who?

Guidon't want anymore excuses. Open the door.

Knock! Knock!

Who's there?

Somber.

Somber who?

Somber over the rainbow.

Knock! Knock!

Who's there?

Hare.

Hare who?

Hare we go again.

Knock! Knock!

Who's there?

Getty.

Getty who?

Getty yap horse, we're out of here.

Knock! Knock!

Who's there?

Kay Jen.

Kay Jen who?

Kay Jen music has a peppy beat.

Knock! Knock!

Who's there?

I Midas.

I Midas who?

I Midas well go home.

Knock! Knock!

Who's there?

Hugh Otto.

Hugh Otto who?

Hugh Otto know. You invited me over.

Knock! Knock!

Who's there?

Toodle.

Toodle who?

Right. See you later.

Knock! Knock!
Who's there?
Mice.
Mice who?
Mice weather we're having, isn't it?

Knock! Knock!
Who's there?
Tom Sawyer.
Tom Sawyer who?
Tom Sawyer sneaking out the back door.

Knock! Knock!
Who's there?
Aware.
Aware who?
Aware. Aware have my little sheep gone?

Knock! Knock!
Who's there?
Tamara.
Tamara who?
Tamara is another school day. Yuk!

Knock! Knock!
Who's there?
Gretta.
Gretta who?
Gretta long little doggie. Gretta long.

Knock! Knock!
Who's there?
Bay B.
Bay B. who
Bay B. Face Nelson.

Knock! Knock!
Who's there?
Adore.
Adore who?
Adore is between us. Open up.

Knock! Knock!
Who's there?
Ellison.
Ellison who?
Ellison the alphabet after K and before M.

Knock! Knock!
Who's there?
Market.
Market who?
Market C.O.D.

Knock! Knock!
Who's there?
Kleenex.
Kleenex who?
Kleenex are nicer than dirty necks.

Knock! Knock!

Who's there?

Habit.

Habit who?

Habit your way, I'll come back later.

....

Knock! Knock!

Who's there?

Oil.

Oil who?

Oil see you later.

....

Knock! Knock!

Who's there?

Michelle.

Michelle who?

Michelle is cracked, said the turtle sadly.

....

Knock! Knock!

Who's there?

I'm Gibbon.

I'm Gibbon who?

I'm Gibbon away free samples.

....

Knock! Knock!

Who's there?

Watson.

Watson who?

Watson your mind, young fella?

Knock! Knock!

Who's there?

Venice.

Venice who?

Venice payday? I'm flat broke.

....

Knock! Knock!

Who's there?

Heidi.

Heidi who?

Heidi Ho everybody!

....

Knock! Knock!

Who's there?

Abbott.

Abbott who?

Abbott you're afraid to open the door.

Knock! Knock!
Who's there?
Barrie.
Barrie who?
Barrie interesting.

Knock! Knock!
Who's there?
Bennett.
Bennett who?
Bennett rains it pours.

Knock! Knock!
Who's there?
Cain.
Cain who?
Cain I please come in?

Knock! Knock!
Who's there?
My Carlos.
My Carlos who?
My Carlos a wheel. I need help.

Knock! Knock!
Who's there?
Clare.
Clare who?
Clare a path! I'm coming through.

Knock! Knock!

Who's there?

For Bryan.

For Bryan who?

For Bryan out loud, open up.

Knock! Knock!

Who's there?

Shelby.

Shelby who?

Shelby right with you, so be patient.

Knock! Knock!

Who's there?

Ray.

Ray who?

No. Who Ray! It's me.

Knock! Knock!

Who's there?

Carmen.

Carmen who?

Carmen get it. I have hot pizza.

Knock! Knock!

Who's there?

Hyphen.

Hyphen who?

Hyphen waiting out here a long time.

Knock! Knock!
Who's there?
Disguise.
Disguise who?
Disguise getting very impatient.

Knock! Knock!
Who's there?
Hiss.
Hiss who?
Hiss anyone else home besides you?

Knock! Knock!
Who's there?
Amos.
Amos who?
Amos stop coming to this house.

Knock! Knock!
Who's there?
Luke.
Luke who?
Luke and see you dummy!

Knock! Knock!
Who's there?
Cheryl B.
Cheryl B. who?
Cheryl B. coming around the mountain when she comes.

Knock! Knock!
Who's there?
I'm Sue.
I'm Sue who?
I'm Sue sorry to be late.

Knock! Knock!
Who's there?
Butcher.
Butcher who?
Butcher money where your mouth is, wise guy.

Knock! Knock!
Who's there?
Rein.
Rein who?
Rein Irish eyes are smiling.

Knock! Knock!
Who's there?
Omar.
Omar who?
Omar Darling Clementine.

Knock! Knock!
Who's there?
Will Lama.
Will Lama who?
Will Lama monkey's uncle!

Knock! Knock!

Who's there?

Hugo.

Hugo who?

Hugo first. I'll follow.

....

Knock! Knock!

Who's there?

Poodle.

Poodle who?

Poodle little mustard on my hot dog.

....

Knock! Knock!

Who's there?

Sharon.

Sharon who?

Sharon gossip is fun. Have you heard this rumor?

....

Knock! Knock!

Who's there?

Ray.

Ray who?

Ray to go dude.

....

Knock! Knock!

Who's there?

Butch.

Butch who?

Butch your arms around me and give me a big hug.

Knock! Knock!
Who's there?
Alfred.
Alfred who?
Alfred the needle if you sew up the rip.

Knock! Knock!
Who's there?
Gus.
Gus who?
That's what you have to do. Guess.

Knock! Knock!
Who's there?
Danielle.
Danielle who?
Danielle at me. Speak softly.

Knock! Knock!
Who's there?
Cowl.
Cowl who?
Cowl get even with you for this.

Knock! Knock!
Who's there?
Dale.
Dale who?
Dale be heck to pay if you don't let me in.

Knock! Knock!

Who's there?

Hiam.

Hiam who?

Hiam here on police business. Open up!

Knock! Knock!

Who's there?

Gandhi.

Gandhi who?

Gandhi kids come out to play?

Knock! Knock!

Who's there?

Hardy.

Hardy who?

Hardy har har! The joke is over. Let us in.

Knock! Knock!

Who's there?

Nobel.

Nobel who?

Nobel so I knocked instead.

Knock! Knock!

Who's there?

Dee.

Dee who?

Dee heck with you! I'm leaving.

Knock! Knock!

Who's there?

Whirl.

Whirl who?

Whirl try again later.

Knock! Knock!

Who's there?

Ireland.

Ireland who?

Ireland you five bucks if you promise to pay me back.

Knock! Knock!

Who's there?

Ali

Ali who?

Ali bama is a fine state.

Knock! Knock!

Who's there?

Bruno.

Bruno who?

Bruno me. I live next door.

Knock! Knock!

Who's there?

Dot Burnett.

Dot Burnett who?

Dot Burnett I'm tired of this dumb game.

Knock! Knock!

Who's there?

Dairy.

Dairy who?

Dairy goes! After him, men!

◄ ◄ ◄ ◄ ◄ ◄ ◄ ◄ ◄ ◄ ◄

Knock! Knock!

Who's there?

Burton.

Burton who?

Burton up your coat. It's cold outside.

► ► ► ► ► ► ► ► ► ► ► ► ► ► ►

Knock! Knock!

Who's there?

Almond.

Almond who?

Almost a very good mood.

◄ ◄ ◄ ◄ ◄ ◄ ◄ ◄ ◄ ◄ ◄ ◄ ◄

Knock! Knock!

Who's there?

Wilda.

Wilda who?

Wilda plane be landing soon?

► ► ► ► ► ► ► ► ► ► ► ► ►

Knock! Knock!

Who's there?

Z.

Z who?

Z you in the morning.

Knock! Knock!

Who's there?

Olive.

Olive who?

Olive the Springtime, don't you.

▶ ▶

Knock! Knock!

Who's there?

Jester.

Jester who?

Jester minute. I'm still thinking.

◀ ◀ ◀ ◀ ◀ ◀ ◀ ◀ ◀ ◀ ◀ ◀ ◀ ◀ ◀ ◀ ◀

Knock! Knock!

Who's there?

Rock it.

Rock it who?

Rock it ships fly into space.

▶ ▶ ▶ ▶ ▶ ▶ ▶ ▶ ▶ ▶ ▶ ▶ ▶ ▶ ▶ ▶ ▶ ▶ ▶

Knock! Knock!

Who's there?

Skip.

Skip who?

Skip it! I'll go next door.

◀ ◀ ◀ ◀ ◀ ◀ ◀ ◀ ◀ ◀ ◀ ◀ ◀ ◀ ◀ ◀ ◀ ◀

Knock! Knock!

Who's there?

Kent.

Kent who?

Kent you see who I am?

Knock! Knock!
Who's there?
Pig.
Pig who?
Pig me up at five o'clock.

....

Knock! Knock!
Who's there?
Otto.
Otto who?
Otto know.

....

Knock! Knock!
Who's there?
Juno.
Juno who?
Juno how long I've been waiting out here?

Knock! Knock!
Who's there?
Howard.
Howard who?
Howard you like to buy some magazines?

....

Knock! Knock!
Who's there?
Ernie.
Ernie who?
Ernie got scraped when she fell on the sidewalk.

....

Knock! Knock!
Who's there?
Canopy.
Canopy who?
Canopy ever grow up to be a string bean?

....

Knock! Knock!
Who's there?
Ham Bacon.
Ham Bacon who?
Ham Bacon you to let me in.

....

Knock! Knock!
Who's there?
Wilder.
Wilder who?
Wilder out let's order pizza.

Knock! Knock!
Who's there?
Ozzie.
Ozzie who?
Ozzie a bad moon rising.

....

Knock! Knock!
Who's there?
Osborne.
Osborne who?
Osborne on the 4th of July.

....

Knock! Knock!
Who's there?
Winnie.
Winnie who?
Winnie gets home, he's in for a big surprise.

....

Knock! Knock!
Who's there?
I lecture.
I lecture who?
I lecture dog out when I came in.

....

Knock! Knock!
Who's there?
Oil.
Oil who?
Oil paint your picture if you'll pose for me.

Knock! Knock!
Who's there?
Dot com.
Dot com who?
Dot com home, we miss you.

....

Knock! Knock!
Who's there?
Freeze.
Freeze who?
Freeze a jolly good fellow, which nobody can deny.

....

Knock! Knock!
Who's there?
Hour.
Hour who?
Hour you feeling? Better, I hope.

....

Knock! Knock!
Who's there?
Venice.
Venice who?
Venice the next train to Rome?

....

Knock! Knock!
Who's there?
Hubie.
Hubie who?
Hubie a good boy while we're gone!

Knock! Knock!
Who's there?
Al.
Al who?
Al in favor, say aye!

Knock! Knock!
Who's there?
Aussie.
Aussie who?
Aussie you tomorrow, mate.

Knock! Knock!
Who's there?
Snow.
Snow who?
No. Snow what and the Seven Dwarfs.

Knock! Knock!
Who's there?
Closure.
Closure who?
Closure mouth and open the door.

Knock! Knock!
Who's there?
Gwen.
Gwen who?
Gwen are you going to open this darn door?

Knock! Knock!
Who's there?
Vicious.
Vicious who?
Vicious a fine howdy do for a visitor.

Knock! Knock!
Who's there?
Data.
Data who?
Data nice boy.

Knock! Knock!
Who's there?
Kenya.
Kenya who?
Kenya kids come out to play?

Knock! Knock!
Who's there?
Althea.
Althea who?
Althea later, dude.

Knock! Knock!
Who's there?
Rut.
Rut who?
Rut do you want me to say?

Knock! Knock!
Who's there?
Megan.
Megan who?
Megan dinner is a lot of work.

Knock! Knock!
Who's there?
Ride.
Ride who?
Ride you tell a fib about me?

Knock! Knock!
Who's there?
Will Hugh?
Will Hugh who?
Will Hugh marry me?

Knock! Knock!
Who's there?
Japan.
Japan who?
Japan my trampoline and bounce around.

Knock! Knock!
Who's there?
Reveal.
Reveal who?
Reveal you deserve a promotion.

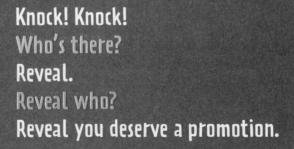

Knock! Knock!
Who's there?
Lassie.
Lassie who?
Lassie what's on the cable channels.

Knock! Knock!
Who's there?
Jamaica.
Jamaica who?
Jamaica a snack for us?

Knock! Knock!
Who's there?
Hygiene.
Hygiene who?
Hygiene! What's new
with you, Gene?

Knock! Knock!
Who's there?
Marcella.
Marcella who?
Marcella is flooded.
Can I borrow a mop?

Knock! Knock!
Who's there?
Habit.
Habit who?
Habit you're afraid to open the

Knock! Knock!
Who's there?
Wagons.
Wagons who?
No. It's wagons ho!

....

Knock! Knock!
Who's there?
Mo.
Mo who?
Mo lasses is very sweet syrup.

Tall Tales

A boy in Rhode Island had a fever so high his little sister popped corn on his forehead!

....

There's a catfish in the Mississippi River that's so big the only way to hook it is to use a python for bait!

....

A comedian in New York City has been banned from telling his best joke because it's so funny some people have died laughing.

....

The soil in parts of Massachusetts is so rocky local worms have to carry tiny jackhammers.

....

There are trees in Washington state that grow so high birds wear oxygen masks to build their nests in the top branches.

....

There was a fish in the North Atlantic who was so smart the school he swam in was made up of Harvard and Yale graduates.

The F.B.I. just captured a gangster so notorious that instead of deporting him to his native country they blasted him into space to live in a space station.

Then there was the circus snake that tried to tie itself into a bow and ended up with a knot in its stomach.

A woman in New York waxes the floors in her home so often her house has slide rules.

A sheriff in a quiet Western town got so bored he finally held up the bank in his own town, tracked himself down, and locked himself in jail.

There's a hotel in Canada that's located in such a remote region that its doorman is a Sasquatch and its greeter is Smokey the Bear.

There's an intersection in Rome that has so many cars merging at the same place they hired an octopus to direct traffic.

Either Africa has the biggest mice in the world or the local elephants have developed a passion for cheese.

In a city in Italy they make macaroni so big and long that if it goes stale they use it as drainpipes.

In Alaska the lightning bugs are so big that if you catch them in your bare hands you get a shock.

A Texas oilman owns a limo so long that when he drives it cross-country, the front end and rear end are in different zip codes.

Gophers in Alaska are so big construction companies hire them to dig train tunnels.

Trees in Montana grow so tall when their leaves fall in October, they don't hit the ground until December.

A young girl in Alabama is so thin when she stands sideways at her desk in the morning her teacher marks her absent.

Bugs grow so big in Alaska that people have to swat them with tennis rackets.

Squirrels in New Hampshire are so forgetful they have to draw tiny maps in order to find the nuts they bury in the fall.

There's a farmer in Russia who is so big he makes the Green Giant look like a leprechaun.

A New Yorker on a plane was boasting to the Texan seated next to him. "In New York City they start putting up a fifty-story building one month and have it finished by the next month." "Humph! That's nothing," replied the Texan. "In Dallas, I've seen them lay the foundation for an apartment building in the morning and when I drive by the same spot that night they're already evicting tenants for non-payment of back rent."

A star in Hollywood received so much fan mail the postal authorities let her open her own branch office.

There is a performer who does such good impressions of Hollywood stars his wife has no idea who she's married to.

There's a new hairspray so strong people who use it have to have their hair cut with a chain saw.

Lobsters in Maine grow so big lumberjacks put them on leashes and let them snip down tree trunks with their claws.

A farm in Oklahoma is so big when a young couple goes out to milk the cows their grandchildren bring back the milk.

A rich couple in California has so many credit cards that they use them to play Canasta.

Horseflies are so big in Texas that cowboys don't swat them, they rope them, saddle them and ride them in air rodeos.

There's an Arab oil baron who is so rich he keeps a small sports car in the trunk of his huge limo just in case he gets a flat tire.

Mosquitoes are so big in some parts of the Amazon that people who get bit need immediate blood transfusions to stay alive.

There's a Mexican chili pepper so hot only fire-breathing dragons are allowed to eat them.

There's a sultan so rich when he plays golf he hires a millionaire as his caddy.

A dog in New Jersey is so talented that instead of rolling over he does magic tricks.

And then there was a guy in Vermont who was so unlucky black cats wouldn't cross his path.

Bullfrogs grow so big in Florida that farmers put rings through their noses.

STELLLAAAA!

A baby born in Wisconsin was so big his wealthy parents fed him with a silver shovel.

There's a place at the North Pole that gets so cold at night that people who live there huddle around their refrigerators to keep warm.

There's a dog in Hollywood who is so smart that he auditions for speaking parts in movies.

There's a Hollywood mansion so huge the owner travels from his bedroom to the kitchen in a golf cart.

There was a high school football player in Maryland so dumb that when his coach told him to run a naked reverse, he stripped off his uniform.

There was a comedian from Pennsylvania whose material was so bad they made a laughing hyena frown.

There was a Texas oilman so rich he bought a university so his dumb son could attend college.

A guy in Nevada is so lazy he traded in his Dachshund for a Great Dane so he wouldn't have to bend over to pet his dog.

The soil in Iowa is so rich farmers plant toothpicks in the spring and harvest fence posts in the fall.

In Texas they make waterbeds so big the owners keep pet dolphins in them.

▷ ▷ ▷ ▷ ▷ ▷ ▷ ▷ ▷ ▷ ▷ ▷ ▷ ▷ ▷ ▷ ▷ ▷ ▷

Hailstones are so big in Buffalo, New York that three of them piled together make a snowman.

◁ ◁ ◁ ◁ ◁ ◁ ◁ ◁ ◁ ◁ ◁ ◁ ◁ ◁ ◁ ◁ ◁ ◁ ◁

There's a new supersonic jet so fast that you get in one end of the plane and by the time you walk to the other end, you're already landing at the place you wanted to go.

▷ ▷ ▷ ▷ ▷ ▷ ▷ ▷ ▷ ▷ ▷ ▷ ▷ ▷ ▷ ▷ ▷ ▷ ▷

The mail delivery in one state is so slow people mail their Christmas cards on the 4th of July in order to have them delivered by December 24th.

◁ ◁ ◁ ◁ ◁ ◁ ◁ ◁ ◁ ◁ ◁ ◁ ◁ ◁ ◁ ◁ ◁ ◁ ◁

A couple of Arctic explorers were swapping stories. "One night it was so cold where we were the flame on our candles froze and we couldn't blow them out until the sun came up." "That's not cold," countered the other explorer. "It was so frigid where we were, when we tried to talk our words instantly froze into ice cubes. We had to fry the ice cubes in a hot pan to hear what we were saying.

▷ ▷ ▷ ▷ ▷ ▷ ▷ ▷ ▷ ▷ ▷ ▷ ▷ ▷ ▷ ▷ ▷ ▷ ▷

A teenager in Nebraska is growing so fast his shadow can't keep up with him.

◁ ◁ ◁ ◁ ◁ ◁ ◁ ◁ ◁ ◁ ◁ ◁ ◁ ◁ ◁ ◁ ◁ ◁ ◁

Then there was the school librarian who was so strict, she taped student's mouths shut.

▷ ▷ ▷ ▷ ▷ ▷ ▷ ▷ ▷ ▷ ▷

There's a Texas billionaire so rich he lines the bottom of his birdcages with hundred dollar bills.

◁ ◁ ◁ ◁ ◁ ◁ ◁ ◁ ◁ ◁ ◁

Then there was the elevator operator who was so dumb he didn't know which way was up.

There's a new jumbo jet so big it has a taxi service between first and second-class.

There's a Texas oil baron so rich he hires the Pope to say grace over his Thanksgiving dinner.

Scientists in Egypt have developed a new camel that has a bucket seat on its back instead of humps for easier riding.

Pearls are so big in the waters off a secret island in the South Seas that natives use them as baseballs.

There's a gambler who is so lucky that when he walks into a casino they automatically hand him a fistful of money.

There is an earthworm bodybuilder so strong it challenges birds to a tug of war and always wins.

There is a schoolteacher so smart computers ask her to check their spelling.

There's an Ivy League football team that is so smart it never has to huddle up because every player always knows the right play to run on every down.

Then there was the absentminded daredevil who went over Niagara Falls in a special barrel and left the barrel on shore.

There is a park in New York City that is so dangerous the muggers demanded police protection.

A bus driver in New Jersey was so snobby he wouldn't allow passengers to get on his bus without an engraved invitation.

A grandfather sneezed so hard he launched his teeth into outer space. They are now orbiting earth.

In some parts of Australia the fleas grow so big kangaroos hitch rides on them.

Scientists have developed a new advanced watermelon that spits out its own pits when you buy it.

My neighbor's poodle is so neat she buries her bones in plastic bags to keep them clean.

There is a lumberjack who is so tall that when he trips and falls his friends all shout, "Timber!"

There is an Army general who is so respected when he goes to a restaurant everyone stands at attention while he gives his orders.

There's a new breed of super squirrel so strong its jaws are powerful enough to crack nuts and bolts.

There's a special rhino that lives in London, England and has a foghorn.

A boy in Miami had a fever so high anyone who sat close to him got sunburn.

An early pioneer was talking about the famous echo mountain. "Once I camped there for a night," said he. "I crawled in my tent and before I sacked out I stuck out my head and yelled, Time to wake up you old buffalo! Then I went to bed and fell asleep. Eight hours later the echo came back loud as ever and woke me up."

There was a private school so wealthy it had tollbooths at the ends of its hallways.

I once had a cat that was so finicky she'd only eat her food if she saw me taste it first.

There was once a watchdog that was so ferocious he wouldn't let his owner into the house after dark.

And then there was the woman who was such a messy housekeeper she had to hire a detective and a bloodhound to track down where her kids were.

I went to a restaurant where the food was so bad the waiters tipped the customers if they stayed for the entire meal.

The other day I went to a Broadway play that was so bad the author's mother and father walked out after the first act.

Global warming is so bad last that winter the Abominable Snowman came down with a case of heat stroke.

There was an oil baron in Texas who was so rich the bank used to call him to borrow money.

Some luxury cars get such bad mileage it takes a full tank of gas to warm up the engine on a cold day.

My pet dog is so spoiled that when I tell him to sit he jumps in my recliner and puts up his feet.

I knew a guy whose name was so long he had it tattooed on his arm so he could remember how to spell it.

Wee Willie Winkie ran through the town in his nightgown and got arrested for indecent exposure.

Jack be nimble. Jack be quick. He jumped over the candlestick and they rushed him to the hospital because he had second-degree burns on his backside.

The Old Woman who lives the shoe couldn't pay her rent so her landlord booted her out.

Mary stole the Golden Fleece and now she's on the lamb.

Little Jack Horner sat in a corner and with the help of a slick lawyer sued his parents for child abuse.

Humpty Dumpty had a great fall, but a lousy winter. He went skiing and cracked his skull.

Jack and Jill didn't go up the hill. They just bought bottled water instead.

Hey Diddle Diddle, the cow jumped over the moon but her landing on the surface was faked by NASA.

Bobby Shafto's gone to sea. He joined the Navy because he heard girls love a man in uniform.

The Three Little Kittens lost their mittens and didn't get any pie. Who cares? Their mom can't bake anyway ... she's a cat!

Little Miss Muffet sat on a tuffet until her new living-room furniture

Along came a spider and sat down beside Miss Muffet so she called an exterminator who whacked the pesky bug.

Jack and Jill went up the hill. Jack fell down and broke his crown. He sued Mother Goose and settled for an undisclosed settlement. Mother Goose has admitted no wrongdoing.

The Three Blind Mice had laser surgery and now they see fine.

Little Tommy Tucker sings for his supper on American Idol.

There was a crooked man, who walked a crooked mile, campaigning for a seat in Congress and he got elected.

Rub a dub dub. Three men in a sauna bath. Times have changed.

To market, to market, to look at all the food we can't afford to eat and to buy a can of cheap tuna.

Baa baa black sheep. We told you to stay away from that oil spill.

Old King Cole was a merry old sole until he went on a strict diet and became a cranky old guy.

Old Mother Hubbard went to the cupboard to see what she could pop into the microwave.

Then there was the Western Marshall whose draw was so lightning fast that every time he pulled a gun there was a crack of thunder.

In Arizona there was an outlaw so strong he used to hold up banks and shake the money out of them.

Maybe you heard about the tiny quarter horse that was only worth a nickel.

There was an Indian medicine man that was so good at performing the rain dance he could make it drizzle just by tapping his foot in time to music.

In Nevada there was an unlucky cowboy who lost his shirt playing poker and had to ride his horse bareback.

Then there was the frontier circus that didn't circle their wagons when attacked. Instead they formed into three rings.

Then there was the cowboy who took boxing lessons because he wanted to punch cattle.

CHAPTER 7

LAST LAUGHS

Why did the king go to a doctor?
He had a royal pain in the neck.

RIGHT BACK THERE!

Knock! Knock!
Who's there?
Tower.
Tower who?
Tower that you love her.

Bill: My wallet is always full of big bills.
Jill: Yeah. Unpaid big bills.

ATTENTION: **Beware of bully bodybuilders. They like to throw their weights around.**

Harry: I always get sick the night before I go on a trip.
Larry: So why don't you leave a day earlier?

Lady: **I'd like to try on that bathing suit in your front window.**
Salesgirl: **I'm sorry ma'am. You'll have to use the dressing room.**

Lady: I like to buy a live piranha.
Pet Store Clerk: Why do you want a piranha?
Lady: Because my cat's been eating my goldfish and I want to teach her a lesson.

Where did the Sheik go for a haircut?
To the berber shop.

What did the polite receiver say to the quarterback?
Please pass me the football.

Millie: My face is my fortune.

Tillie: Tsk! Tsk! Another child born into poverty.

....

What did the Munchkin order in the seafood restaurant?

A little bit of sole.

....

What part of the castle did Sir Artist protect?

The drawbridge.

....

Show me a bald businessman ... and I'll show you a guy with no overhead.

....

Show me an unemployed ghost ... and I'll show you a job haunter.

....

Knock! Knock!

Who's there?

Tolbert.

Tolbert who?

Tolbert Ernie is outside.

....

If money grew on trees everyone would rake in the dough.

....

KOOKY QUESTION: Do Oz Munchkins have short lifespans?

....

What do you get if you cross an oyster and a philosopher?

Pearls of wisdom.

....

Molly: What creature reproduces more rapidly than any other animal on earth?

Dolly: I don't know.

Millie My face is my fortune.

Molly: A zucker.

Dolly: What's a zucker?

Molly: I don't know, but there's one born every minute.

Knock! Knock!

Who's there?

Wallace.

Wallace who?

Wallace go on my permanent record?

What do you call a fake buck?

An artificial hart.

How do sailors clean their clothes at sea?

They throw them overboard and they wash ashore.

What do you get if you cross a giant with a poker player?

A big deal.

Jack: **I'm tired of paying high taxes.**

Mack: **Why don't you write a letter to Washington?**

Jack: **What good will that do? He's dead.**

SPIN CYCLE COMING UP!

Knock! Knock!

Who's there?

Murray Lee.

Murray Lee who?

Murray Lee we roll along.

What do you call a 300-pound background actor?
Extra large.

what do you get if you cross an artist with a card player?
Draw poker.

What happened after the lottery player picked his nose five times?
He was a pick-six winner.

Which runs faster hot or cold?
Hot. Anyone can catch cold.

What do you find in the windows of a king's castle?
Royal panes.

what do you get if you cross soda and a sorcerer?
A fizz wiz.

Knock! Knock!
Who's there?
Victoria.
Victoria who?
Victoria's secret boyfriend.

what do you call a Munchkin victory over the Giants in football?
A huge upset.

A critic started to walk out of a Broadway play after the first act. The play's producer stopped him on the way to the exit. "Why are you leaving so early?" asked the producer. "There are still two acts to go." "I know," grumbled the critic as he made for the door, "but I'm pretty sure the person who penned that awful first act also wrote the other two."

Captain: Are you happy now that you're in the Army?

Private: Yes, sir.

Captain: And what were you before you were in the Army?

Private: Much happier.

What magazine do dogs and golfers read?
Cur and Driver Magazine.

Knock! Knock!

Who's there?

Hi Ray.

Hi Ray who?

Hi Ray work slows down traffic.

KOOKY QUESTION: **Do tired birds sleep on feather beds?**

What game do Arab children like to play?

Hide and Sheik.

What pill is a body builder?
Extra-strength aspirin.

Judge: Haven't I seen you someplace before?

Prisoner: Yes. I gave your daughter singing lessons.

Judge: Ten years in solitary confinement.

What do you get if you cross the second letter of the alphabet and a clock?

B on time.

What did the book manuscript say to the bellboy?
Page me.

◄ ◄ ◄ ◄ ◄ ◄ ◄ ◄ ◄ ◄ ◄ ◄

Which letter of the alphabet would like to go to the prom?
I would.

► ► ► ► ► ► ► ► ► ► ►

Knock! Knock!
Who's there?
White.
White who?
White until the light changes to green.

◄ ◄

A man walked into the office of a TV producer who specialized in weird reality shows. "I have an act that might interest you," the man said to the producer. He reached into his coat pockets and took out a mouse and a lizard. The man put them on a table. As the producer watched in astonishment, the lizard began to play a miniature guitar and the mouse began to sing. When the critters finished performing the producer clapped loudly. "That was amazing, said the producer to the man. "But if there's anything phony about this act, you'd better tell me right now." The man gulped. "Okay," he admitted, "I'll come clean. The mouse can't really sing. The lizard is a ventriloquist."

► ► ► ► ► ► ► ► ► ► ► ► ► ► ► ► ► ► ► ►

KOOKY QUESTION: Does the superhero known as "The Flash" get old quick?

◄ ◄ ◄ ◄ ◄ ◄ ◄ ◄ ◄ ◄ ◄ ◄ ◄ ◄ ◄ ◄ ◄ ◄ ◄

Why was Ms. Giant mad at Mr. Giant?
They had a big argument.

► ► ► ► ► ► ► ► ► ► ► ► ► ► ► ► ► ► ►

Student Driver: What's the easiest thing to run into?
Instructor: Debt.

What did the diet police give the man for overeating?
A meal ticket.

Knock! Knock!
Who's there?
Whitey.
Whitey who?
Whitey or lefty does it really matter?

Where did Santa go to buy potatoes?
He went to Idaho-ho-ho!

Knock! Knock!
Who's there?
Wally.
Wally who?
Wally's thinking, let's hum a tune.

What kind of cars do ghosts drive?
Eek-conomy cars.

What do you get when a large water
fowl gets stuck in wet earth?
Mudder Goose.

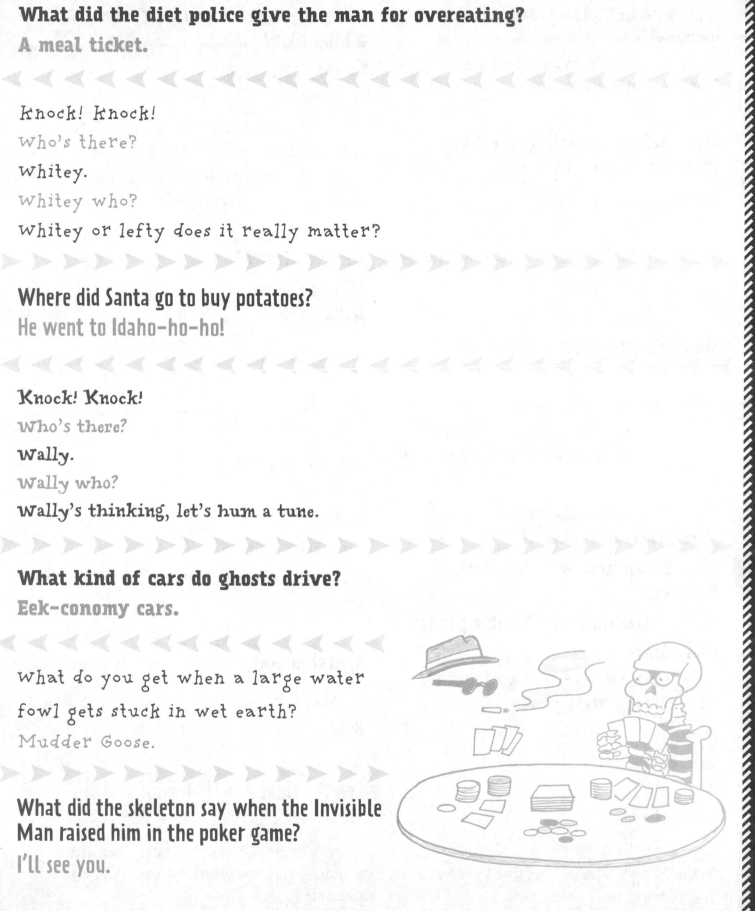

What did the skeleton say when the Invisible Man raised him in the poker game?
I'll see you.

Tillie: What's the weather like outside?

Millie: I don't know. It's raining so hard I can't see out.

....

How did the coach grade his quarterback test?

It was pass or fail.

....

What do most horror stories have?

A cemetery plot.

....

What do you call a gangster story?

Words to the wise guys.

....

KOOKY QUESTION: Do English zombies always keep a stiff upper lip?

....

Man: Can you direct me to the First National Bank?

Boy: I can and will for five dollars.

Man: Five dollars? That's pretty high pay.

Boy: I know, but bank directors are always well paid.

....

Knock! Knock!

Who's there?

Van Hugh.

Van Hugh who?

Van Hugh open the door, you'll be surprised.

Who do you get if you cross a hen and a Munchkin?

Chicken Little.

....

Prisoner: How can I be a forger? I can't write my own name.

Judge: Writing your name is not what you're charged with.

....

Knock! Knock!

Who's there?

Hole.

Hole who?

Hole up your hands and come out quietly.

....

Knock! Knock!

Who's there?

Lotta.

Lotta who?

Lotta folks out here are getting angry.

....

Knock! Knock!

Who's there?

Ben.

Ben who?

Ben the rules and let me in.

....

KOOKY QUESTION: Why would a young person want to feel like his old self?

Why do Munchkin doctors always lose their tempers?
Because they have little patients.

....

Mr. Brown: Is Smithers a good employee?

Mr. Green: Let me put it this way. Every month he puts in a good day's work.

....

NUTTY BOOK NOTES:

THE NAKED TRUTH – a book with no cover.

TRUMPETS & FLUTES – Reed this book!

1,001 INSULTS – you can't put it down.

ALL-TIME BASEBALL SCORES – a run for your money.

THE STORY OF GPS – you can't go wrong.

LOCKS & SAFES – a winning combination.

THE END OF THE BLACK CAT – a dark tale.

THE STORY OF SODA – here comes the fizz.

SPELLS – an enchanting book.

....

What do you get if you cross a leopard and a penguin?
An animal in a polka-dot tuxedo.

Knock! Knock!
Who's there?
A. Monty.
A. Monty who?
A. Monty always gets his man.

....

What do convicts put on their prison beds?
Rap sheets.

....

Did you hear about the gangster who was so crooked that when he got whacked, they didn't bury him they just screwed him into the ground?

....

KOOKY QUESTION: Is a French poodle a luxury cur?

....

What musical instrument did the steer play?
A bull horn.

What do you call an ape from Athens?
A Greece monkey.

How did the Canadian Mountie paint his house?

He put on a coat of red.

Dolly: Are you using your bicycle today?

Molly: Yes. I'm sorry, but you can't borrow it.

Dolly: No problem. What I really want to borrow are your roller blades.

Knock! Knock!

Who's there?

Wise.

Wise who?

Wise Sally in there and I'm not.

Knock! Knock!

Who's there?

Oak.

Oak who?

Oak-lahoma is a fine state.

Knock! Knock!

Who's there?

Ida.

Ida who?

Idaho is a good state, too.

Employee #1: Why didn't you laugh when the boss told us that joke?

Employee #2: I don't have to. I'm quitting tomorrow.

Show me a muddy hobo ... and I'll show you a guy who's dirt poor.

Why did the giant go to a psychiatrist?
Because he had big problems.

Why are giants so happy?
Because they know how to live large.

Why couldn't the Tin Man pitch for the Oz baseball team?
His throwing arm was a bit rusty.

What do you get if you cross a millionaire with a kangaroo?
An animal with very deep pockets.

Knock! Knock!
Who's there?
Hanover.
Hanover who?
Hanover the keys or else.

How much does a deer counter earn?
About twenty bucks an hour, which is a lot of doe.

Lolly: Does it cost a lot to visit Munchkin land?
Molly: No. It's a small price to pay for the experience.

SIGN IN A PARACHUTE FACTORY: Our business has a lot of ups and downs.

When can a house fly?
When it's a mansion with wings.

Jed: Did you catch all those fish by yourself?
Fred: No. Some worms helped me.

Knock! Knock!
Who's there?
Vest.
Vest who?
Vest Virginia.

Dork: What's kleptomania?
Mork: It's a disease.
Dork: Is it catching?
Mork: No. It's taking.

What do you say if the Statue of Liberty sneezes?
God Bless America!

Who takes care of Andy Bee and Opie Bee? Aunt Bee.

SIGN ON AN ANGER MANAGEMENT CENTER:
It's a mad, mad, mad, mad world!

Then there was the hit man who hated windy weather so much he tried to shoot the breeze.

Taxi Driver: I forgot to start the meter so I don't know how much to charge you.

Lady: That's okay. I forgot to bring money so I couldn't pay you anyway.

Al: Why did the crook break the glass window?
Sal: He was a pane killer.

Knock! Knock!
Who's there?
Rick.
Rick who?
Rick Shaw.

Knock! Knock!
Who's there?
Elsie.
Elsie who?
Elsie if anyone is watching us.

How do you find an Army camp? Follow the base path.

What did the judge say to the crooked lawyer?
Defend yourself.

Millie: Why did you run on duck feathers?

Tillie: The commercial said to hurry on down.

....

What do you get if you cross Davy Jones' locker with a retail store?

A place that gives deep discounts.

....

How does Plumber Cat fix a leaky sink?

He uses his tool kit.

....

Knock! Knock!

Who's there?

I Gabe.

I Gabe who?

I Gabe you my answer already.

....

DAFFY DEFINITION:

Transatlantic cable – the bottom line.

....

Movie Usher: How far down do you want to sit?

Man: All the way down. I'm very tired.

....

What's the last thing you take off before getting into bed?

Your feet. You take them off the floor.

....

Where does a shrub play baseball?

In the bush leagues.

....

Knock! Knock!

Who's there?

Garden.

Garden who?

Garden the door must be a boring job.

Knock! Knock!
Who's there?
Les.
Les who?
Les talk man to man.

What do you call mice that cheer for a sports team?
Pep squeaks.

How do Munchkin umpires check their calls?
They use instant wee-play cameras.

Dolly: Grandpa finally got Grandma to stop biting her nails.
Molly: How did he do that?
Dolly: He hid her false teeth.

SIGN IN A SILENT CLOWN CLASS – Mime your own business.

What do you get if you cross a contented cat and a golfer?
Purr for the course.

ATTENTION: Writers have lots of read and write blood cells.

Knock! Knock!
Who's there?
Oral.
Oral who?
Oral quiz time.

Knock! Knock!

Who's there?

Vowel.

Vowel who?

Vowel play is suspected in this case.

YOU HAVE THE RIGHT TO REMAIN SILENT!

Knock! Knock!

Who's there?

Wilma.

Wilma who?

Wilma Prince ever come?

Customer: How much are your fifty dollar shoes?

Clerk: Twenty-five dollars a foot.

Why did the fish go to jail?

It robbed a riverbank.

What did the nose say to the ear?

Are you trying to pick a fight with me?

What brand did the Catholic sisters use on their ranch?

Bar-Nun.

ATTENTION: Dumb Polly wants a wise cracker.

Basketball Coach: We're going to win this game.

Basketball Player: I hoop so.

What do you get when a jet flies through a flock of birds?

Shredded Tweet.

Knock! Knock!
Who's there?
Seesaw.
Seesaw who?
Seesaw you sneak out last night.

Knock! Knock!
Who's there?
Sour.
Sour who?
Sour your parents doing these days?

What happens if you break an hourglass?
Time slips through your fingers.

Where does a calendar keep an account?
In the daylight savings bank.

Teacher: Fenster! How many times am I going to have to keep you after school for misbehaving?
Fenster: Fifty-two.
Teacher: Huh? Why fifty-two?
Fenster: That's how many days are left until summer vacation.

Mary: **What are you going to be when you graduate from college?**
Harry: **An old man.**

ATTENTION: Golfers are people with holes in their heads.

Rodney dozed off in the back row of his third grade classroom while his teacher lectured her students about trees. "Rodney," the teacher called out to her sleepy pupil. "What do we call the outside layer of a tree?" Rodney yawned and sputtered. "W-What?" "Bark, Rodney," snapped the teacher. "Bark!" "Woof! Woof! Woof!" blurted out the startled student.

Knock! Knock!
Who's there?
Olga.
Olga who?
Olga round to the side door.

Cowboy: **Why are you only wearing one spur?**
Dude: **I figure if one side of a horse starts running, the other side will go along too.**

Son: **Hey Mom! You know that antique vase you've always worried about me breaking?**
Mother: **Yes. What about it?**
Son: **Your worries are over.**

Benny: **I started my life without a penny in my pocket.**
Lenny: **Big deal. I started life without a pocket.**

Why did the giraffes park in lover's lane?
They wanted to neck.

Knock! Knock!
Who's there?
Sayer.
Sayer who?
Sayer sorry.

Knock! Knock!
Who's there?
Noah.
Noah who?
Noah body.

What did the wrinkled pants say to the stuffed shirt?
I'm depressed.

Doe: Here come some deer hunters.
Buck: Keep quiet. Don't get yourself in a stew.

Knock! Knock!
Who's there?
Avenue.
Avenue who?
Avenue tried to get in here once before?

SIGN ON A BASEBALL PITCHER'S LOCKER: I'm just a delivery man.

Ken: **I have a gift for music.**
Len: **What kind?**
Ken: **Gift rap.**

ATTENTION: Peter makes Neverland movies in Panavision.

....

ATTENTION: **Tinker Bell likes diamond rings.**

A town in the Midwest was so small Sheriff Tom Brown also doubled as the local dogcatcher. Late one night Mr. Brown got a frantic call from Old Miss Gray. "Mr. Brown, I need your professional services at my house right away." "Yes, ma'am," said Mr. Brown. "Do you need Sheriff Tom Brown or Dogcatcher Tom Brown?" There was a short pause. Then Miss Gray replied, "Both! The neighbor's pit bull has a robber trapped in a tree in my yard."

....

Knock! Knock!
Who's there?
Vera Orphan.
Vera Orphan who?
Vera Orphan I stop by for a visit.

Knock! Knock!
Who's there?
Champ.
Champ who?
Champ who your hair once a week.

....

Why did the cow go to court?
She was involved in a dairy case.

....

What did the editor say to the hippie author?
Write on, dude.

....

ATTENTION: **Better to have loved a short girl than never to have loved a tall.**

....

Where did the farm girls have cheerleading practice?
In the root cellar.

....

What do you call a woman who teaches classes about giraffe throats?
A neck-ed lady.

....

Knock! Knock!
Who's there?
Shaq.
Shaq who?
Shaq well before using.

....

Show me a kitten born in Warsaw ... and I'll show you a polecat.

Chester: **See that guy. He's from Turkey.**

Lester: **What's his name?**

Chester: **I don't know, but his fez is familiar.**

....

Billy: A fly ball hit my baseball cap in the game today and I didn't even feel it.

Father: Why not?

Billy: I loaned my cap to Tommy.

....

ATTENTION: **Try our new Sasquatch hotdogs. They're much bigger than a footlong.**

....

Dude: **What do you use that rope for?**

Cowboy: **I use it to catch cattle.**

Dude: **What do you use for bait?**

....

Knock! Knock!

Who's there?

Row.

Row who?

Row out the barrel, we'll have a barrel of fun!

....

Which letter of the alphabet never makes any noise?

B quiet.

Man: **What do you prescribe as a cure for cowardice?**

Doctor: **Go on a strict diet of hero sandwiches.**

....

Why shouldn't you lose your temper?

Because no one else wants it.

....

what did the shepherd say after the wolf went away?

I'll sheep good tonight.

....

What do kings want most during a drought?

A long rain.

....

Knock! Knock!

Who's there?

Hugh **Otto** Bea.

Hugh **Otto** Bea who?

Hugh **Otta** Bea ashamed of yourself.

....

Who is the smartest pig in the world?

Albert Einsty.

What do you get when you tell bird jokes?
Cheep laughs.

Cowboy: I broke three wild horses this morning.
Dude: The next time you go riding, be more careful.

Knock! Knock!
Who's there?
I'm Fonda.
I'm Fonda who?
I'm Fonda your entire family.

Knock! Knock!
Who's there?
Dee James.
Dee James who?
Dee James Gang rides again. Yahoo!

Show me an Australian wearing jockey shorts ... and I'll show you down underwear.

Did you hear about the soccer goalie that was accused of accepting kickbacks?

What do you call an athlete who is a prizefighter?
A jock-in-the-boxer.

Why will a person never starve in the desert?
Because of the sand which is there.

What do you get if you cross an author and a broncobuster?
A rodeo writer.

Knock! Knock!
Who's there?
Bitter.
Bitter who?
Bitter days are coming.

Knock! Knock!
Who's there?
Hunger.
Hunger who?
Hunger down and prepare to be attacked.

Lenny: **My mother gave me five dollars for being good today.**

Jenny: **Humph! And all this time I've been being good for nothing.**

Knock! Knock!
Who's there?
I bid.
I bid who?
I bid you farewell.

What famous skeleton did Leonardo Da Vinci paint?
The Bony Lisa.

Why are your secrets always safe with egotists?
Because they never talk about anyone but themselves.

What are the most fragile things in the world?
Promises. People almost always break them.

Why did the chimp buy jogging shoes?
It wanted to join the human race.

What do you get if you cross a hen and a hand?
Chicken fingers.

Knock! Knock!
Who's there?
Wire.
Wire who?
Wire you being so stubborn?

Knock! Knock!
Who's there?
Karma.
Karma who?
Karma home, it's getting late.

What do you get if you cross a cobbler's store and hog food?
A shoe slop.

What happened when David hit Goliath?   He knocked him stone cold.

Little Melanie came home from her first day of school and scowled at her mother. "I'm never going back there!" she grunted. "Why not?" asked her puzzled mom. "I can't read. I can't write. And the teacher won't let me talk! So what's the use?"

Molly: Do you want to hear a funny story about a giraffe's neck?

Dolly: That depends. How long is it?

Knock! Knock!

Who's there?

A Poe.

A Poe who?

A Poe boy looking for a handout.

Teacher: Name four animals that belong to the cat family.

Boy: Mother Cat, Father Cat, and two baby kittens.

ATTENTION: Munchkin salesmen who have no confidence sell themselves short.

Then there was the bald grizzly that wore a bear rug.

What did the robber glue say to the pig farmer?

Stick up your hams.

Kate: My sister married a nice Irish boy.

Mary: Oh really?

Kate: No. O'Reilly.

Knock! Knock!
Who's there?
Louis N.
Louis N. who?
Louis N. my patience.

....

Knock! Knock!
Who's there?
Nelda.
Nelda who?
Nelda bell doesn't work.

....

Game Warden: Why haven't you caught anything?

Boy: I'm fishing with a naked hook and maybe the bass and trout are bashful.

....

Why can you trust an Invisible Man dressed in a business suit?
Because he has nothing up his sleeve.

....

SIGN ON A CHICKEN COOP: Employees must wash their hens.

....

What do you get if you cross a judge's chambers and a sea vessel?
A courtship.

....

Knock! Knock!
Who's there?
Slipper.
Slipper who?
Slipper a dollar through the mail slot.

....

What do cheerleaders do at a poker tournament?
Deck cheers.

Knock! Knock!
Who's there?
Roland.
Roland who?
Roland down a hill is fun.

. . . .

Bill: **What do you get if you cross a dinosaur and a skunk?**
Will: **I don't know, but you can smell it coming from miles away.**

. . . .

who writes fairytales about poker games?
Mother Deuce.

. . . .

Who insulted the cardinal?
A mockingbird.

. . . .

Knock! Knock!
Who's there?
Owl.
Owl who?
Owl many times do I have to tell you to stop answering the door?

. . . .

why did the giraffe go to the skin doctor?
It had a mole on its neck.

. . . .

Why did the skin doctor tell the giraffe not to worry?
The mole on its neck was really a gopher.

. . . .

What's black and has big ears and a trunk?
An elephant dipped in chocolate.

Knock! Knock!

Who's there?

Ann April.

Ann April who?

Ann April pound on his chest and break down your door.

Knock! Knock!

Who's there?

Beau Hen.

Beau Hen who?

Beau Hen Arrow.

Knock! Knock!

Who's there?

Candidate.

Candidate who?

Candidate be changed to Saturday night?

Knock! Knock!

Who's there?

Thatcher.

Thatcher who?

Thatcher was a funny story.

How can you tell a girl mummy from a boy mummy?

One is wrapped in pink and the other is wrapped in blue.

Tim: Did you hear about the funny fungus?

Slim: Oh no. Not another mold joke.

What do you get if you cross your mouth and a whip?

A tongue lashing.

Knock! Knock!

Who's there?

Chair.

Chair who?

Chair up and don't be so gloomy.

What book about crows did Jack London write?

The Caw of the Wild.

Why did Charles Dickens' chicken cross the road?

To get to the author's side.

How do you get a tired shepherd to relax?

Give him a sheeping pill.

What do you get if you cross a boxer and a suitcase?

A punching bag.

What did the pimple say to the zit?

It's time for us to break out.

What happens if an inchworm is afraid of heights?

He just can't measure up.

Knock! Knock!

Who's there?

Oliver.

Oliver who?

Oliver relatives are unfriendly, too.

Knock! Knock!

Who's there?

Polk.

Polk who?

Polk her in the eye if she looks through the peephole.

◀ ◀

Father: Why do you get such bad grades in school?

Son: I can't think of any answer.

Father: That explains it.

▶ ▶

Mrs. Turtle: The zoo has a lot of visitors today. Don't you want to see them?

Mr. Turtle: No. I'm through sticking my neck out for people.

◀ ◀

GOOD LUCK TURNS TO BAD LUCK WHEN...

Lightning misses you and hits a nearby tree ... and the tree falls on your house.

You get a 100 on a surprise quiz ... and the teacher decides not to count the grade.

The prettiest girl in school says she'll go to the prom with you ... and then she shouts April Fool's!

The best looking boy in your class finally calls you ... and then apologizes for dialing the wrong number.

You win an all-expense-paid trip to Hawaii ... and you already live in Honolulu.

You find a hundred dollar bill ... and it turns out to be counterfeit.

The roaches in your house move out ... only because termites are moving in.

You hit home runs in your first two times up ... and the baseball game is called off because of a sudden cloudburst.

School is called off because of a snowstorm ... and you spend the day shoveling out your driveway.

You finally get great tickets for your favorite band's concert ... and the group unexpectedly cancels the tour.

◄ ◄ ◄ ◄ ◄ ◄ ◄ ◄ ◄ ◄ ◄ ◄ ◄ ◄ ◄ ◄ ◄

YOU TELL 'EM...

You tell 'em Simon, I'll Legree.

You tell 'em Dickens, Oliver friends are waiting.

You tell 'em Mark, it's a well Twained audience.

You tell 'em, Mary, Shelley introduce you now.

You tell 'em, Oscar, Wilde horses couldn't drag you away.

You tell 'em, Victor, Hugo dude.

► ► ► ► ► ► ► ► ► ► ► ► ► ► ► ► ►

Knock! Knock!

Who's there?

Liver.

Liver who?

Liver alone and let's go home.

◄ ◄ ◄ ◄ ◄ ◄ ◄ ◄ ◄ ◄ ◄ ◄ ◄ ◄ ◄ ◄ ◄

Why didn't the Western marshal hang the outlaw giraffe?

He couldn't find a tree tall enough.

► ► ► ► ► ► ► ► ► ► ► ► ► ► ► ► ►

Knock! Knock!

Who's there?

Kobie.

Kobie who?

Kobie or not kobie, that is the question.

◄ ◄ ◄ ◄ ◄ ◄ ◄ ◄ ◄ ◄ ◄ ◄ ◄ ◄ ◄ ◄ ◄

Which bone tells a lot of jokes?

The humorous.

What do you call a well-behaved boa constrictor?

A civil serpent.

How do you deal with a spoiled kid who wants ice cream?

Good humor him.

Knock! Knock!
Who's there?
Wayne.
Wayne who?
Wayne is good for the front lawn.

Teacher: Have you ever read any books by Samuel Clemens?

Girl: No teacher. My favorite author is Mark Twain.

What do you get if you cross a turtle and an ATM?

A machine that shells out cash.

ATTENTION: Batman's ghost is a caped crime frighter.

Which famous author was also a gangster?

Robber Louis Stevenson.

Knock! Knock!
Who's there?
Kit.
Kit who?
Kit out of my way. I'm coming through.

Uncle: Did the Devil make you kick the neighbor's boy in the seat of the pants?

Nephew: Yes, uncle. But punching him in the nose was my own idea.

SIGN ON A CARPENTER'S SHOP: We build New England beach houses. We're a cottage industry.

Uncle Al: I don't mind running into debt. It's running into creditors that embarrasses me.

....

What did the coach tell the athlete who fell in love with the hurdles event?

You'll get over it.

....

Why didn't the bones keep today's appointment?

Because they were too marrow-minded.

....

What did one shepherd say to the other when the wolf pack attacked?

Don't give up the sheep.

....

Knock! Knock!

Who's there?

Wheeler.

Wheeler who?

Wheeler bicycle up onto the porch.

....

DAFFY DEFINITION:

Medicine Ball – a gala dance for sick people.

Waiter – a person who believes money grows on trays.

Punter – A gridiron athlete who foots his bill.

Palm Tree – A handy plant to have around.

Spider – a hairy yo-yo with legs that catches bugs.

....

Teacher: Who was Oliver Wendell Holmes?

Boy: He was a famous detective who had a best friend named Dr. Watson.

What do you call insects that live in an ant farm?

Tenants.

....

Dina: I heard that all of King Arthur's soldiers suffered from insomnia.

Gina: Wow! Now that's a lot of sleepless knights.

Ms. Tippy Toe — Ballerina.
Mr. Sal A. Mander — Reptile expert.
Mr. Ivan Dere — Travel agent.

A traveler staying in a cheap hotel room called the desk clerk to complain. "There's a mouse on my bed," the man grumbled. "What are you going to do about it?" "Relax," instructed the desk clerk. "The snake that lives under your bed will snap him up."

What kind of ghoul do you find in a store?
A shop creeper.

Knock! Knock!
Who's there?
Roger.
Roger who?
Roger over and out.

Knock! Knock!
Who's there?
Alby.
Alby who?
Alby glad when this job is finished.

SIGN ON A PLUMBER'S SHOP: Repair your sink or swim.

What do you get if you cross candy and your father's sister?
A chocolate-covered aunt.

Why did the little light bulb skip a grade?

He was a bright boy.

◄◄◄◄◄◄◄◄◄◄◄◄◄◄◄◄◄◄◄◄◄◄◄◄◄◄◄◄◄

Lady: I'm walking to reduce.

Man: You're going the wrong way.

What do you get if you cross a pony and a vegetable?

Horse radish.

How do you get a zombie driver's license?

First present your death certificate to the DMV clerk.

Knock! Knock!

Who's there?

Bun.

Bun who?

Bun Voyage.

►►►►►►►►►►►►►►►►►►►►►

Knock! Knock!

Who's there?

Candice.

Candice who?

Candice be the end of Mighty Mouse?

Father: Yong man do you want to marry my daughter?

Young Man: Yes, sir.

Father: Can you support a family?

Young Man: Yes, sir.

Father: Are you sure? There are six of us.

> **Knock! Knock!**
> Who's there?
> **Teller.**
> Teller who?
> **Teller fortune for a dollar.**

Tina: My boyfriend gave me a handful of pearls.

Gina: Why didn't he give you a pearl necklace?

Tina: I don't take gifts if they have strings attached to them.

> Why did the Green Giant tiptoe through his garden?
> He didn't want to crack the eggplants.

Why were Mr. and Mrs. Poster so proud? They had a poster child.

> **Artie: Did you hear the joke about the drought?**
> **Marty: Is it dry humor?**

Knock! Knock!
Who's there?
Raisin.
Raisin who?
Raisin taxes again this year?

DAFFY DEFINITIONS:

Spur – a cowboy's sidekick.

Confession – a pray-tell ritual.

Knock! Knock!
Who's there?
The Beast.
The Beast who?
The Beast is yet to come.

Knock! Knock!
Who's there?
Swarm.
Swarm who?
Swarm in the summer
and cold in the winter.

Knock! Knock!
Who's there?
Retch.
Retch who?
Retch for the sky, pardner.

Lucky: I don't mind going to jail.
Ducky: Why not?
Lucky: At least I don't have to worry about anyone raising my rent.

ATTENTION: The first pair ate the first apple.

Boss: Why are you asking for a raise?

Employee: Because somehow my family found out other people eat three times a day.

....

Benny: I paid fifty cents apiece for these new jokes.

Lenny: I'm sure you'll get some cheap laughs.

....

What do you get if you cross a band member and a cheerleader?
Musical cheers.

....

Knock! Knock!

Who's there?

Albino.

Albino who?

Albino lottery tickets from you.

....

Knock! Knock!

Who's there?

Arab.

Arab who?

Arab my pitching arm when it feels sore.

....

Why did the fish jump out of the lake and into the air during a rainstorm?

He was tired of baths and wanted to take a shower.

....

Knock! Knock!

Who's there?

I'm Shad.

I'm Shad who?

I'm Shad to see you go.

ATTENTION: Fireflies have big egos. They think they're hot stuff.

DAFFY DEFINITIONS:

Speech Writer – a person who puts words in other people's mouths.

Light bulbs – watts cooking.

Desert – a waterless beach.

Basketball – an overweight volleyball with a tan.

Maple – the sweet sap of the tree family.

ATTENTION: The cost to repair tornado damage is spinning out of control.

Teenage girl: Mom, the girl next door has a prom dress just like mine.

Mother: I guess that means you want another prom dress.

Teenage girl: Well it would be easier than moving to a new school district.

"I spent my youth as a cowboy in the Old West," Tex bragged to the other folks at the senior citizen center. "In fact, I roped and broke every wild mustang in New York City." "Humph!" grunted a retired businessman. "There are no wild mustangs in New York City." Tex grinned. "Not anymore there ain't pardner," said he.

How much did the psychiatrist charge his elephant patient?

Two hundred dollars for the visit and eight hundred dollars for the broken couch.

ATTENTION: Financial success is relative. The more financial success, the more relatives.

Why did Bambi join the Air Force during World War II?

He wanted to be a bombadeer.

Knock! Knock!
Who's there?
Zeno.
Zeno who?
Zeno evil. Hear no evil.

Lady: I want a skirt to wear around the house.

Salesgirl: What size skirt does your house wear, ma'am?

Jenny: How did you do in history class?
Benny: Terrible, but I'm great when it comes to dates.

Wife: How'd you do in the marathon today?
Husband: Fine. I would have finished first if two hundred runners didn't finish ahead of me.

Dork: What's today's date?
Mork: Check the newspaper in your back pocket. The paper has the date on it.
Dork: That's no help. It's yesterday's paper.

Ken: Where did you get those big blue eyes?
Jen: They came with my face.

What do you get if you cross a staircase and talking birds?
Step parrots.

Knock! Knock!
Who's there?
Dial.
Dial who?
Dial be a hot time in the old town tonight.

Man: My daughter is at an awkward age. She's too old for an allowance and too young for a credit card.

What do you shout when skunks smell good?

Scents be praised!

What do you get if you cross a rude kid and a watch?

A clock that tocks back.

Girl: Would you like to buy a dictionary?
Boy: No. I have one. And when you've read one, you've read them all.

Knock! Knock!

Who's there?

Kennedy.

Kennedy who?

Kennedy in math keep you out of college?

Knock! Knock!

Who's there?

Roman.

Roman who?

Roman or we'll never get across this lake.

What did the jogger say when the music started to play?

Dancing runs in my family.

What do you get if you cross a Corvette and an elephant?

A sports car with a huge trunk.

What do you get if you put vanishing cream on a clock?

Something that disappears in a minute.

◄ ◄ ◄ ◄ ◄ ◄ ◄ ◄ ◄ ◄ ◄ ◄ ◄ ◄ ◄ ◄ ◄

Sara: Have you heard the rumor about Donna's new boyfriend?
Clara: Hear it? I started it.

► ► ► ► ► ► ► ► ► ► ► ► ► ► ► ► ►

SIGN ON A COBBLER'S SHOP — I'm an old-time heeler.

◄ ◄ ◄ ◄ ◄ ◄ ◄ ◄ ◄ ◄ ◄ ◄ ◄ ◄ ◄ ◄ ◄

Hal: Does your teenage daughter like having her own credit card?
Cal: Yes. She gets a charge out of it.

► ► ► ► ► ► ► ► ► ► ► ► ► ► ► ► ►

Tourist: I just drove my car from one end of New York City to the other.
Cop: Sightseeing?
Tourist: No. Looking for a parking place.

◄ ◄ ◄ ◄ ◄ ◄ ◄ ◄ ◄ ◄

Knock! Knock!
Who's there?
Barton.
Barton who?
Barton down the hatches, mateys!

► ► ► ► ► ► ► ► ► ►

Knock! Knock!
Who's there?
Putt.
Putt who?
Putt your shoes on and come outside.

◄ ◄ ◄ ◄ ◄ ◄ ◄ ◄ ◄ ◄ ◄ ◄ ◄ ◄ ◄ ◄

Why did the corn farmer go to the tattoo shop?
He wanted to get his ears pierced.

What do you get if you cross a stomach with a cell phone?

A belly ring.

⟨ ⟨ ⟨ ⟨ ⟨ ⟨ ⟨ ⟨ ⟨ ⟨ ⟨ ⟨ ⟨ ⟨ ⟨ ⟨ ⟨ ⟨ ⟨

SIGN ON A POULTRY FARM: Hardboiled eggs are great for lunch and hard to beat.

⟩ ⟩ ⟩ ⟩ ⟩ ⟩ ⟩ ⟩ ⟩ ⟩ ⟩ ⟩ ⟩ ⟩ ⟩ ⟩ ⟩ ⟩ ⟩

Lady: Is golf a rich man's game?

Caddy: Heck no. There are plenty of poor players.

⟨ ⟨ ⟨ ⟨ ⟨ ⟨ ⟨ ⟨ ⟨ ⟨ ⟨ ⟨ ⟨ ⟨ ⟨ ⟨ ⟨ ⟨ ⟨

Zeb: **Did that tornado damage your barn?**

Zeke: **I don't know. I haven't found it yet.**

⟩ ⟩ ⟩ ⟩ ⟩ ⟩ ⟩ ⟩ ⟩ ⟩ ⟩ ⟩ ⟩ ⟩ ⟩ ⟩ ⟩ ⟩ ⟩

What do you call an angler named Rodney?

A fishing Rod.

⟨ ⟨ ⟨ ⟨ ⟨ ⟨ ⟨ ⟨ ⟨ ⟨ ⟨ ⟨ ⟨ ⟨ ⟨ ⟨ ⟨ ⟨ ⟨

FLASHING SIGN ON A BUS TERMINAL: Don't walk!

⟩ ⟩ ⟩ ⟩ ⟩ ⟩ ⟩ ⟩ ⟩ ⟩ ⟩ ⟩ ⟩ ⟩ ⟩ ⟩ ⟩ ⟩ ⟩

Jack: My doctor told me I shouldn't play golf.

Mack: Oh! When did you play with him?

⟨ ⟨ ⟨ ⟨ ⟨ ⟨ ⟨ ⟨ ⟨ ⟨ ⟨ ⟨ ⟨ ⟨ ⟨ ⟨ ⟨ ⟨ ⟨

SIGN ON A BIKE SHOP: Peddlers allowed.

⟩ ⟩ ⟩ ⟩ ⟩ ⟩ ⟩ ⟩ ⟩ ⟩ ⟩ ⟩ ⟩ ⟩ ⟩ ⟩ ⟩ ⟩ ⟩

ATTENTION: Adult Education will continue as long as children need help with their homework.

⟨ ⟨ ⟨ ⟨ ⟨ ⟨ ⟨ ⟨ ⟨ ⟨ ⟨ ⟨ ⟨ ⟨ ⟨ ⟨ ⟨ ⟨ ⟨

Why did the battery leave the hospital happy?

All of his tests were negative.

Rudy was going on a long business trip to the Orient and wanted to give his girlfriend, Brenda, a gift before he left. Rudy went to Brenda's house with a cute puppy. Brenda's little brother let Rudy in the house and followed him as he walked up to Brenda. "Oh how adorable!" Brenda sighed as Rudy handed her the puppy. "Every time you look at him," said Rudy, "I want you to think of me." Brenda stared at the doggie's face and replied, "But, Rudy," he doesn't look anything like you." Then Brenda's little brother added his own two cents. "That's because," the little boy mocked, "you're looking at the wrong end."

Knock! Knock!
Who's there?
Ashley
Ashley who?
Ashley if Grant was a good general.

Who helps Captain blue jay fly the plane?
His crow pilot.

What's the difference between ammonia and pneumonia?
One comes in bottles and the other comes in chests.

Zack: I'm a pauper.
Jed: Congratulations. Is it a boy or a girl?

Mugsy: How was the play they put on in the prison?
Bugsy: It was a cell out.

Jenny: Isn't it great to be alive.
Penny: It certainly beats the alternative.

Why did the jump rope graduate from high school early?
She skipped a lot of grades.

ATTENTION: Monks wear holy socks.

What do you get if you cross a giraffe and a clock?
The neck of time.

What do you get when a rabbit sneezes?

Hare spray.

Knock! Knock!

Who's there?

Selkirk.

Selkirk who?

Selkirk your collectables. Kirk pays fair prices.

Why did the crowd boo the boring magician?

He was up to his same old tricks.

Captain: Why are you wearing two wristwatches, soldier?

Private: Because the sergeant wants us to do everything double time.

NOTICE: Even if you're on the right track, you may get run over by a train if you don't watch out.

Ace: **They sent me to jail for something I didn't do.**
Duke: **Really?**
Ace: **Yeah. I didn't pay my taxes.**

A snobby lady went into a pet store. "I want a very high class pet," the lady said to the clerk. The clerk showed her a beautiful cat. "This feline has an impeccable pedigree," said the clerk. "Is that so?" scoffed the lady. "How impeccable?" "Well, lady," replied the clerk. "I this cat could talk, she wouldn't bother to speak to either of us."

Knock! Knock!

Who's there?

Iva Tennessee

Iva Tennessee who?

Iva Tennessee to forget my own name.

Knock! Knock!

Who's there?

Shy Anne.

Shy Anne who?

Shy Anne Wyoming.

Why are corn farmers good musicians?

They play by ear.

How do you get a doctor to make house calls?
Marry one.

What did the psychiatrist do on the poultry farm?
He took care of the eggs that were cracking up.

KOOKY QUESTION: Do Eskimos like mushed potatoes?

SWIFTIE: "Do I have to drink this in one swallow?" Tom gulped.

...IN SICKNESS OR IN HEALTH...

What did the shepherd say when the sheep won the raffle?

Lucky ewe.

Teacher: Are you an avid reader?
Girl: I don't know. What kinds of books did Avid write?

Knock! Knock!
Who's there?
Earl E. Earl E.
Earl E. Earl E. who?
Earl E to bed and Earl E. to rise.

SIGN ON A BOWLING LEAGUE BULLETIN BOARD: Get your kids off the back streets and into our alleys.

Why did the girl exit the bus by walking backwards?
She heard some people say they wanted to grab her seat.

Jack: I heard you're a golfer. What's your handicap?
Mack: My wife wants me to spend more time at home on the weekends.

Teacher: Can you define pugilism and pugilist?
Boy: Those are fighting words where I come from.

Why did the psychiatrist refuse to treat the kangaroo?
Because the kangaroo kept jumping on his couch.

Then there was the rich farmer who dressed his scarecrows in tuxedos.

Reporter: I heard you are the only survivor of the shipwreck. How is that?
Man: I missed the boat.

Zack: Do you know what this is?
Mack: It's an envelope.
Zack: No. It's the only letter not found in the alphabet.

A tourist went into a crowded hotel in Mexico. "I'm sorry, sir," apologized the desk clerk. "We're all filled up. I couldn't get you a room if you were President Obama."

The tourist sighed in dismay. "I'm not President Obama," he said softly. "But can't you find a room for Juan Moore?"

Man: I hear your son earned a master's degree last year.

Father: That's so. And this year he's one of the smartest guys on line at the unemployment office.

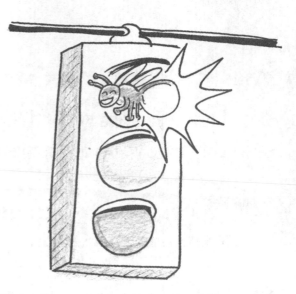

Knock! Knock!
Who's there?
Justine.
Justine who?
Justine case you forgot, I'm your brother.

Why is it hard to drive golf balls?
They don't have steering wheels.

TONGUE TWISTERS:
Shave a thin cedar shingle.
Surely the sun shall shine soon.
Blue black bug's blood.
Timmy Tomkins tripped Tommy Timkins.

Mr. Firefly: What do you want to be when you glow up?
Little Firefly: A traffic light.

What did the arthritis say to the rheumatism?
Let's get out of this joint.

Knock! Knock!
Who's there?
Knight Lee.
Knight Lee who?
Knight Lee news shows are boring.

What kind of buildings have oars sticking out of their sides?
Row houses.

Why is the Abominable
Snowman single?

Because he gets cold feet when
it comes to marriage.

What kind of work is the Raven?
Edgar Allen Poetry.

Which Charles Dickens' book is about a tornado?
Oliver Twister.

Do new automobiles grow on trees?
No. They come from plants.

Knock! Knock!
Who's there?
Assisi.
Assisi who?
Assisi a guy who's not very tough.

....

Knock! Knock!
Who's there?
Axel Lee.
Axel Lee who?
Axel Lee, I'm a stranger in these parts.

....

Knock! Knock!
Who's there?
Barnett.
Barnett who?
Barnett down men.

....

ATTENTION: Apply for a Munchkin credit card. Use it when you're short on cash.

....

Patient: Doctor, it hurts when I walk on my right foot. What should I do?

Doctor: Try hopping around on your left foot.

....

Why did the corn farmer take soap into the field?
His wife told him to wash his ears.

....

What did the cornstalk say to the angry farmer?
Don't yell in my ear.

....

ATTENTION: Miners always expect coal weather.

Which letter of the alphabet is a pirate?

The one with the I-patch.

What do you get if you cross a magician and a golf course?

A lot of tricky holes.

Knock! Knock!

Who's there?

Liv.

Liv who?

Liv and let Liv.

Man: Has your son's college education proved to be of value?

Father: Yes. It cured his mother of bragging about him.

Tina: How was your boat ride with your new boyfriend?

Nina: Humph! He not only lied about the size of his boat, but he also made me row.

Mother: Why is your i-Pod in the refrigerator?

Son: I wanted it to play some really cool music.

Ted: Have you heard the joke about the flu germ?

Ed: No. And stop spreading it around.

What did the crow say to the blue jay?

Do you mind leaving? I'm trying to make a personal caw.

Coach: What's one way a player can show he's a good loser?
Young Hockey Player: By not punching the winners in the nose.

Then there was the mummy crook that had a long wrap sheet.

ATTENTION: Bambi likes to play truth or deer.

Then there was the bald rabbit that wore a hare piece.

Billy was walking his new dog, Rover, when he bumped into Martha. "What a dumb looking pooch," Martha remarked. "Dumb?" grunted Billy. "Rover is the smartest dog in the world and I can prove it. Watch this." Billy stuck out his finger pretending it was a gun and pointed it at Rover. "Ka-pow!" Billy shouted. Rover just sat there panting. "I told you he was dumb," snorted Martha. "He didn't even play dead." "Humph!" countered Billy. "You're the one who's dumb. Rover knows a finger can't shoot him."

Knock! Knock!
Who's there?
Rayburn.
Rayburn who?
Rayburn all over town looking for you.

Teacher: Alexander Graham Bell invented the telephone. What did his assistant Mr. Watson do?
Boy: He sent out the phone bills.

Then there was the well-bred hunting dog that thought it was impolite to point.

Bill: Does your wife jog?
Will: No. She just runs up lots of expenses.

What did the Queen say to the Ace?
I've heard a great deal about you.

What did the English gentleman say to the cowboy's leather pants?
Hello, old chaps.

What did the gardener say when he caught a burglar stealing his grass seed?
I'll have the lawn on you.

How do you keep a baseball pitcher from crying?
Use bawl control.

What does Sir Lancelot get if he doesn't show up on time for dinner?
A late-knight snack.

Knock! Knock!
Who's there?
O. Shay.
O. Shay who?
O. Shay can you see by the dawn's early light.

Judy: **I'm homesick.**
Rudy: **But we are home, dear.**
Judy: **I know and I'm sick of this place.**

What did the horse say to the saddle?

Do you want to go for a ride?

▶ ▶ ▶ ▶ ▶ ▶ ▶ ▶ ▶ ▶ ▶

Why did the zombie win the beauty pageant?

She was drop-dead gorgeous.

◀ ◀ ◀ ◀ ◀ ◀ ◀ ◀ ◀ ◀ ◀

DAFFY DEFINITIONS

Ice – water cooler.

Moot Court – a legal practice.

▶ ▶ ▶ ▶ ▶ ▶ ▶ ▶ ▶ ▶ ▶

Knock! Knock!

Who's there?

Hugh Quack.

Hugh Quack who?

Hugh Quack me up!

◀ ◀ ◀ ◀ ◀ ◀ ◀ ◀ ◀ ◀ ◀ ◀

What goes up to your front door, but never comes in?

The sidewalk.

▶ ▶ ▶ ▶ ▶ ▶ ▶ ▶ ▶ ▶ ▶ ▶

Uncle Al: **Did you hear about the patient with the split personality who was so stuck up she wouldn't speak to herself.**

◀ ◀ ◀ ◀ ◀ ◀ ◀ ◀ ◀ ◀ ◀ ◀

ATTENTION: SpongeBob sponges off of his friends.

▶ ▶ ▶ ▶ ▶ ▶ ▶ ▶ ▶ ▶ ▶ ▶ ▶

A young man looked at his girlfriend and took a deep breath. "I have something to confess," said he. "While we've been going out, I've been secretly seeing a psychiatrist." The girl kissed her boyfriend on the cheek and smiled. "It doesn't matter," she told him. "While we've been dating, I've been secretly seeing a lawyer and a football coach."

Lacy: What are you giving your parents for Christmas?

Stacy: A list of the gifts I want.

◄ ◄ ◄ ◄ ◄ ◄ ◄ ◄ ◄ ◄

What is a floor polisher's motto?
Rise and shine.

► ► ► ► ► ► ► ► ► ► ►

What did one wall say to the other?
I'll meet you at the corner.

◄ ◄ ◄ ◄ ◄ ◄ ◄ ◄ ◄ ◄

SASSY SIGNS

ON A PLANETARIUM – Now show-
ing! A cast of thousands! Every one a star!

ON A FROZEN FOOD COUNTER – The best meals you ever thaw.

IN A BUTCHER SHOP – We'll never give you a bum steer.

ON A TOW TRUCK – We meet all of our customers by accident.

ON A DATING SERVICE – We fix broken hearts.

ON A NEW LAWN – Your feet are killing me.

ON A CLASSROOM DOOR – Time passes ... will you?

ON A STORE – Say hello to our good buys.

◄ ◄ ◄ ◄ ◄ ◄ ◄ ◄ ◄ ◄ ◄ ◄ ◄ ◄ ◄

The teacher asked her students to name the nine great Americans. All of the students had turned in their papers except Marty. The teacher walked up to Marty's desk. "Can't you finish your list?" she asked him. "Not yet," Marty replied. I'm still undecided about the first baseman."

► ► ► ► ► ► ► ► ► ► ► ► ► ► ►

Teacher: We're going to watch a DVD about life on the bottom of the ocean.

Student: Oh boy. A dive-in movie.

◄ ◄ ◄ ◄ ◄ ◄ ◄ ◄ ◄ ◄ ◄ ◄ ◄ ◄

Mike: When I die I'm going to leave you everything I have.

Judy: Thanks for nothing.

Benny: My Uncle Hugo is running for Congress.

Lenny: Honest?

Benny: No, but that's not stopping him.

....

Penny: I have a sore backside from doing homework.

Jenny: How can homework give you an aching behind?

Penny: I spent three hours going over my riding lessons.

....

What does Big Foot use when he sprains his ankle?

A hairy cane.

....

Jack: What do you do at the lantern factory?

Mack: I work on wick ends.

....

Why can't a dog go into a yard?

Because it has four feet, not three feet.

....

Juan: I'm half of a famous baseball double-play combination.

Don: Oh! So you're in with the out crowd.

....

Rudy: Do you want to hear a joke about mud?

Trudy: No. I don't like dirty stories.

Knock! Knock!

Who's there?

Dee Rufus.

Dee Rufus who?

Dee Rufus leaking. Get it fixed.

....

Rudy: This part of the movie is real scary. You'd better close your eyes real tight.

Judy: I can't. I'm afraid of the dark.

....

Man: My daughter's feet are killing me. She keeps buying new shoes!

....

What did the angry horse say to the nagging cowboy?

Quit riding me.

....

Knock! Knock!

Who's there?

Pully.

Pully who?

Pully Anna.

....

Why is a horse like a good friend?

They both listen to your woes.

....

Where was the zombie on his family tree?

He was the dead wood.

Knock! Knock!

Who's there?

T. Phineas.

T. Phineas who?

T. Phineas thing happened to me on the way home.

....

Psychiatrist: **Lie down on my couch. Get nice and comfortable. Just relax. Now tell me what's your problem?**

Patient: **I'm a couch potato.**

....

Boy: **I'm a guy with a disposable income.**

Girl: **So why can't you afford to take me out for dinner.**

Boy: **My income has already been disposed of.**

....

What did Mr. Mason say to Mr. Dixon?

I guess we have to draw the line somewhere.

....

What do you get if you cross a miser and a friar?

A cheapmonk.

....

Knock! Knock!

Who's there?

Tarawa.

Tarawa who?

Tarawa-wa-boom-de-yah!

What do you get if you cross an engagement ring and a musical group?

A wedding band.

Then there was the judge who held her husband in contempt.

....

Miles: **Did you hear about the tree surgeon that ended up in the hospital?**

Giles: **No. What happened?**

Miles: **He fell out of one of his patients.**

....

Father: **Where did you get that fifty-dollar bill?**

Boy: **I found it on the sidewalk.**

Father: **Are you sure it was lost?**

Boy: **Absolutely. I saw a lady searching high and low for it.**

....

KOOKY QUESTION: **Do architects like to play bridge?**

knock! knock!
Who's there?
Taras.
Taras who?
Taras sticky when it's hot.

Sara: **What's socialized medicine?**
Clara: **It's when a doctor dates a nurse.**

Doctor: I'm tired of being a dentist.
Nurse: What's wrong with being a dentist?
Doctor: Every day is the same old grind.

What is a kitten after it's five days old?
Six days old.

Why is an egg like a bronco?
Because neither is useful until it's broken.

What did the police chief say to Bruce Wayne?
I have bat news for you.

What do you get if you cross a cowboy with Robin Hood?
A guy with bow legs.

Judge: **Why did you steal that purse?**
Mugger: **I was feeling ill and I thought the change would do me good.**

Watson: How did you solve the case of the missing sheep, Holmes?

Holmes: It was sheer luck, my dear Watson.

Politician: It's a small world.

Taxpayer: Then why does it cost so much to run it?

Knock! Knock!

Who's there?

Sadie.

Sadie who?

Sadie magic word and win a prize.

Knock! Knock!

Who's there?

Tubby.

Tubby who?

Tubby or not Tubby.

Knock! Knock!

Who's there?

My Tea.

My Tea who?

My Tea Mouse.

Jill: Money makes the world go round.

Bill: Right now it's spinning out of control.

Marina: My new boyfriend is such a hypochondriac last weekend we went for a drive in the country in an ambulance.

ABBREVIATED HUMOR

Which state never feels well?

Il.

Which state is a father?

Pa.

Which state is a number?

Tenn.

Which state is an unmarried woman?

Miss.

Which state is very clean?

Wash.

Which state has a iron will?

Ore.

Which state is very religious?

Mass.

Which state is a doctor?

Md.

Which state did Noah move to?

Ark.

What do you get if you cross a lollipop and a boxer?

A sucker punch.

Knock! Knock!

Who's there?

Daisy.

Daisy who?

Daisy works. Nights he goes out.

What do you get if you cross a baseball batter and a bad driver?
A person who hits a lot of things with his car.

Why did the dork jog around his bed?
His doctor told him to catch up on his sleep.

What did the cabbage farmer say to the acrobat?
Watch me stand on my head.

Why did the kangaroo lose her job as a cashier? She kept pocketing the change.

Knock! Knock!
Who's there?
Wade.
Wade who?
Wade for me under the oak tree.

Knock! Knock!
Who's there?
Takoma.
Takoma who?
Takoma party bag when you leave.

In Texas, what do they call a cowboy who is 6' 4" tall?
Shorty.

Who repairs shoes in an orchard?
A peach cobbler.

....

Why did the ship cross the road?
To get to the other tide.

....

Temper Tantrum — the call of the riled.

I.Q. Test — an intelligent life form.

Genius — someone who was brained at birth.

Pilot — an uppity person.

Hot air — a major cause of inflation.

....

Knock! Knock!
Who's there?
Juan Torres.
Juan Torres who?
Juan Torres pants. Can you sew them?

....

ATTENTION: **Are basketball players the kind of athletes who bounce back from injuries?**

....

Knock! Knock!
Who's there?
Seoul.
Seoul who?
Seoul sister.

....

Mork: I can't call the zoo.
Dork: Why not?
Mork: The lion's busy.

Knock! Knock!

Who's there?

Chester?

Chester who?

Chester minute I'll be right there.

. . . .

Where does a cowboy play golf?

On the driving range.

. . . .

Knock! Knock!

Who's there?

Alphabet.

Alphabet who?

Alphabet me you'd say that.

. . . .

Danny Dorky opened his lunchbox in the cafeteria and sighed. Stan Smith, the guy sitting next to him asked, "What's wrong?" "I have a cheese sandwich for lunch," Danny Dorky lamented. "And I hate cheese." The next day the same thing happened. For two more days in a row, it was the same story. Finally, Stan Smith turned to Danny Dorky and said, "If you don't like cheese sandwiches, tell your mom to make you something else for lunch." Danny Dorky looked at Stan Smith and said, "Oh, I make my own sandwiches."

. . . .

Knock! Knock!

Who's there?

Tai.

Tai who?

Tai a yellow ribbon round the old oak tree.

Knock! Knock!

Who's there?

Stalin.

Stalin who?

Stalin me won't work. Open up!

KNOCK KNOCK

What do you get if you cross a grizzly with Bambi and a cowboy?

A bear buck rider.

ATTENTION: David delivered a slingin' telegram to Goliath.

ATTENTION: Do basketball players wear long underwear?

ATTENTION: Do funny jockeys like to horse around?

Knock! Knock!

Who's there?

Sydney.

Sydney who?

Sydney Australia.

Knock! Knock!

Who's there?

Gino.

Gino who?

Gino body ever asked me that before.

KOOKY QUESTION: Can a musician play cards?

Patron: This chili tastes funny.
Waiter: I hope it doesn't give you laughing gas.

Knock! Knock!
Who's there?
Bee Cider.
Bee Cider who?
Bee Cider who else is coming to the party?

Why couldn't the publisher print books on his press?
Because it was a cider press.

Knock! Knock!
Who's there?
Dots.
Dots who?
Dots all dere is folks.

Who wrote Tom Sawyer and goes toot toot?
Mark Train.

Boy: **Lady, will you give me ten bucks so I can see my grandparents?**
Lady: **Where are your grandparents, little boy?**
Boy: **At the movies.**

A father read that overweight middle-aged men shouldn't shovel snow because it might give them a heart attack. After the first snowstorm of the winter, the father took a shovel and went up to his lazy teenage son. "Marty," said the father, "will you please shovel the sidewalk and the driveway?" Of course the father was prepared for an argument. When the boy jumped up, grabbed the shovel, and replied, "Sure, Pop! No problem," the father was so shocked he instantly suffered a heart attack.

Ron: **Why is that turtle crying?**

Lon: **He's just a young weeper snapper.**

▶ ▶ ▶ ▶ ▶ ▶ ▶ ▶ ▶ ▶ ▶ ▶ ▶ ▶ ▶

What did the choir leader cook on the barbecue grill?

Hymnburgers.

◀ ◀ ◀ ◀ ◀ ◀ ◀ ◀ ◀ ◀ ◀ ◀ ◀ ◀ ◀

Knock ! Knock!

Who's there?

Vera.

Vera who?

Vera good. Never open the door for a stranger.

▶ ▶ ▶ ▶ ▶ ▶ ▶ ▶ ▶ ▶ ▶ ▶ ▶ ▶ ▶

Who prepares Bugs Bunny to step on a movie set?

A Hollywood hare dresser.

◀ ◀ ◀ ◀ ◀ ◀ ◀ ◀ ◀ ◀ ◀ ◀ ◀ ◀ ◀

Why did the football players go trick or treating?

Because they were wearing face masks.

▶ ▶ ▶ ▶ ▶ ▶ ▶ ▶ ▶ ▶ ▶ ▶ ▶ ▶ ▶

What does an unmarried football player wear?

A bachelor pad.

◀ ◀ ◀ ◀ ◀ ◀ ◀ ◀ ◀ ◀ ◀ ◀

Jenny: **What do you do at the fitness center?**

Lenny: **I work in middle management.**

▶ ▶ ▶ ▶ ▶ ▶ ▶ ▶ ▶ ▶ ▶ ▶

Beautician: **Would you like a surfer hairstyle?**

Girl: **What's that like?**

Beautician: **It has lots of waves.**

What kind of a rock can move?
A stepping stone.

◄ ◄ ◄ ◄ ◄ ◄ ◄ ◄ ◄ ◄ ◄ ◄ ◄ ◄ ◄ ◄ ◄

Beautician: **I'd like to insult your hair.**

Girl: **What do you mean?**

Beautician: **I'm going to tease it.**

► ► ► ► ► ► ► ► ► ► ► ► ► ► ► ► ►

Beautician: How about a rude hairstyle?

Girl: What's that?

Beautician: I'll cut you short.

◄ ◄ ◄ ◄ ◄ ◄ ◄ ◄ ◄ ◄ ◄ ◄ ◄ ◄ ◄ ◄ ◄

What do you get if you cross a dentist and a wedding?
A brushing bride.

◄ ◄ ◄ ◄ ◄ ◄ ◄ ◄ ◄ ◄ ◄ ◄ ◄ ◄ ◄ ◄ ◄

Matt: Did you make a New Year's resolution?

Pat: Yes. I swore not to be so insulting to people from now on.

Matt: You're such a hothead. Just how long do you expect that resolution to last?

Pat: Humph! All year you ignorant moron!

► ► ► ► ► ► ► ► ► ► ► ► ► ► ► ► ►

What did the motorist say to the mechanic?
Give me a brake will ya?

◄ ◄ ◄ ◄ ◄ ◄ ◄ ◄ ◄ ◄ ◄ ◄ ◄ ◄ ◄ ◄ ◄

What happened to the nervous corn farmer?
He went stalk raving mad.

► ► ► ► ► ► ► ► ► ► ► ► ► ► ► ► ►

What is Robin Hood's secret agent number?
Double Bow Seven.

Wizard: I can remove wool from sheep just by waving my wand.

Shepherd: Now that's sheer magic.

....

Hal: You've been making fun of my new toupee all night.

Sal: Do you want me to knock it off?

....

How did the cavalry troop get into trouble?

They overcharged everyone.

....

And then there was the angry poker player who always had a chip on his shoulder.

....

Why did the cop join the Army?

He wanted to be a private investigator.

....

A husband and wife went to see a marriage counselor to improve their relationship. "The only problem we have," began the husband, "is that in the five years we've been together we've never been able to agree on anything."

The counselor then looked at the man's wife to hear what she had to say. "It's six," she corrected. "We've been together for six years."

What baseball team did Babe Pig play for?

The New Pork Yankees.

....

What did the owl say to the skunk?

Who do you stink you are?

....

Why was Sir Lancelot carrying a bat and glove?

He had a knight baseball game.

....

Show me a mixed-up author ... and I'll show you a writer who can't make heads or tales out of anything.

Wife: **It's pouring rain. You can't play golf today. Now what are your plans?**

Hubby: **I'll just putter around the house.**

Tim: That girl has been singing the national anthem for two hours.

Slim: I won't stand for this any longer.

....

Mrs. Mouse: Mickey, did you take a shower?

Mickey: Yes, Mom. Now I'm squeaky clean.

....

Why couldn't the bee get a good job?

He didn't have a hive school diploma.

....

What did the ladies say when they finished making their basket?

Weave done it.

....

SIGN ON A GOLF COURSE: Putt an end to your worries.

....

A minister prepared to address the crowd of people gathered in his church. "Brothers and sisters," he began. "Today my sermon is about liars. Now last week I advised you all to read the 30th chapter of Matthew before today. How many did that?" About half of the people in church raised their hands. The minister smiled. "You're just the people I want to talk to," he said. "There is no such chapter."

What do you get if you cross someone who knits with a storyteller?

A person who appreciates a good yarn.

....

SILLY SIGN:

ACME ORCHARDS – We sell fruit off the tree. Come in and take your pick.

....

What do you get if you cross a senior citizen skunk and Santa Claus?

Old Scent Nick.

....

Tim: I get sick all the time.

Jim: Seriously?

....

CRAZY QUESTION:

Does a kangaroo carry a pocket watch?

Mr. Jones: I wrote a get rich quick book.

Mr. Smith: Will I get rich quick if I buy it and tell my friends about it?

Mr. Jones: No, but I might.

NOTICE: Employees at the U.S. Mint went on strike because they claim they're overworked. Now they want to make less money.

What instrument did the fish play in the rock band?
Bass guitar.

Why couldn't the Munchkin give CPR?
He was short of breath.

Show me a guy whose toupee catches on fire ...
and I'll show you a man who's really hot headed.

Craftrsman: **Do you want to learn how to make a hunting knife?**

Student: **Yes. If it doesn't take too long to come to the point.**

Don: Did you hear about the movie star dog that wore braces?

Juan: No.

Don: His name was Rin Tin Grin.

What university do all I.R.S. agents graduate from?
I.O.U.

Tim: I graduated from bottling school with honors.

Jim: What kind of honors?

Tim: I graduated Phi Beta Capper.

Show me a depressed football tackle ... and I'll show you a down lineman.

Show me a lawyer who plays tennis ... and I'll show you a person who makes a lot of court appearances.

Show me a baseball hurler who walks to the back of the mound ... and I'll show you a pitcher who's over the hill.

What does a mother hen do before she deposits her babies in the coop?

She signs her chicks.

A lawyer sent an overdue bill to one of his clients. The attorney attached a note to the bill that read: This bill is now one year old. What do you have to say about this? The client sent back the bill with no cash or check. Instead he attached a note of his own that read, "Well, Happy Birthday!"

How do you burst a pro wrestler's balloon?

Pin him.

What do you do for a sore puck?

Ice it.

What do penguins like to get at parties that people don't?

Chilly receptions.

Monster: But Dr. Frankenstein, I don't want a brain transplant.

Doctor: Isn't there anything I can say to change your mind?

Jill: The leader of our church says prayers in Spanish.

Bill: Maybe he's a foreign minister.

Which soldier is in charge of an oil rig?
The Drill Sergeant.

What do you get if you cross pig food with a hockey player and a comic?
Slopstick comedy.

Why did the quarterbacks throw a clock back and forth?
They were just passing time.

Boy: Why does your dog flinch so much?
Girl: She's a flinch poodle.

Sara: It's a real shame that Adam and Eve got evicted from Paradise.
Cara: I know. They never had a chance to raise Cain in the Garden of Eden.

Why didn't the cop arrest the talking bird?
It only committed a mynah offense.

What do you get when you cross a grocery store and a science lab?
Market research.

Lady: These envelopes are all stuck together.

Postman: Don't blame me. It's a case of mail bonding.

What do you get if you cross a pooch with a pig?
A doggie pork.

There's laughing gas and there's tear gas. The local gas station has both. In fact, it's the same gas. It all depends on if you're selling or buying.

Zack: Did you get a job driving your truck over that frozen lake last winter?

Mack: No. The job fell through.

ATTENTION: The best golf lies aren't found on the course. They're found in the clubhouse.

ATTENTION: Gretel cooked lots of tasty food for her brother. After serving him a giant, three-course meal, she finally had her Hans full.

Mr. Brown: I heard the glue business is very bad.

Mr. Green: That's true. I think we're in for a stick market crash.

....

City slicker at state fair: **Where are the animal pens?**

Farmer: **Just follow your nose, Sonny.**

....

How did Captain Hook cut himself?

He scratched an itch with the wrong hand.

....

Clerk: Would you like to rent a tuxedo sir?

Man: Yes. That'll suit me just fine.

....

Boy: I have a broken arm.

Girl: I have a broken leg.

Boy & Girl: Let's have a cast party.

....

What did the detective say after he packed his trunk?

Case closed.

....

What did the bungee jumper say to the cord?

Remember to snap it up.

....

A teacher told her third grade class it was be kind to animals week. The very next day the same teacher asked her students if anyone did an appropriate good deed. A boy raised his hand. "I did teacher," said Marty Morgan. "I saw a kid kick his dog so I went over and punched the kid in the nose."

....

Vet: What's wrong with your pet snake?

Boy: He's hissterical.

Harry: I'm a psychic healer. I make people feel good by thinking positive thoughts.

Barry: I sure hope you think well of me.

. . . .

Patient: Doc, I'm a compulsive jogger.

Doctor: Are you giving me the old run around?

. . . .

Mary: Gee, you smell good today. What do you have on?

Barry: Clean socks.

. . . .

YOU KNOW YOU'RE IN THE WRONG HOSPITAL IF...

... your doctor's stethoscope is two empty tin cans connected by a string.

... the person taking your medical information asks you to spell your middle initial.

... your X-ray technician has a faint green glow.

... the parking lot attendant makes you pay in advance before entering the hospital.

... a funeral home has leased space there.

... the blood technician comes into your room after sundown and has a cape and fangs.

... you have to sign a no-fault disclaimer before they'll serve you hospital food.

... the interns hold an office pool before every operation.

... your anesthetist is a scary guy holding a big mallet.

... instead of surgical masks, the doctors wear Halloween masks.

... the wheelchairs all have coin-operated meters on them.

Bill: Why do you clean office floors at night?

Will: I'm a late sweeper.

Knock! Knock!

Who's there?

Gus.

Gus who?

Gus I'll try again later.

DAFFY DEFINITION:

Bank foreclosures — a sad case of homeowners losing ground.

Show me a dentist who commits a crime ... and I'll show you a guy about to have a brush with the law.

SIGN IN A DELI: "We're proud of yesterday's heroes."

Why did the pig actor go to Hollywood?

He was looking for pork roles in the movies.

What happened when the pig insulted the girl who feeds him?

She slopped his face.

What do you get if you cross a hockey player with a comedian?

Slapstick humor.

How do you measure the distance between a chicken coop and a pigsty?

Use a barnyard stick.

RHYME TIME:

Mary had a little dragon
She fed him chili in a pot.
The day when he got heartburn,
Boy! Was that dragon's breath hot!

What do you get if you cross an angel with a skunk?
Something that's heaven scent.

Cadet #1: **Our military school hands out student report cards tomorrow.**
Cadet #2: **Oh great! Tomorrow it's D-Day all over again.**

Sara: **What happens if I have an accident on the trampoline?**
Kara: **Don't worry. You'll bounce back from it.**

Chad: Did you hear Mr. Piggy bought a million-acre ranch.

Thad: Wow! Talk about a ground hog.

I won't say snail mail is slow, but yesterday the flower seeds I ordered through the mail arrived as a bouquet.

What do you get if you cross a kangaroo with a saint?

I don't know, but it has a pocketful of miracles.

NOTICE: A person who is impatient has a serious wait problem.

Knock! Knock!
Who's there?
Purdy.
Purdy who?
Purdy soon I'm going home.

HOW'S THE SURFING?

Mr. Banana slipped up.
Mr. Astronaut splashed down.
Mr. Tissue wiped out.
Mr. Cake fell.
Mr. Bank Account lost his balance.
Ms. Swan took a dive.
Mr. Tumbler flipped overboard.
Ms. Math Teacher hung ten.

How do you punish an eye doctor?
Give him forty lashes.

Man: I'd like to sell underwear for your company.
Boss: Okay. We'll need to conduct a brief interview.

Why do music lovers go to Sherwood Forest?
Robin Hood has a very merry band.

What did the Scotsman do when he couldn't find any pants to wear?
He kilt himself.

What do you get when an elephant suffers from heatstroke?
Ele-faint.

Why are gangster fishermen dangerous?
Gangster fishermen carry rods.

◄ ◄ ◄ ◄ ◄ ◄ ◄ ◄ ◄ ◄

Reporter: Can you tell me about your research on Swamp Land?

Scientist: Not now. I'm bogged down in my work.

► ► ► ► ► ► ► ► ► ► ► ► ► ► ► ► ► ►

Why is Mr. Zombie a good reporter?
He never misses a deadline.

◄ ◄ ◄ ◄ ◄ ◄ ◄ ◄ ◄ ◄ ◄ ◄ ◄ ◄ ◄ ◄ ◄ ◄ ◄

What kind of book can help you see in the dark?
A book of matches.

◄ ◄ ◄ ◄ ◄ ◄ ◄ ◄ ◄ ◄ ◄ ◄ ◄ ◄ ◄ ◄ ◄ ◄

Sergeant: Sir, my platoon charged into quicksand. What should I do?
Captain: Hurry, Sergeant! Pull out your troops!

► ► ► ► ► ► ► ► ► ► ► ► ► ► ► ► ► ► ►

Woman: Waiter, I want to complain to the chef about this disgusting meal.

Waiter: I'm afraid you'll have to wait. He's just stepped out for his dinner.

◄ ◄ ◄ ◄ ◄ ◄ ◄ ◄ ◄ ◄ ◄ ◄ ◄ ◄ ◄ ◄

NOTICE: History professors get together to talk over old times.

► ► ► ► ► ► ► ► ► ► ► ► ► ► ► ► ► ►

How old was the young genie's friend?
He was Aladdin his teens.

Cook: What should I do after I season these barbecue ribs, Sarge?
Mess Sergeant: Fire when ready.

....

Why didn't the laundry man go swimming?

Because he was a dry cleaner.

....

RHYME TIME

Ashes to ashes.
And dust to dust.
Mix metal and water
And you'll end up with rust.

....

WACKY THINGS YOU CAN COUNT ON WHEN YOU'RE REALLY, REALLY TIRED AT NIGHT …

… your pet dog will bark to go out.

… your pet cat will scratch at the door to come in.

… police or fire sirens will sound in the distance.

… the neighbors will have a noisy party.

… the other neighbors will have a loud argument.

… if it's a hot night, the air conditioning will break down.

… if it's a cold night, the furnace will break down.

… there'll be a thunderstorm.

… a car will stall outside your house and start to backfire.

… the batteries in your smoke alarms will run down and start to beep.

… if you're a parent, one of your kids will have a nightmare.

… someone outside will scream.

… someone's car alarm will go off.

....

DAFFY DEFINITIONS:

Mud ball – ground round.

Fireman's Fund – a cause for alarms.

Refrigeration – a cool business to be in.

....

What did the crow poker player say to the dealer?

I'll caw you.

What does Santa Pirate say?
Yo ho ho ho!

What happened when the Abominable Snowman became a pirate?

The captain made him his frost mate.

....

What does a maid wear in winter?

A dust jacket.

....

What did the mountain climber say as he clung to a boulder?

I'm off to a rocky start.

....

CRAZY QUESTION:

Do geologists go to rock festivals?

....

Jonah: **I was carving a heart for you out of wood, but I dropped it and it broke into pieces.**

Mona: **Oh well, love is a many splintered thing.**

....

What did the hitchhiker say after he got two rides?

I had thumb luck today.

....

Why did the eye doctor go to the bank?

To check the teller visions.

....

Why did Cop Crow arrest Mr. Robin?

He jaywalked.

What has big antlers and lives in Disney World?

Mickey Moose.

Benny: **Do you know how the ten-cent fairy tale begins?**

Jenny: **No.**

Benny: **Once upon a dime ...**

....

Ken: I once sang the Star Spangled Banner for two hours.

Len: Big deal. I can sing Stars and Stripes Forever.

....

What do you get if you cross the Loch Ness Monster with a great white shark?

Loch Jaw.

Pilot: I'm not sure I can fly a plane as well as I used to.

Navigator: Try taking off a few days.

THE DAFFY DIFFERENCE BETWEEN YOUNG & OLD:

... When you're young, you love birthdays. They don't come soon enough. When you're old, you hate birthdays and wish they'd never arrive.

... When you're young, you're positive old people don't know what they're talking about. When you're old, you're positive young people don't know what they're talking about.

... When you're young, getting up early is a drag. When you're old, you drag yourself upstairs to go to bed early.

... When you're young, you wish Christmas came more than once a year. When you're old, you're glad Christmas only comes once a year because you can't afford it.

Investor: I don't mind that my money doesn't go far today. What troubles me is that it doesn't stay put.

What do you say to a baby wearing designer jeans?

Gucci, Gucci, Gucci!

Show me a developer who makes all of his deals on the side of a hill ... and I'll show you a real estate agent who is not on the level.

How can you find out how long a printing press is?

Use a type measurer.

What is Lassie's favorite state?

Collierado.

What is Lassie's second most favorite state.
Colliefornia.

Farmer #1: I was expecting ten young chickens and my hens hatched out eleven.
Farmer #2: Congratulations! You got a bonus chick!

What famous love story did Santa Claus write?
Romeo Ho Ho and Juliet.

Farmer: I'd like to buy a rooster and two hens and charge it.
Clerk: Yes, sir. Do you have a chicken account with us?

Sally: Why won't you date Mr. Magnet?
Kelly: His looks repel me.

SIGN ON A BLANKET FACTORY: Come in and look around. There's no cover charge.

ATTENTION:

Ms. Perfume Bottle has no scents.

Mr. Scissors can't cut it any longer.

Mr. Knife is a sharp dresser.

Mr. Paste sticks to his story.

Ms. Plate is a hot dish.

Mr. Straw knows how to suck it up.

Bork: I won the International Burping Contest again this year.
Dork: I guess that makes you a repeat champion.

What did the robber say to the soldier?
I won't stand guard for you, but I'll take your watch.

And then there was the bike racer who wore a handlebar moustache.

Cabin Boy: Why is that pirate guarding the treasure?
Captain: He's our chest protector.

What fish lives in Washington, D.C.? The Senate Herring.

Girl: Mom. Johnny has a filthy mouth.
Mother: What do you mean? What did your little brother say?
Girl: Nothing. He's been eating mud pies.

FRACTURED FAIRY TALES

Old King Cole was a merry old sole until he was hooked by a fisherman.

Orville and Wilbur had a sister named Snow Wright who lived with the Seven Dwarfs.

Tom Thumb got arrested for using a five-finger discount at the store.

What did the mosquitoes say after they flew off of Robinson Crusoe?
Let's get together again on Friday.

What do you call a farmer who raises sheep? A shear cropper.

Show me a dork who swallows dynamite ... and I'll show you a guy who's going to get a bang out of life.

What is the favorite music of Irish teenagers?   Shamrock.

What does a dogcatcher play golf with?

Kennel clubs.

Why did the burglar go to Yankee Stadium when it was closed?
He wanted to break into the major leagues.

Judge: Do not tell any jokes in my courtroom, counselor.
Attorney: Is that a gag order, your honor?

What's green, yodels and has holes?   Irish Swiss Cheese.

Athlete: I'd like to insure my tennis serve.
Agent: All we offer is no fault insurance.

Sharon: **I got a new puppy for my boyfriend.**
Karen: **That sounds like a good trade to me.**

Vagrant: If I knew how to make money I wouldn't be in jail.
Counterfeiter: I knew how to make money and that's why I'm in here.

Knock! Knock!
Who's there?
Scold.
Scold who?
Scold outside so dress warm.

....

What do you get if you cross an untidy hobo with a millionaire?
A guy who is filthy rich.

....

Jed: I keep my retirement money hidden in an old pot.
Fred: I have a pension pan.

....

Boss: Did you men build that rickety staircase?
Carpenter: Yes, sir, but it won't happen again.
Boss: Okay. But from now on watch your steps.

....

WACKY WORD POWER

"I've got to find a way to blow off some steam," Robert Fulton.

"Oh go fly a kite!" Mr. Franklin to his son Ben.

"Writing this poem is making me a raven maniac!" Edgar Allen Poe.

"I've got a code in my head," Samuel Morse.

"Some girls lose their heads over me," King Henry the Eighth.

"You boys are both airheads," Mrs. Wright to her sons Orville and Wilber.

"What a revolting development this is," King George of England in 1776.

"There's a hot time in the old town tonight," Nero.

Murphy's Loony Laws: Anything that can go wrong ... will!

THE USED CAR LAW - The minute you drive it off the lot, a used car will start to make a strange, annoying noise no one can explain.

THE WINDY PAPER LAW – If the wind blows papers off your desk and out the window, important papers will be lost forever and useless junk will land near the desk.

THE PIZZA LAW — The place that makes the best pizza is located the farthest from your house and does not deliver.

THE CAR TIRE LAW – Car tires and spare tires always go flat at the same time.

THE SLED LAW - Sled runners turn rusty the minute snow starts to fall.

THE RAINCOAT LAW – Your raincoat can only be found on sunny days.

THE BONUS LAW — An unexpected check or bonus is immediately followed by an unexpected or overdue bill.

THE ELECTRIC LAW – You always discover the live wire you exposed by accidentally touching it.

THE BABY LAW - Infants sleep peacefully all day so they can save up enough energy to cry all night.

THE DOG LAW – Your pet dog never has to go out at night until you're ready to go to bed.

THE TV LAW – The cable always goes out just before the big game or your favorite program starts.

THE KITTY LITTER LAW – The stray cat you adopt is always a pregnant female.

THE PIMPLE LAW – A zit appears on your chin, forehead, or nose before an important date or party.

THE ICE CREAM LAW – Your sister's ice ream cone always lasts longer than the one you're eating.

THE SLIP-UP LAW – If you buy a snowmobile, it'll be the mildest winter on record.

THE SNOW SHOVEL LAW – Minutes after you finish shoveling out your driveway, the snowplow comes by and blocks it.

THE HOMEWORK LAW – The day you finally do all of the assigned homework, your teacher is absent and the sub doesn't collect it.

FOOD FREAKOUT LAW – You wake up in the middle of the night and crave a snack food item you don't have in the house.

THE FIX IT LAW – You never have the exact tool you need to repair something.

THE PRODUCT LAW – Easy-to-assemble products come with tons of instructions. Hard-to-assemble items come with no instructions.

THE NO GPS LAW - The person you ask for directions never speaks English.

THE TOY LAW – The most expensive toys break easily. The cheap toys last forever.

THE LIGHT LAW – Your flashlight always works fine until there's a blackout or a power failure.

THE BUS LAW – School buses only break down on the way home from school.

THE SHOPPERS LAW – The store will run out of the sale item you drove twenty miles to buy just before you get there.

THE BASEBALL LAW - The game is rained out on the day you get free box seats.

THE DRESS LAW – The dress that makes you look great is not on sale. The one that makes you look horrible is.

THE SCHOOL PARENTS LAW – Back to School Night is always held on the evening of a sporting event you're dying to watch.

THE SHOE LAW – The best looking shoes in the store don't come in your size.

THE CLICKER LAW - Somehow the TV remote always gets misplaced.

◄ ◄ ◄ ◄ ◄ ◄ ◄ ◄ ◄ ◄ ◄ ◄ ◄ ◄ ◄

THE KLUTZ LAW – No one notices your best dance moves, but everyone is watching when you slip and fall on your rear.

► ► ► ► ► ► ► ► ► ► ► ► ► ► ► ►

THE GAMER LAW – The new video game you really want always costs a dollar more than you have.

◄ ◄ ◄ ◄ ◄ ◄ ◄ ◄ ◄ ◄ ◄ ◄ ◄ ◄ ◄

THE GAMER LAW II – Just when you save up enough for the video game system you want, a better, more expensive one comes out.

► ► ► ► ► ► ► ► ► ► ► ► ► ► ► ►

DOGGIE DIRT LAW - your pet will always roll in the dirt just minutes after you give it a bath.

◄ ◄ ◄ ◄ ◄ ◄ ◄ ◄ ◄ ◄ ◄ ◄ ◄ ◄ ◄

THE STICKY TAPE LAW – Scotch tape will stick to your fingers, but not to the paper you ripped.

► ► ► ► ► ► ► ► ► ► ► ► ► ► ► ►

THE FIELD DAY LAW – Thunderclouds will clear up two minutes after your school field day has been cancelled.

◄ ◄ ◄ ◄ ◄ ◄ ◄ ◄ ◄ ◄ ◄ ◄ ◄ ◄ ◄

THE KITTY LAW – The stray cat you name Spike or Rocky will have kittens.

► ► ► ► ► ► ► ► ► ► ► ► ► ► ► ►

THE CHRISTMAS LIGHT LAW - Christmas lights will work perfectly until you put them on the tree on Christmas Eve. Then they'll go on the fritz.

◄ ◄ ◄ ◄ ◄ ◄ ◄ ◄ ◄ ◄ ◄ ◄ ◄ ◄ ◄

THE TURKEY LAW – Your doctor puts you on a diet the week before Thanksgiving.

THE GRAVY LAW — You drip gravy on your fifty-dollar shirt instead of your five-dollar tie.

THE PIZZA LAW – You discover the bottom of the pizza you bought is burned to a crisp after you drive all the way home.

SNOW LAW #1 - You wake up and rejoice because a blizzard has dumped ten feet of snow on the ground and school is sure to be cancelled. Then you realize winter break started.

SNOW LAW #2 – You buy the best snow-blower money can buy so you won't have to shovel snow. A blizzard hits and you realize you forgot to buy gas for the snowblower.

SCHOOL LAW #1 — On the exam the teacher always asks the one question you didn't study because you figured she'd never ask it.

SCHOOL LAW #2 – The principal always sees the kid who hits second and not the kid who hits first.

DATING LAW - Pretty girls always have strict fathers and big, tough brothers.

GUARANTEE LAW – Everything breaks down the week after the guarantee expires.

COLD LAW — The refrigerator and the air conditioner break down on the hottest day of the year.

HOT LAW – The furnace breaks down on the coldest day of the year.

FISHING LAW #1 – The person who hates fishing the most catches the biggest fish.

FISHING LAW #2 – Your line gets tangled up in the tree limb that's too far away to get tangled up in.

THE ALARM CLOCK RULE – The alarm clock that never rings on workdays, always rings loudly on weekends.

THE CAR CURSE – The automobile that always gets you to work on time, breaks down on the way to the beach.

THE LID LAW – The jar lid a big strong guy can't twist off is always opened by a girl or a little kid.

THE COMIC'S LAW – The joke you paid a comedy writer a hundred bucks for gets booed while the one your seven-year-old son wrote gets a laugh.

THE LITTLE LEAGUE RULE #1 – The longest fly ball you ever hit always goes foul.

THE LITTLE LEAGUE RULE #2 – You hit a homerun when no relatives come to the game and strike out when every family member you have is in the stands.

THE MONEY LAW – Banks only lend money to people who really don't need it.

THE TAX LAW – The more money you make, the less taxes you pay.

THE LOST LAW – Anything you lose will stay lost until you don't need it anymore or buy another one.

Stupid Sentences

Drink this medicine encase you feel sick.

After the party our house was amass.

That low price is asbestos I can do.

Adjust don't care what you do.

This is the warship I ever sailed on.

Open fire soldiers. It's usher them!

If you drink a glass of warm milk, you will go to sleep the miniature in bed.

My jeans have ripped knees, but no tears on deceit.

If a boy comes over to your house, you'd better vitamin or he'll go home mad.

Teenagers should show proper respect folder people.

The reason I came on Wheel of Fortune is because I want to window.

After you hit a baseball you have Toronto first base.

Guess what? I avenue baby brother.

Mount Everest is so high you have to be a little crazy to climate.

When a cat is very thirsty elapse up all of his milk.

You can go to college, but festival you have to graduate from high school.

Those shoes are nice, but have you tried ammonia to see if they fit right?

I'm hungry. Let's gopher a pizza.

The marshal got in a shootout with some outlaws and now he has a bulletin his arm.

The patient is doing well thanks to the curious taking now.

Why did you get insulate last night?

The fodder you jog the more tired you get.

You supply the frankfurters and I'll bring a Canada best sauerkraut money can buy.

Take this Madison and you'll feel better soon.

The way to win a prize at a game of chance is to piccolo number

I stay home because symptoms I don't feel like going out.

I felt terrific yesterday, but today adjust don't feel so hot.

The lady's pet chimp grabbed her hand embitter on the finger.

Jack and Jill were cistern brother.

I avenue job as an English teacher.

Rebus hurry or we'll miss the train.

Going on carnival rides symptoms makes me dizzy.

Your kitchen flourish kind of dirty.

I Santa letter home to your parents.

When you bet cash on a horserace, sometimes you window.

The bull wouldn't go in the barn, but the coward.

The surfer who wiped out yelled, "Alp! Alp! I'm drowning!"

This old tugboat is the worship I've ever been on.

The foreman told us to loathsome crates on the truck.

My lazy teenage son satyr all day playing video games.

Pick that paper off the floor and commonplace it in the trashcan.

If you plant bulbs in September in junior flowers will grow.

My brother didn't want the last pancake so I edit.

London an airplane takes a lot of practice.

You ankle looks fine, but does journey hurt?

I've been garden the prisoner all night, Marshal.

The teacher told me to open my ears and to clothes my mouth.

Johnny thinks his football team has a chance to go awl the way.

She's either tenor eleven years old.

My father likes to relax in front of his TV on the daisies he off from work.

The Army doctor said, "Send in tumor men."

Joe got caught on barbed wire and tourist pants.

About Applesauce Press

What kid doesn't love Applesauce?

Applesauce Press was created to press out the best children's books found anywhere. Like our parent company, Cider Mill Press Book Publishers, we strive to bring fine reading, information, and entertainment to kids of all ages. Between the covers of our creatively crafted books, you'll find beautiful designs, creative formats, and most of all, kid-friendly information on a variety of topics. Our Cider Mill bears fruit twice a year, publishing a new crop of titles each spring and fall.

"Where Good Books Are Ready for Press"

Visit us on the web at
www.cidermillpress.com
or write to us at
12 Port Farm Road
Kennebunkport, Maine 04046